CLARISSA FARR is an  non-executive director and Girls' School for eleven years, Clarissa led one of the country's top academic schools, also becoming a regular correspondent for *The Times* letters page and a commentator on wider educational issues. She now works in international education. A member of the board of the African Gifted Foundation, which is transforming the lives of African girls in maths and science, Clarissa is also a Governor of The Royal Ballet School and a Fellow of Winchester College. As a Trustee of the British Museum, she chairs the Friends Advisory Council, which represents the Museum's 75,000 members around the world.

'In 2017, after more than 10 years at St Paul's Farr decided to leave. This elegantly written book shares the wisdom she deployed there and the lessons she learnt. It is about the importance of good teachers and the influence a school community can have on the lives of children'
Sunday Times

'[Farr] has certainly shown her talent here as the teller of a good story . . . part memoir, part love letter to the mad, wonderful world of schools and school leadership, Farr brings to life her own experiences and interweaves them with wider reflections upon education in the UK today . . . a warm and witty book'
Times Educational Supplement

'An urgent call to improve the way we help young women prepare for this complex world written by someone with oodles of experience and a load of passion for good education'
George Osborne

'This is a crucial book of the moment: the best-informed education insider laying out how schools should work. Farr's writing is graceful and considered: she's honest about the highs and lows of her own career, as well as unspoken topics such as dealing with over-protective parents. An insightful, useful book: excellent for parents and teaching professionals alike'

David Bodanis, bestselling author of *E=mc2*

'Clarissa Farr was the doyen of headmistresses in the early 21st century. Wise, courageous and compassionate, a true leader from a world where many heads struggle to lead'

Sir Anthony Seldon, Vice Chancellor,
University of Buckingham

'In this topical and moving book, Clarissa Farr bridges the gap between a traditional education and the 21st-century internet revolution. With an astounding lightness of touch that is only available to a true master, Clarissa looks at the importance of school, community and education . . . And somehow manages to guide us towards thinking about helping our girls find an existential resilience. With the onslaught of increased mental illness and a rapidly changing and challenged world, they are going to need it'

Julie Lynn Evans, author of *What About the Children*

Clarissa Farr

The Making of Us

Why School Matters

WILLIAM
COLLINS

William Collins
An imprint of HarperCollins*Publishers*
1 London Bridge Street
London SE1 9GF
WilliamCollinsBooks.com

First published in Great Britain as *The Making of Her* in 2019 by
HarperCollins*Publishers*
This William Collins paperback edition published in 2020

1

Image on page 212 from Christopher Alexander, Murray Silverstein, Sara Ishikawa,
A Pattern Language Towns, Buildings, Construction (Oxford University Press, 1977)

A catalogue record for this book is available from the British Library

ISBN 978-0-00-827132-9

Set in Adobe Garamond Pro 11/15 pt by
Palimpsest Book Production Limited, Falkirk, Stirlingshire

Printed and bound in Great Britain by CPI Group (UK) Ltd, Croydon CR0 4YY

MIX
Paper from
responsible sources
FSC
www.fsc.org
FSC™ C007454

This book is produced from independently certified FSC™ paper
to ensure responsible forest management.

For more information visit: www.harpercollins.co.uk/green

Remembering my parents, Alan and Wendy Farr

Contents

Foreword

Coming back from teaching to my office, I find an intricate, pop-up paper sculpture made from the insides of a book perching like a curious bird on my desk, with a note from the artist. Meanwhile, a shock netball match result against a team we were *certain* to beat reverberates around the building. A tutor reports that a head of peacock-blue hair has materialised in the Lower V (surely it was brown yesterday?) and we discuss whether this requires a response. On results day, a girl is face down on the marble concourse after it emerges she has a near-disastrous GCSE profile of nine A*s and one A. Four of our youngest girls come to see me to ask if I can be filmed saying the first word that comes into my head when they say 'Paulina' ('independent'). And just after Christmas, my urgent attention is required by parents whose daughter has been offered a place at the *wrong* Oxbridge college. What, Ms Farr, are you going to do about it?

Such are the fragments that make up the life of a headmistress – but how to capture them? The headlong nature of schools means I could do little more than fire off the occasional letter to *The Times* from my iPhone while heading towards the Great Hall of St Paul's to take assembly, scribbled notes flying. And even if I could set them down, would anyone be interested?

School. The word conjures a world at once so familiar as to be hardly worthy of comment (much less a book) but at the same time often attended with emotion: for some, affection and nostalgia, for a few, sadly, hostility and anger. There are those for whom school was a mixed or even traumatic experience, those for whom it was mainly rather dull and, equally, there are some for whom nothing has ever been quite as much fun since.

This book is for anyone who has been to school. I invite you to go back in time to that unique and personal world, to walk the academic year with me and to reconnect in memory with the teachers, places and habits that were yours. This isn't meant as therapy, you understand: how would I presume to offer that? I have been lucky: happy for the most part at school in Somerset (I've expunged the memory of diving into the freezing outdoor pool in April) and apart from the equally icy coldness of the billowing, black-clad nuns at my convent primary school, my school days were far from traumatic. But whatever our recollection of school, to revisit that impressionable time is to understand better who we have become and why. And the more we can turn our education to good account in the present, the more we can help our children, whose adult lives will be so different from ours, to do the same.

School came to mean something different when I became a teacher – not through a high-minded desire to serve the next generation but because, while putting the finishing touches to my MA dissertation, I was, somewhat pretentiously, obsessed by the novels of Henry James. 'Live! . . . Live all you can; it's a mistake not to,' he writes in *The Ambassadors* – and I wanted to do so. This meant finding an excuse to go on reading James while being paid and, if possible, persuading my students of the unrivalled brilliance of these works. In practice as a teacher I rarely touched on his labyrinthine novels – most of my pupils would have been escaping through the doors (or windows) before I reached the end of the first, attenuated, periodic, excruciatingly Jamesian sentence. Instead, I was surprised to find I liked the company of my students for its own sake: their quick-wittedness, their irreverence, their refusal to be impressed.

I began my working life in the ordered world of Farnborough

Sixth-Form College. The students were barely younger than I was and teaching Chaucer's *Miller's Tale* as a twenty-two-year-old young woman to a class peppered with eighteen-year-old boys provided challenges I hadn't been trained for (no, they might *not* kiss me – not even once – at the end of term). I was able to learn some of the craft of teaching with A-level students who had chosen their subjects and were eager to learn. This was not a given in all classrooms, as I found out later when I moved from this ambrosial world to the spin-dryer that was Filton High School in Bristol, a city comprehensive. There it was period eight, last of the day, with a bottom-set class of adolescents, that everyone dreaded, but I learned there everything I know about classroom control and how to discipline a rowdy room through timing and silence.

Three years in the Far East followed as I finally shed my West Country tethers, arriving at Sha Tin College in glittering, clattering Hong Kong. When the prospect of becoming a gin-and-tonic-swilling expat palled, I returned to the gloomier skies of England's heart and Leicester Grammar School, where at the time, Richard III was still safely buried under a city centre car park. There I began my life in senior management, with the monitoring of skirt lengths, the removal of nail varnish and timetabling in my wide-ranging portfolio. I moved into girls' education (much easier for an ambitious woman wanting to get to the top than staying with co-education, at that time) as deputy head at my mother's old school, Queenswood in Hertfordshire, in 1992. When the headmistress, Audrey Butler, retired four years later, I was chosen to succeed her. My father, rarely a man to waste words on optimistic sentiment, beamed with pride: his girl was obviously as bossy as he was – what joy! Ten years followed, during which I also married and had two children, before the chance of running the schools' equivalent of Manchester United came up. Elizabeth Diggory was to retire from St Paul's. The stars were aligned, the timing was perfect and I came to lead my first and only London day school in September 2006.

Drawing upon my own experiences as a pupil, teacher, head-mistress and mother, I have in mind as I write those who are parents of teenagers, particularly those bringing up girls. After twenty-five years in girls' education, I have well-founded respect and admiration for the young women of this age group (though a few of them have almost driven me nuts) – with their optimism, their intelligence, their determination and their wonderful sense of humour. Whether or not the 'girls' school movement', as it was once grandly called, survives – and that must be a question, despite the growing body of research defending the need for girls to be educated separately – there has to be continued attention paid to the education of girls, if the special talents and gifts they offer are to be brought out for the world's greater benefit.

As a leader in education, seeing many common preoccupations across the sectors, I am also writing for anyone responsible for the work of others, where the task is to encourage a group of people to cohere behind a shared vision. Schools are exceptionally complex, with so many constituencies to read and keep happy: governors, staff, parents and students past, present and future, the general public, the government, the inspectorate and, for most independent schools while they remain charities, the Charity Commission. But the central elements of effective leadership are readily recognisable and transferable, so I offer observations from my own experience, including my mistakes, for the parallels others may smilingly draw with their own.

Finally, this book is for any person who wants simply to reflect on their own life, their opportunities and choices, and the unique path we each follow as we gradually make and remake ourselves: the inexorable process of becoming the person we are destined to be.

September

Sunday	Monday	Tuesday				
1	2	3				7
8	9	10	11	12	13	14

You can't remake the world
Without remaking yourself.
Each new era begins within.
It is an inward event,
With unsuspected possibilities
For inner liberation.

– Ben Okri, 'Mental Fight'

TO DO
- write first assembly
- agenda for govs strategy day
- set up meeting about senior scholarship
- do online shop
- Postpone dentist (parent meeting)
- pay car tax

BRUTON SCHOOL FOR GIRLS
SUNNY HILL

NAME *Clarissa Farr*   Term *Autumn* 1959

FORM *LIVH.*   Number in form   23

Age *11yrs 6mths.*   Average Age *12yrs 9mths.*

Term Average   3+   Number above and below   1/6

Examination Average   Number above and below

[A Good; B Average; C Weak; D Poor]

Absences   8   Honourables   3   Detentions   –

Next term begins: Boarders *7th Jan.*   Day Girls

Half term *Feb 13th – 16th.*

Next term ends: Boarders *18th March.*   Day Girls

Man can do nothing
without the make believe
of a beginning.
— George Eliot

CHAPTER I

September

Back to school – 'the make-believe of a beginning'

The bank holiday weekend is over, summer is waning and as the season turns, the soft, slanting afternoon light reminds us it's time to be getting ready for the new term. For some weeks, vast electronic billboards looming over city roads have borne the cheerful exhortation 'Back to School!' The angelic, tousle-headed children, pictured wearing their Teflon-coated school trousers with improbably white shirts and artfully skewed ties, seem to think that none of us can wait for the holidays to be over. Real children, alert for any shopping opportunity, badger their parents for new stationery, with its cellophane-wrapped, freshly minted smell and brightly coloured promise: pristine pads of hole-punched paper, rainbow post-it notes, neat geometry sets, rulers, rubbers and writing equipment in every shape and colour. For them, the time soon comes to pack your bag, board the school bus, find your locker in the cloakroom and print your name neatly on a fresh exercise book. For parents, after the flurry of gathering everything, once the term starts, a little silence falls. And for the teachers and the head, the task is to get the whole glittering enterprise launched once again. As a new academic year begins, everyone has their own hopes and aspirations and perhaps some anxieties too: this is when the foundations are laid for the school life that unfolds, month by month, and which I will sketch through the pages of this book.

A book, a chapter, a school life: what does it mean to start something – and is a beginning ever truly that? 'Men can do nothing without the make-believe of a beginning,' writes George Eliot, as the opening words of *Daniel Deronda*. Something in us needs that sense of starting afresh to give us purpose. We want to separate what has gone before from what is to come, to shape and construct the future. Perhaps it reflects our fundamental optimism – and nowhere is that felt more powerfully than in a school, where young people are looking to their future and all the possibilities it holds. With their ingrained temporal structure of a year divided into three terms, terms divided into weeks, weeks into the daily timetable, and each day into its lesson compartments, schools provide regular opportunities for that act of renewal. At the same time the annual starting point is odd: why September? If like me you have spent your life in education, you are hard-wired to see the month that ushers in autumn, two-thirds of the way through the calendar year, as its beginning. Children are no longer employed in the fields during the summer months gathering in the harvest, yet the academic year still starts here. The long annual summer holiday in July seems at first a release from the remorselessness of the school year. But all too soon for children set free, the axis turns and the new term looms. Even now after so many years I feel a certain habitual apprehension at this time – will all go well with those first few days? Going back to school is a bit like getting out for that morning run: the thought of it is the worst bit – once you've done it you remember how you enjoy it and, each year, there is a moment to begin again. Japanese children return to school in April, when the spring cherry blossom offers the most natural sign of new beginnings. Different traditions but the same effect: a page turned and a fresh start.

The first day arrives and the school buildings that have been eerily quiet – only the noise of a distant drill from some maintenance work breaking the silence – are suddenly filling with voices. Younger children make their way through the school gates carrying their too-new rucksacks, eyeing the older ones who, oblivious, are nonchalantly removing earbuds. Parents, dismissed, wave goodbye and hesitate, feeling a mixture of anxiety and relief. Inside, teachers are already in their classrooms, noticeboards cleared, preparing for the arrival of their classes. As a young teacher, I would print up my long blue mark book with the names of the pupils in each of my classes on the left-hand side, the double spread of squared cream paper ready to receive the recorded marks that would build up like a secret code of letters and herringbone strokes across the page as the year wore on. A whole blueprint was contained in those thick, pristine pages: the yet-to-be-written history of your world, of your life as a teacher, and of the progress of pupils in your care.

What are your recollections of going back to school? It's a question that often prompts strong reactions. Whether or not we enjoyed them at the time, our school days are formative: whatever our path in life, especially if we are parents contemplating the schooling of our own children or if we become professional teachers, our own experience of being a pupil is never far below the surface, inevitably colouring our views. However long ago it was, we have a reservoir of stored memories of our early lives and our time at school which can shed light on how we have developed into our adult selves. You might be surprised to find just how fresh those early memories are, once you invite them to the surface. Affection and a certain nostalgia may sweeten the picture, but all those injustices or near misses come straight back too. Sadly, some are seriously scarred by the memories, and it's a pity that we hear so many more of those stories than the happier ones. Whatever it was like, it's now a part of you.

Given how much we read about people who were miserable at school, I feel lucky that for me it was for the most part a happy experience. This has been continually influential in my work because I know, from first-hand experience, that there are few things so grounding and reassuring to a child as feeling you truly belong to your school community. When school takes on that unforced comfortable familiarity, the buildings themselves, the favourite corners where you linger with your friends, the routes and corridors you traverse at full tilt (unless a teacher is coming), your lessons, the teachers themselves, your friends, the soundscape of bells and clatter, the smell of the polish even: these things make up your entire world. There is no sense of being in some anteroom, peering in from the sidelines of an adult world waiting for real life to begin. This is it and you are the centre of it. When pupils feel at home at school in this way, they are at their most naturally confident and this is when the best learning is done. As a head, I simply wanted every child to know that feeling; so creating the conditions for it informed everything.

Of course, there are always some children who find it more difficult to integrate, even though often they may very much want to belong. In a high-achieving intellectual environment (where you test for many things but not emotional intelligence) there are more pupils than you might think who, despite their prodigious gifts, find the social contact with others difficult. And there are always a few who stubbornly resist, at odds with their school, rejecting its values and authority. *They* will not allow their individuality to be diluted, to be lured into some institutional conformity and suffer agency capture! They would be the grit in the oyster. But over time, a little pearl would often secrete itself around these too. For on the whole, especially when joining a new school at age eleven, children don't want to be different or to stand out; they want to be accepted, and the first few weeks are all about fitting in and becoming part of the tribe. Pupils learn to belong by watching, adapting and through myriad small adjustments that often go under adult radar. Their 'pack' is their form, or tutor group, and this is the unit in which they first find their feet.

The importance of helping new pupils feel secure and grounded in their year group was a priority for me as a head because of something that happened to me, no doubt from the best of intentions, when at school in my first senior school year.

I had joined my senior school, Sunny Hill (known more formally as Bruton School for Girls), set on a rolling green hilltop outside Bruton, Somerset, in 1968. Aged ten, I was placed in Miss Reed's first-form class. The youngest children in the school, we were taught in a long wooden hut with a gabled roof and its own small garden, rickety windows and walls pockmarked by drawing pins where our pictures, stories and poems were proudly displayed. Miss Reed, a tiny person with the bright brown eyes of a mouse, had the appearance of someone who spent her weekends taking bracing walks along cliff paths. That first term I quickly made friends and felt both absorbed and stimulated by everything we did; it was one of the happiest of my school days. But then everything changed.

One morning at the start of the second term, Miss Reed called me up to her desk. 'I've something to tell you, Clarissa,' she said, eyes twinkling. 'You're being moved up a year. The work will be more stretching. And it's also that you're more mature than the others . . .' Mature! What was that? My world had just fallen apart. When was I to start? Well, there was no time like the present: it would be at once. Miserably, I said goodbye to my friends and was escorted down unfamiliar corridors to the alien, too-bright world of my new form room, where at the desk next to mine a sturdy girl with a pale-brown fringe and sensible glasses called Margaret Morgan had been told to look after me. Margaret was politely kind, but after a few days she admitted one break-time how she was missing spending time with her best friend, Cecily Krasker, and gratefully went off to find her. Sitting alone on a wall, I hoped I didn't look too conspicuous and longed for the bell to ring so that I could return to the anonymity of the class.

Untethered from the lovely security of Miss Reed's class and my friends, I was lost. I dreaded the long lunch hours where I would drift around, trying to attach myself to one group of girls or another. They were kind enough, but nobody really wanted me: friendships had formed a year ago and this new, younger girl was an awkward thing. I felt childish next to these impossibly mature thirteen-year-olds who had started to wear bras and have periods. Once only interested in the fascinating world of discovery that was the first-form classroom, now I was ashamed of my failure to reach these very different milestones. At last, after much hinting, my mother did allow me to have a bra and there was a mortifying trip to the local outfitters, where she and the well-padded assistant exchanged amused glances as an infinitesimally small garment was selected. We bought two, neatly packed in cardboard boxes, like clothing for a doll. One on, one in the wash, the assistant said efficiently. The anxiously awaited arrival of my periods – a rite of passage in the lives of all young girls – came to me long after it had ceased to be a newsworthy matter to our class generally, accompanied by a silent relief that, alone in the bathroom at home, I shared with no one.

Children adapt and are often more resilient than we expect. I eventually settled in to the new class and by the following year, had made friends and was starting to enjoy academic work again. From that unnecessarily rocky start I went on to have six more happy years at the school. In my penultimate year, unlooked-for success was secured as a result of a chance meeting between my grandmother and the headmistress in a local tea shop. Miss Cumberlege (I will come back to her later), seeking no doubt to make polite conversation, said to my grandmother: 'Clarissa seems to be doing very well at school . . .' to which my grandmother replied magnificently: 'Doing well? Clarissa could run an Empire!' No doubt on the strength of this I was soon appointed one of the four head girls. So all ended well, but that early experience of being moved up always seemed a pointless emotional setback, never more so than when I emerged at the other end of the school having taken my A levels at barely seventeen, too young to go to university. I spent an unremarkable gap year working in our local pub and interrailing around Europe. Perhaps I was just doing a bit more growing up: it felt as if I'd been forced through things too quickly.

Whoever we are, our experience of school informs our values and our adult view of the world. Having been very young in the year, I'm now particularly alive to that predicament in school children and how it affects them in ways that may go undetected by the adult radar. Children live their school lives amongst their peers and experience much that the adults around them, however well intentioned, will never know (one reason why bullying and unkindness can be so hard to detect). Age matters hugely in early adolescence: however intellectually advanced a pupil is, if her (or his) emotional and physical development are not aligned with that of peers, especially around puberty, then being fast-tracked through the system may well do more harm than good. Parents can be impatient for their children to achieve academic milestones, but to what end? Of course they need to be stimulated but this can happen in so many lateral ways; they also need time to grow and be themselves, to develop at their own pace amongst friends and peers with whom they feel at home. This is what creates confidence and provides the secure foundation for their self-esteem throughout life.

Even where things appear to go smoothly from the outside not every child settles into a new school easily. As the one-time head of a boarding school, I know something about homesickness, that most physical feeling, creating a dull ache in the middle of you as if there is a gap there, exactly the shape that home and all that is familiar should be. It can be felt by children in day schools just as fiercely – a school day when you feel left out or lonely or overwhelmed can seem to last forever. But for many, just like my own period of unhappiness, it almost always passes. At Queenswood

I can recall only one girl out of the many hundreds of boarders whose homesickness seemed to have no cure, and this had more to do with anxieties about an unstable home situation than with being at school. While not all children will necessarily adapt to and enjoy boarding, parents who are sympathetic listeners while staying positive about the new experience and waiting for time to do its work are likely to see their child settle happily. I've often smiled to myself on hearing older girls recalling their own difficult initial experiences, as a way of helping younger pupils through those early weeks. Self-possessed young women now, and with the wisdom of experience, they had the air of having left such worries far behind.

For many children, the start of senior school is exciting. There might be apprehension at first, but the expectation of a new beginning soon takes over. There is so much to learn: new friends to make, new teachers to meet, new habits and traditions to learn about. All part of becoming a member of this new community. To promote the building of confidence, at St Paul's we deliberately kept our forms or tutor groups small, around twelve (two joined together made a teaching group) so that it would be easier for the children to make friends quickly and get to know their pastoral or home-room tutor. As a London school with a scattered catchment area, we also grouped the children as much as possible by geography, so that you would be likely to find two or three girls in your group who lived reasonably close. Over the first few weeks, there would be careful attention paid to helping everyone settle in and make friends, including a much anticipated one-day visit to an outdoor activity centre, with team-building exercises and plenty of opportunity to get extremely wet and muddy, which the staff looked forward to nearly as much (or so they claimed afterwards . . .) By half term, most would feel completely at home in their new school.

It isn't just the pupils who have to adapt, however. Their parents face challenges too. If you are a parent on the brink of seeing your child move to secondary school, you may well have conflicting emotions: excitement at the new opportunities opening up mixed with fear that you will suddenly feel redundant and pushed away. All those years of having fragile artwork and sticky cookery pressed into your hands at the school gates, of checking satchels for squashed letters about the next school trip or dress-up day, of hearing in detail what Miss Eyelash said about hedgehogs – all this is about to give way to a new, more grown-up experience for your child, and also for you. If for pupils it's about fitting in, for mum and dad it's about building trust in the school and letting go, especially when the children leave the normally smaller and cosier environment of their prep or primary school and, at age eleven, transfer to senior school. Parents wonder what their role will be, now that the children no longer seem eager to share every detail of their day, but look past the too-familiar face at the school gate to something or someone more interesting, answering the eager question 'So what did you do today?' with a shrug of the shoulders and that familiar adolescent brush-off: 'Oh, stuff'.

For the leadership team at the school, carefully building a relationship not just with the new pupil but also with their parents is vital, for it's the school which is the newcomer in this triangular relationship. Schools are used to doing the talking – to setting out the expectations – and this is important; but first, establishing the relationship with a family means being ready to listen and learn, demonstrating trust in and respect for parents' knowledge and experience by encouraging them to share as much as possible about their child. Almost all parents secretly believe (some not so secretly) that their own children are the most wonderful young people in the world. I know mine are. Parents love any opportunity to talk about these remarkable individuals they have created and nurtured. What topic could possibly be of greater interest? A parent's view of their child is at once the most informed and also the most subjective, so as new families joined St Paul's, I would invite the parents to write me a letter about their daughter. Note this was to be a letter: the importance of the subject matter meant this was going to be something you would take time to think about, not a form to be filled in hurriedly or a dashed-off email (even though some would inevitably arrive electronically). I asked parents simply to tell me as much as they could about their daughter's personality and interests, about the family and about any unusual experiences she might have had that it would be useful for us to know about. These might be special triumphs or achievements (many parents delighted in providing a long list of those) and equally, they might be difficult life events; it would all help us understand her better. Most parents appeared thoroughly to enjoy the process and put great thought into it: each new pupil came alive on the page in the voice of her mother or father: 'We came to parenthood late and Hattie has continued to amaze and astonish us since the day she was born. She cannot wait to start senior school', or 'Lola has a very strong sense of right and wrong and finds it hard to stand by and watch any unkindness amongst other children', or 'Maisie has a very close relationship with her grandmother and they love making up stories together; she is a quiet child and is therefore somewhat apprehensive about being at a larger school', or occasionally: 'We sometimes feel quite exhausted after a weekend with Zainab. She is looking forward to interviewing her new teachers for the magazine she has recently started writing in her bedroom.' And so on. Sometimes I learned about difficulties, perhaps of loss or separation, that these not-quite-eleven-year-olds had already weathered. How important for us to have this context, to understand them better as we took charge of their education and care. The letters gave parents at the outset an unhurried and respected voice as well as underlining the importance we attached to their special, uniquely experienced perspective. Of course, they also gave insight into the dynamics of families and their values and what circumstances we might be engaging with as time went on: families separated across the world because of work commitments perhaps, families where there was only one parent or sometimes families caring for a sibling with disability or an elderly grandparent. Reading these letters, filled with unashamedly partisan love and with hopes and aspirations for a daughter's future, I hoped the parents would keep copies, to read again to their daughter as she left school in seven years' time. 'Tell me about your daughter' was perhaps the most powerful conversation opener I ever employed, and it was where each individual girl's story at senior school would begin.

Having invited them to write those important letters, during our welcome tea party I would explain to the crowd of slightly apprehensive new parents that we would be encouraging the girls' independence right from the start. So soon? their faces said. My own mother's maxim was that as a good parent you should make your child independent of you 'as early as possible' and this very practical and sound advice, especially for working mothers, I have always kept in mind. As parents, they would not be told every little thing, because this was a stage where the pupils would be encouraged to take responsibility for themselves and sort out some of their own challenges. There are many things for the girls to adjust to on starting life in a new, bigger school, with more pupils and teachers, more subjects to get used to and a totally new way of doing things, I would tell them. But we would all be there to help. For example, if as a pupil you are too busy attending lots of exciting after-school clubs to get your homework done (a very familiar problem to many an eager new eleven-year-old) this is a thing to talk to your tutor about. You don't need to rush to involve your mother or father. At this I would see the parents looking hesitant: surely it was up to them to know everything, to smooth away all the snowdrifts blocking their path? No, I would say firmly. Education is about learning to solve problems for yourself, even though that adjustment and releasing of parental control is very hard.

For us parents, this learning to let go is a lifelong counter-intuitive lesson (I'm still working on it and my children are in

their early twenties) and we are greatly helped in the adjustment
if, at the secondary stage, the school makes the effort to forge an
effective and trusting relationship with us. As a head I was always
aware that mutual trust could only be built up over time, but the
school needed to make clear that this was a priority. Reminding
parents that as a parent myself I was not unaware of the adjustment
they were having to make, at that same welcome tea party I would
talk about the exciting journey we were embarking on together,
entering into partnership in the care and education of their children, and how important it was that we established good channels
of communication – and then kept them open. During your
daughter's time with us there will be ups and downs, I warned
lightly. The teenage years are coming! If you are having difficulty
adjusting to that bored sigh when you ask what your daughter
did at school, wait until you are getting the adolescent eye roll
accompanied by '*Hello* . . . ?' when you make some well-
intentioned but hopelessly inept remark about modern social mores
or popular culture.

School and home need to work together – or at least in trusting
partnership. With long experience of teenagers, we have dealt with
most things: absenteeism, amnesia about homework deadlines,
absconding, arson . . . one could go on through the alphabet but
you get my point. We try always to operate from the principle
that the school is a place to learn about boundaries but wherever
possible to have the chance to start again and do better. But of
course we know that having heard your daughter's own account
of events, you may not necessarily always see things as we do. If
as parents you are unhappy about the way we handle something,
try not to talk about the school critically in front of your daughter
at home, but come and talk to me or your daughter's tutor.
Children are naturally loyal – both to their school, and to their
parents. The girl who has heard her parents running the school
down at home cannot then look her headmistress in the eye: an
invisible line has been crossed; something is wrong in her world.

I have seen this on a few occasions and it always saddens me to see the girl removed from that happy circle of security and unsure of the way back. We need to build up, to see her through good times and bad, that precious, triangular relationship of trust and respect between pupil, parents and school. This is incredibly important to the security and stability of your daughter. Once it has been damaged, it can be very difficult to repair. If you promise not to criticise us at home, I would end with a wry smile, I promise I will not say to your daughter: 'I hear your mother has been complaining again, Anya!' If the parents felt they had had a talk from the headmistress, well, they had. Better that than have communication breakdown later when, inevitably, it would be the girl who suffered.

So how to be a good 'new' parent? Remember that whatever school meant to you, your child is writing her own story. Get used to the fact that you will not know everything: be sure to forge a good relationship with your child's most important adult at school – probably the tutor – which means not expecting daily personal bulletins on progress, but a relationship of trust where you would feel comfortable to be in touch if you had a genuine concern or worry. Respect the fact that your child will choose her own friends, develop her own opinions and explore her own interests: this is her education after all . . . Encourage and enjoy her growing independence, for just as she develops her separate life from you, just as surely she will want, in her own time, to share parts of it too.

In thinking about ourselves as former pupils and now as parents, projecting our own memories of school onto the fresh experience of our children, we have always to keep in mind that the world today is very different from the world in which we grew up ourselves. It sounds so obvious. The generation growing up in schools today – sometimes called Generation Z or the post-millennial generation – have for one thing never known a world without the internet, the iPhone and the iPad. Using technology

comes naturally to them and they are used to the freedoms it
brings: the ability to find out information instantly, the ability
to connect with others unlimited by time and space and the
ability to create virtual identities which appear to be untrammelled
by the responsibilities of normal life. In cities especially, children
tend to be both less connected to their immediate communities
and less interested in national politics while at the same time
being better informed about the macro, global problems of
inequality, poverty and climate change. Following the financial
crisis of 2008 and the revaluation of financial power, together
with the loss of respect for certain industries such as banking,
there is now a more general questioning of the authority of
institutions. This generation does not find virtue in patience; with
the answer to anything a screen touch away, students value speed
over accuracy. However, while they may be able to source information very fast, they are less equipped to discriminate as to
whether sources are trustworthy. When you take a book out of
the school library, you pretty much know it is worth reading or
it wouldn't be there. Look up something online and you don't
necessarily have that assurance. The prevalence of mental ill health
in young people points amongst other things to the darker side
of the fast-moving and technological world they inhabit, and the
sense of being alone which prevails within the virtual world of
cyber connectivity. All that said, Generation Z are fired with a
great sense of social responsibility: they grasp the fact that if the
species is to survive, they will need to turn a competitive world
in which wealth is more and more unequally distributed into a
collaborative one where shrinking natural resources are shared.
Many opt to volunteer their time in projects which have social
benefits either at home or abroad (almost every girl in the top
year was doing this by the time I left St Paul's) and they look
forward to careers which will be more varied and less linear than
those their parents have experienced. (I will return to specific
aspects of this wider context and the Generation Z mindset in

later chapters.) The point to emphasise here is that the prevailing characteristic which they and therefore schools need to grapple with is a climate of much greater uncertainty and unpredictability. This provides challenge and opportunity and we have to prepare them for both. To lead fulfilled lives and contribute to society they will need more than their natural optimism and enviably short memory for things that went wrong. They will need creativity and imagination, the ability to work with others and to apply their knowledge in new situations, and they will also need resilience and grit. Increasingly therefore, these are qualities we are actively addressing in our schools.

At the start of the year, for the school itself, with all the hopes and aspirations of so many people to meet and manage, creating the make-believe of a beginning offers special challenges – for leadership and for teamwork. I often thought of the process in terms of flying a large, fully loaded passenger aircraft. As the head, you're the pilot: you climb aboard, settle into your seat and check the controls, remove your peaked cap and taxi down the runway. The great machine, loaded with its freight of people, luggage and expectations, gathers speed, and then by a miracle of engineering, with much shuddering and thanks to laws of physics that few understand, the whole thing climbs into the skies and becomes airborne. At St Paul's, with almost 250 staff and over 740 pupils, that point came when the first staff meeting, the first assembly, and the arrival and induction of new staff and pupils were all comfortably ticked off. At last I would put away my file with its dividers marked 'beginning of school year' and think to myself: okay, so far so good. Now we climb to cruising altitude.

Leaders need to tell stories, and good stories have a beginning that makes you want to read on. The start of a new academic year provides various opportunities as a head for using a public forum – of which the school assembly is one example – to set the tone and mood, and engage everyone with excitement for the challenges ahead. That's how you would speak to the girls, but then there are the staff to think about. In speaking to any large audience it's important that each person feels you are speaking directly to them. Keeping the analogy of the story in mind, everyone listening to you is a character in the adventure you are about to begin and great things are only achieved when teams of people work together, each person seeing what it is that they (and only they) can contribute to the whole. I made sure that the opening staff meeting of the year was attended by everyone – not only teachers, but the cleaning and catering staff, business managers, those who worked in the offices, together with technicians and groundsmen too – we were one team, all contributing to the unfolding story of one school.

There was always a lively receptivity at that meeting and I was often struck how after the much-needed summer break everyone looked so startlingly young and refreshed. The last time we were all together in June, people were utterly exhausted: now they had bright eyes and outdoor faces, ready for anything. News of summer projects flowed; particularly enjoyable were the pithy accounts of school trips: 'We made only a *passing* visit to the accident and emergency department at the hospital in Rome this year', or 'The ground staff at Heathrow were pleasantly surprised that we had only to make *one* dash back through the airport to retrieve a passport from the seat pocket.' The publication of public exam results (consistently excellent at St Paul's and therefore a highlight of this meeting, though not vaunted externally) meant thanks to everyone: if you taught or fed the pupils, or mended their computers or cleaned their classrooms, you shared that success. The school took the decision some years ago to withdraw from the regular round of published league tables to take the emphasis away from this crude measure of educational quality, but it didn't stop us enjoying privately working out where we would have been placed had we submitted our data and the director of studies would enjoy regaling us with our theoretical placing amongst our keenest competitors. Whoever you were, this was your moment to feel proud of being part of the success story. After an hour, people would edge along the rows of cinema-style chairs to head for coffee in the staffroom, feeling surprisingly good: valued, happy to be back, ready for all that the term might bring.

The next day, there was the first assembly of the school year, which was my opportunity to welcome those who were new. Standing at the carved wooden lectern in the centre of the stage in Gerald Horsley's Great Hall, this was a new beginning for everyone, I would remind them. For the girls new to the school, seated cross-legged on the shiny floorboards at the very front of the hall in clothes picked out with more care than they ever would be again, it marked the start of life as a Paulina and all that meant in terms of pride and identity. For new staff, the beginning of a fresh chapter in their career; and for other students, a shift in their position in the seven-year narrative of school life. How immensely grown up it must feel, to be twelve and entering the 'UIV', (Upper IV – the equivalent of year 8 at St Paul's) and not to be a MIV (Middle IV – year 7) any more, with the senior girls looking at you fondly as if you were a small fluffy animal. How significant to be entering the VI (year 11) and know that you were in the run-up to GCSE just a few months away. Or even more exciting, to have entered the Senior School (sixth form) with the privilege of sitting on the red upholstered seats on the balcony of the hall, a position affording you a critical view of events below and one to which you had been aspiring for a full five years.

It was also an important moment to begin setting the tone and values for the new pupils, and to begin on some of the themes for modern life. What did it mean to have arrived at St Paul's? I would often use a recent event as a parallel story. In September 2008, for example, the Beijing Olympics provided the perfect subject. Here's what I said to the girls that morning:

> I'm speaking especially to those of you who are new Paulinas and
> I hope the rest of you will find some echoes in what I'm saying.

We're probably all feeling a bit uncomfortable this morning: we've had to get up earlier; we've abandoned our flip-flops for proper shoes, the floor of the hall is every bit as hard as we remembered although it is a bit shinier (thank you Mr Radford and maintenance) and the summer holidays are rapidly receding.

Those of you who are new are in unfamiliar surroundings – which is a bit daunting. What you'll gradually do, starting today, is find your place within this new world of school. There will be questions in your mind: how do I find my way around? Who will my friends be? How will I fit in with my class and my year group? Will the work be hard? How will I find the music rooms for my piano lesson? Probably all of us remember asking those questions on the first day and now wonder why we worried about them.

St Paul's will encourage you to feel at home and also help you become independent. We'll encourage you to think for yourself, to develop and test your opinions, to pursue your own interests. Most people find the school a very open, friendly and supportive place. I hope you'll find it so too. Those of you who are old hands, please lend the newcomers all the help you can.

I hope you've all had a great holiday. Whatever you have been doing over the past few weeks, most of you will have watched some of the Olympic Games happening in Beijing. I know some of you were lucky enough to go out to China to watch. If you've been following, you will know that:

- 204 countries took part
- 10,500 athletes competed in twenty-eight sports ranging from athletics to BMX cycling and beach volleyball
- Team GB won nineteen gold medals, the most since a hundred years ago when the games were here in London at White City.

We all have a natural desire to strive for success, but even for Olympic athletes, such success does not come easily. In swimming, for example, the Dutch athlete Marten Van Der Weijden, who won the open water event, was six years ago in hospital with leukaemia. He said: 'My illness taught me to think step by step, to think about the next hour, to be patient – the same strategy I chose here to take my moment, to take the lead.' That was a truly inspirational win. Natalie du Toit, of South Africa, a top-flight international swimmer who lost a leg in a motorcycle accident in 2001, competed in the same event. She said: 'I want to do everything on merit – this is not just a free ride.' And things did not always come easily either to Michael Phelps, USA, who won eight gold medals (the greatest number ever in a single Olympics). He had struggled at nursery school with attention deficit disorder.

So, whether you were supporting Team GB, or another country's athletes, you couldn't fail to be aware of the sheer hard work, the hope and ambition; the connection between effort and excellence. Simon Barnes, writing in *The Times*, said of the British team that they were not just winning gold medals, but they were 'setting the agenda for excellence'. Perhaps as we look forward to the year ahead, we can – in our own way – do that too.

You are all here because you have shown through competition that you have outstanding talent and outstanding potential. That should not make you smug or complacent because it gives you a responsibility – to make as much of those gifts as you possibly can. You will enjoy some great teaching here, but what you make of your potential will be to a large extent up to you. What we do together, in this school, is to aim as high as we can; to use our capability in the best way – not just when things go well, but when we stumble and things get harder too.

I would return to this idea of managing our own expectations of ourselves repeatedly when talking to both the students and staff, through the year. In some ways it became one of the most important messages of all in the constant task of balancing a stretching, challenging and exciting education with the fact that we all have edges to our capability and striving for excellence has to be tempered with an awareness of our individual limits. A happy balance is found when demands are great enough for energy and confidence to flow but not so great that they tip us over into stress and anxiety. In a school like St Paul's, where the pupils are prodigiously talented, that balance, I found, had to be struck and restruck. Aspirations should be set high while being tempered with the active building of self-esteem and confidence, especially in girls who, in my experience, are inclined (partly because of the high standards they set themselves) to doubt themselves more than they should. Equally, that confidence mustn't spill over into complacency or arrogance. One girl said to me privately, 'I hate it when people say how clever we are . . .' She felt it as a pressure, an unhelpful label. Only through the constant conversation could that balance be achieved and kept in fruitful equilibrium.

School assemblies, whether at the start of the year or not, rather than being merely 'a hymn, a prayer and a bollocking' – as one distinguished headmistress colourfully described them – can inform and set the tone, convey values and ethos as well as sometimes amuse and entertain. That is why I fought to keep the whole-school assembly (three times a week by the time I left the school) and would defend its value fiercely. Assemblies have been the vehicle through which I've conveyed some of the most important, and sometimes most difficult, messages during my two headships, including on three occasions, tragically, telling the school about the death of a pupil or member of staff. One of these was the death of my predecessor, Elizabeth Diggory, who survived the return of cancer for only eight months of her retirement.

Elizabeth, an elegant and gracious woman, shyer than her height and bearing made people think and perhaps someone who did not altogether relish standing up and addressing 700 or so difficult-to-impress teenagers, once told me that assemblies, these ten-minute gatherings of the whole school at 8.40 in the morning, were times when the Paulinas 'expected to be entertained intellectually'. Privately resolving that this sense of entitlement would be something to coax them out of, I used the early assemblies of my headship not so much for any grand pronouncements or displays of intellectual skill but to introduce myself as a person. It was important as part of getting to know each other to show that the 'high mistress' was not just a formal figurehead in academic dress, only slightly more animated than the portraits of her predecessors lining the walls, but an individual with interests, tastes and opinions and importantly, flaws – someone you might get to know. At the start of my first term, for example, it had been twelve months since the news of my appointment had become public. Plenty of time for myths of various kinds to precede me, not all of which I scotched straight away. I came from a school in Potters Bar, Hertfordshire: where was that exactly – in the *Midlands* somewhere? Was it true that I planned to introduce *uniform* into this highly individualistic school, where the pupils all choose their own clothes? Did I *really* run marathons? While allowing certain myths to continue – the uniform one added a certain frisson – I talked to the girls and staff about my interests, my experiences – and occasionally my mistakes. Over the first few years, this involved forays into Thomas Hardy's novels (my best attempt at a Dorset accent); a challenge to one of my predecessor's adages that a Paulina should be taught to 'think and not cook' (they can of course do both), which involved baking a loaf of bread on the stage in my trusty Panasonic bread machine (the fire alarm having been briefly disabled); and an account of my re-education by the City of London Police following a speeding fine. Whether these stories 'entertained intellectually' was for others to say: what I hope they did was to give some sense of the high mistress as a human being, with preferences, foibles and failings, just like anyone else.

The various rituals of the start of the year almost done, I always felt relieved to feel the term begin to get into its rhythm. But the patterning of the academic year and the frame that it gave to everything we did was always there. What other kind of life is marked by such a formal structure? In the UK, three 'terms' are divided by three holidays still – in most schools – aligned tradi-tionally to the Christian calendar: we have the Christmas holidays, the Easter holidays and then the long summer break. In the midst of each term there are the half-term holidays, sometimes lasting for a week but in many cases for two in the autumn. A regular and predictable pattern, published by most schools a year in advance. Before the current move by some families towards taking holidays in term time, when flights and accommodation are gener-ally far cheaper, this was an absolute red line that could not be crossed. As high mistress I would write a letter to parents at the start and end of most terms and one of my crisper efforts included the words: 'Thank you for *not* asking me if you can leave two days early at the end of term because the flights are less crowded.' But even then it did not entirely work. And my cause certainly wasn't helped when I made my own mistake about holiday dates shortly after Adam, my son, started at a new school. Thinking to celebrate my mother's birthday, I had booked a five-day trip to Venice for my mother, myself and the children at summer half term. Half term is always a week, isn't it? Only at my son Adam's school, I discovered a week before departure, that half term was actually only two days. Paralysed with embarrassment, I picked up the phone to launch a major charm offensive on the deputy head. 'I thought it would have real educational value, Carl,' I wheedled, hoping desperately this wasn't going to go right round the staffroom the minute I put the phone down. 'That's all right, Clarissa – these things happen,' came the reply after a short pause, during which I realised Carl had been stifling amusement sufficient for his broad grin not to be audible down the phone. We went to Venice: the sun shone, the water slapped against the jetty outside the hotel. I still have the picture of my mother sitting on the steps of Santa Maria della Salute and of Adam in his gondolier's hat. But I didn't make that mistake again, and I always remembered to be particu-larly respectful to Adam's deputy head. Unsurprisingly, I have since been a little more tolerant of the occasional 'diary moment'.

An aspect of the school year which causes more widespread problems for parents is the dogged idiosyncrasy of individual schools. A year or so ago I read a very sensible letter from a grandfather who was concerned about the strain on his daughter, struggling as she was to juggle the demands of the slightly different term and holiday dates of her four school-aged children. I'm no mathematician but you can quickly work out that this poor woman was racing round trying to avoid the Carl conversation over no fewer than forty-eight potential dates during the year. And that's before she started trying to take account of the extra holidays, special half-days and INSET (in-service training) days that are squeezed in to confuse parents by these 'constantly on holiday' teachers. It shouldn't be beyond independent schools in the same city – London, say – to agree to have the same holiday dates, should it? Try suggesting it. I somewhat naively did so at a regional heads' meeting, where people looked at me with that indulgent incredulity reserved for those asking why Oxford and Cambridge colleges can't adopt consistent admissions procedures. Feeling the weight of centuries of baroque and inexplicable process settle like a vast smothering tapestry over my head, I said no more.

We have the formal structure of years and terms. And then there is the shape of each day. As Larkin puts it with beautiful simplicity:

What are days for?
Days are where we live.
They come, they wake us
Time and time over.
They are to be happy in:
Where can we live but days?[1]

In a school, the regular set pattern of each day is often punctuated and symbolised by the ringing of bells for lessons and break time. Some might think this restrictive: imagine being an adult and still having your day determined by a bell every half an hour or so. In my experience, as a teacher, it's a way of making sure you have the most exceptionally productive day. You might long for a precious free period to get your marking done, but it isn't possible to find you've wasted over half an hour noodling around on your phone if you have twenty eager faces in front of you ready to discover the Russian language and you only have *that particular thirty-five minutes* in which to help them do so. A class cannot be kept waiting! And again, there is comfort in the familiar regularity. We conducted an experiment at St Paul's to see whether to change the shape of the school day, but after a lengthy and highly consultative process, we decided more or less to keep things as they were. There was something in the rhythm and pattern that seemed balanced, as if we were biologically adapted: the changed day felt by turns piecemeal and baggy, lacking in proper flow – just wrong, somehow.

Living to the discipline of the academic year, week and day has its frustrations and constraints. At the same time, it provides a familiar rhythm from which we can draw confidence, security and comfort. I believe that the pattern and structure which we become used to at school meets a more fundamental and lifelong human need: to feel ourselves located, grounded, placed in relation to the world around us. To lack that – and sometimes in life if we are untethered from our moorings and face periods of confusion or loss – produces a feeling very like the homesickness we might recall from childhood. In a world of expanding possibilities and greater uncertainty we are fortunate that in schools, our children's lives still have this regular pattern: its cycle of peaks and troughs of concentration, anticipated special days and traditional events, giving the school year a safe and familiar rhythm. And just as a school encourages ambition and challenges its pupils to take intellectual risks and aim high, it balances this with a longer perspective, with patience and compassion. If you mess things up, there will be a chance to start again: next half, next term, next year.

October

Sunday	Monday	Tuesday
		1
6	7	8

16	17	18	19

TO DO
- Write open day speech
- Collate results of alum surv
- Talk to girls about Colet D
- Apple recipe from Fred?

It isn't true that one never
Profits, never learns:

Something is gathered in,
Worth the lifting and stacking;
Apples roll through the graders,
The sheds are noisy with packing

- 'In The Huon Valley' by James

Dads4Daughters

All women together ought to let flowers fall upon the tomb of Aphra Behn, for it was she who earned them the right to speak their minds.

– Virginia Woolf

Being a confident young woman threaten
a lot of people — men and women. In w
that kind of confidence is celebrated.

Gender issues in the workplace,
St Paul's alumnae survey 2016

CHAPTER 2

October

A question of gender – still vindicating the rights of women?

The leaves are turning, the wind is gusting and I arrive in the office having lost yet another umbrella. As October starts, the academic year is well underway, corridors are humming with conversation and everyone is settling into the familiar rhythm of the term. In the admissions department, thoughts are already turning to next academic year, this being the month of open days for families considering applying to the school, so it's time to brush up my speech for the prospective parents. It's also the annual service in St Paul's Cathedral, known as Colet Day, held jointly with St Paul's Boys' School, where each year we celebrate our foundation. Two reasons for me to be reflecting on John Colet's vision for education, the case for single-sex schools, the education of girls in particular and what happens when girls will *not* be girls: in other words, the wider issue of gender identity schools are facing today.

Dean of St Paul's, member of the Worshipful Company of Mercers and pioneering educationalist, John Colet used the fortune he inherited from his father to found St Paul's boys' school in 1509. At this time, the height of the Renaissance in England, Colet counted among his friends the great Dutch scholar Erasmus, who assisted both with writing textbooks and a Latin grammar for the school and with appointing staff. Colet also knew Thomas More, another progressive thinker and advocate of the education of women – his own daughter Margaret Roper becoming a distinguished classical scholar and translator. Amongst the early high masters of St Paul's was Richard Mulcaster, appointed in 1596, who wrote extensively on education, advocating proper training for teachers and the development of a curriculum determined by aptitude rather than age. He too thought women should have access to formal education, including attending university. Another contemporary, Robert Ascham, became tutor to Queen Elizabeth I and was the author of *The Scholemaster*, published in 1570 after his death and which, as well as being a treatise on how to teach Latin prose composition, explored the psychology of learning and the need to educate the whole person. These were forward-thinking men. Widely travelled himself, Colet believed that education generally and his school in particular should be for the children '*of all countres and nacions indifferently*' and that it should, as the humanists of the Renaissance believed, concentrate on developing the life of the mind through the study of Latin and Greek and the scholarship of antiquity, all of this becoming more achievable with the advent of printing. Colet was ambitious for his school as an institution of learning but also as an instrument of social change. Given this and the cultural climate in which the school was founded – a time of burgeoning exploration, discovery and scholarship – it is perhaps surprising that it took another 400 years for the Mercers' Company to establish a girls' school. But in 1904 they did, and as I was fond of telling prospective parents, by the early twenty-first century, we had more than made up for the time lost, the two schools by then equally established and known for their breadth of education and academic excellence. As a result of a developing bursary programme, they were also no longer just the preserve of the wealthy, but educating a widening range of bright children from across London, reflecting the cultural diversity of a capital city.

To the contemporary Paulina, with her characteristic wit and taste for unexpected juxtapositions, John Colet is part embodiment of her love of tradition and part teen icon. Colet's unblinking black bust, staring straight out and dressed in austere sixteenth-century clericals, presiding over the long, black-and-white chequered corridor known as 'The Marble', often appears in the background of selfies, with added sunglasses or perhaps a Father Christmas hat. 'John Colet rocks!' the girls exclaim with affectionate irreverence. And Colet's legacy is extraordinarily alive in the two schools today, where his vision finds fresh and contemporary expression. I feel sure that the addition of the girls' school is something of which he would have wholeheartedly approved.

Colet Day itself is a high point in the calendar anticipated with great excitement. The vast cave of St Paul's Cathedral with its unnerving acoustic (open your mouth and you think you are singing on your own – very disconcerting) is packed with proud parents and in the front rows, under the echoing dome, the two schools sit, flanked by their tutors. A monumental rustling as the organ swells and the service begins, the clergy processing and everyone rising to their feet, anticipating the ritual that is to come. Moving to the lectern to speak my allotted words (the high master and high mistress alternate their lines each year, in careful observance of equality) I wonder again about the respective characters of these two schools, with their brother and sister relationship of familial closeness and sibling rivalry, and whether one day they will become one. For the time being, Colet Day brings the two schools together in symbolic unity and the question dissolves unspoken in the air.

Whatever form schools take in the future, the length of time it has taken us to take seriously the education of girls must remain one of history's great opportunity costs. We can reflect that despite the efforts of early pioneers, for all the women who have risen to prominence in the world, there are so many more whose capability and contribution have rested either unsung, unrealised or unfulfilled.

That's half the potential of any single generation. And when we talk about the education of women today, even though so much progress has been made, there is still always an underlying sense that we are righting a wrong, catching up with something which has been given insufficient importance and which now therefore needs special explanation or attention. As part of this, we are also still working out how women fit into the public, professional world and therefore to what kinds of roles they are best suited: are they bringing something different from men to strategy, to leadership, to getting things done? Should the fact of your gender be celebrated or ignored? While the debate continues, at school level the emphasis is overwhelmingly on integration. Worldwide, the modern default school model that is regarded as more 'natural' is not single-sex education but having boys and girls learning alongside one another in a co-educational setting. Single-sex schools might have been all right a hundred years ago, when girls were only just progressing from being taught refined accomplishments by governesses in the safe and sequestered setting of their homes, but that time has passed. This is the twenty-first century. Aren't single-sex schools just an anachronism, encouraging outdated ways of thinking and walking out of step with the real world?

This is a question that cannot be sidestepped with sentimental appeals to custom and tradition. If single-sex education is to have a future, for girls or indeed for boys, it has to be not merely nice, but necessary. This means being based on something more than a nostalgic affection for how things used to be when time stood still and a school was its own little citadel, shut off from the real world like Hogwarts or St Trinian's. Boys' schools, perhaps because many are so long established, have not often felt the need to explain overtly the advantages they offer boys. Why would you, if you've been going strong for hundreds of years and produced many of the people (men) who have been the opinion formers and leaders of their day? And perhaps too with the prevailing attention being on addressing the needs of women, it hasn't been easy for them to do so. As more and more boys' schools admit girls to buttress their finances and academic profile, and boys-only establishments become a rarity, a few are now advancing their unique proposition with more clarity. Girls' schools on the other hand have been in campaign mode from the start: the only way to educate girls properly is to educate girls only. But is it? Any movement championed by women for women faces challenges, not least having to weather being caricatured by some as shrill, desperate, unfeminine or just downright hoydenish – think of the suffragettes. At the same time advocates for girls' schools have not always helped themselves by choosing the most robust and persuasive grounds on which to prevail. I'm a passionate believer myself in women's education and empowerment, but not every argument for having girls educated separately is necessarily convincing and we do ourselves no good by appearing to grasp any new 'proof' instrumental to our cause.

I'm particularly dubious, for example, about there being a scientific, biological justification for girls' schools. In a no doubt well-intentioned attempt to ensure their immortality, a body of so-called 'science' has developed arguing that girls *need* to be taught separately because they are neurologically different – they literally have differently wired brains and therefore it follows that they require teaching in special ways that would be wasted on boys but can make differently wired girls flourish. We can call this the 'nature' argument. A few years ago, for example, advocates of girls' schools latched with great enthusiasm onto the work of the American psychologist JoAnn Deak and her book *Girls Will Be Girls*. Here was the 'proof' the girls' school movement had been looking for. Along with a great deal of very sensible and pragmatic advice about the raising of daughters, Deak – renowned, as the cover blurb says, for her knowledge of 'what makes girls tick' – makes this claim: 'brain research now clearly shows that the structure of the male and female brain is different at birth, apparently the result of oestrogen or testosterone shaping it in utero.

In other words, female brains have more neurons in certain areas than male brains as a result of having more estrogen bathing them during fetal development.'[1] Bathed in oestrogen in the womb, the female brain also has a predisposition for effectiveness in certain cognitive areas: language facility, auditory skills, fine motor skills and sequential/detailed-thinking. Deak goes on to argue that the amygdala, the emotional centre of the brain, is especially sensitive in females, making them experience more frequent and more intense emotions. Given the biologically different nature of the male and female brains, both genders, she advises, need to spend time on activities that are *counter* to their neurological grain. To grow into properly balanced individuals, little girls should spend more time with building blocks and little boys in the drawing corner, and so on. You can see at once how its central point – that girls are wired differently – could be used by advocates of girls' schools to propose an entire curriculum and approach to learning that would be uniquely girl-centred, justified – indeed essential – because the science says they need it.

Not everyone is so convinced by this correlation. The idea that men and women are biologically different in more ways than the obvious is explored with some vigour by Cordelia Fine in her wonderfully acerbic book, *Delusions of Gender*. The clue is in the title: Fine ruthlessly demolishes what she sees as the dubious scientific proofs of the neurological differences between men and women and the so-called male and female brains. Distinguishing between the brain as a biological structure and the more complex notion of the mind, and surveying hundreds of years' worth of evidence which has been used to build the concept of 'neurosexism', she points to the fact that in a world where we love referencing gender differences and learn to do so from very early childhood, time and time again those differences are seen to be derived as much – or more – from our own preconceptions, born of social customs about the characteristics of gender, as from any actual physiological evidence. In other words, for her it's about nurture rather than nature.

Fine argues that men and women behave and perform certain tasks differently, and might presumably also learn differently, not so much because of any intrinsic neurological difference but because they are fulfilling a social expectation. Society and the self thus become reciprocally defining – the one informs and reinforces the other. Here for example is what she has to say about housework and who does it:

In families with children in which both spouses work full time, women do about twice as much childcare and housework as men – the notorious 'second shift' . . . You might think that, even if this isn't quite fair, it's nonetheless rational. When one person earns more than the other then he (most likely) enjoys greater bargaining power at the trade union negotiations that, for some, become their marriage. Certainly, in line with this unromantic logic, as a woman's financial contribution approaches that of her husband's, her house-work decreases. It doesn't actually become quite equitable, you understand. Just less unequal. But only up to the point at which her earnings equal his. After that – when she starts to earn more than him – something very curious starts to happen. The more she earns, the more housework she does . . .

What on earth could be behind this extraordinary injustice in which she returns home from a hard day at work to run the vacuum cleaner under his well-rested legs? A few popular writers have made some creative suggestions. John Gray, author of the *Men Are From Mars, Women Are From Venus* books, has recently made a valiant stab at arguing that performing routine housework chores is actually selectively beneficial to women, including – if not especially – those with demanding jobs. His idea (which to my knowledge has not been empirically tested) is that because the modern woman has removed herself from her traditional home sphere with its babies, children and friends on whom to call with a pot roast, she has dangerously low levels of oxytocin coursing through her blood. (Oxytocin is a mammalian hormone associated with social bonding

and social interactions.) Thankfully, however, 'nurturing oxytocin-pro-
ducing domestic routine duties like laundry, shopping, cooking and
cleaning' are available in plentiful supply. Phew! Such chores,
however, have a very ill effect on men. For them, the priority is
testosterone-producing tasks – for without the stimulating rush of
that sex hormone, men become little better than limp rags (and
not even ones that wipe themselves along the countertops).[2]

This fascinating debate will go on, but I'm inclined to agree with
Cordelia Fine that the perceived differences in behaviour – and
as part of that, learning preferences – are more to do with cultural
and social influences than biology. In my experience, generally
speaking, there are certain ways in which girls and boys *tend* to
differ in their habits and behaviours. I say *tend*. Of course I know
more about the girls – based on twenty-odd years of leading girls'
schools I can say for example that the girls I have known are often
inclined to be self-critical, to be more concerned than their brothers
about getting things right first time, to be dutifully good at planning and completing things (which is why they sometimes do
better when assessed continuously and less well if taking exams).
They are also sensitive to social dynamics and can read the subtext
of conversations and behaviours very skilfully. This of course is
linked both to why they value and nurture lasting friendships as
well as why they are also so much better than boys at bullying.
Where boys are inclined just to hit one other, girls can torture
one another slowly over weeks using only gestures of their eyebrows,
making the behaviour so much harder to detect and pin down. I
also know that generalising is dangerous and there are many girls
at St Paul's who would pull me up for stereotyping and say they
didn't recognise themselves here. But actually these are my general
observations, based on the 25,000 or so girls I have known. The
question for us here is not so much whether they are different
from boys – which in my opinion they are – but more how does
that difference come about? Are girls born different, or is it that

society makes them so because of its expectations? What actually can we say to justify educating girls (and therefore boys) separately?

In many ways, when I hear recent leavers from St Paul's who are now making their way in professional life talk about their experiences, it is more and more clear to me that girls' schools are indeed oddly out of step with some of the 'realities' of the so-called modern working world. In a well-regarded modern company, for example, a Paulina in her thirties told me recently how she was surprised at having to fend off the unwelcome advances of a more senior male colleague at work who would approach her desk, stand too close and suggest drinks after hours. When I asked why she didn't tell him to get lost, she replied that as he controlled her promotion prospects and her pay, she had to be very careful. Another told me that when the male staff packed up on Fridays early to go and play football and she asked to join them, she was told that wasn't how it worked and she might like to go and have a manicure instead. We may be providing a stimulating intellectual experience and nurturing a love of scholarship, but as regards preparation for life and work, our messages – our assumptions – about equality are by some standards hopelessly off-message. Because it turns out that the real world has a long way to go and still needs a great deal of cleaning up.

The disconnect is simple: at a school like St Paul's (or Queenswood, or Sunny Hill where I was a pupil, or at most girls' schools I'm aware of), girls learn an instinctive, fundamental confidence that far from being girl specific, *has nothing to do with their gender*. As one alumna wrote in a survey carried out amongst the 25–35-year-olds who had been to St Paul's, 'We commanded respect in our very nature.' Note that masculine-sounding word 'commanded' which she uses without self-consciousness. Paulinas, along with other girls' school-educated young women, *assume* that their opinions are of intrinsic interest, and are even happy to revise those opinions, as one inspection report memorably suggested, '*if* convincing evidence is put before them'. They take themselves seriously in the best way: they have never been taught to 'play nicely' because they are girls, to assume they will be less talented at science and maths, to defer to male opinion because it is more loudly expressed, or to assume they are being educated to be the wives of top men. If they are articulate, confident and full of opinions (as they tend to be) they do not expect to be treated as if this were unusual and slightly unfeminine, or actually rather admirable, given they are only girls. They enjoy sport, but generally prefer to play it rather than be WAGs on the touchline, watching their brothers and boyfriends play rugby. If the school play is *Macbeth*, they assume it is not beyond the talents of one of them to play the main part – in fact to play *all* the parts. In short, they think they can do pretty well anything, because at school, they can.

When they emerge into a workplace and a wider society which rather lags behind in that everything is still pretty much weighted in favour of men, where organisations work according to male tastes, behaviours and preferences, they just don't get it. One former head girl, who visited St Paul's to address the students about her career in the decade since leaving, put it this way: 'I just had no idea that it would be *so* much more challenging making your career as a woman – at school, it never occurred to us – everything seemed possible.'

Everything seemed possible because it was. Despite some progress, the realities in the so-called 'wider world' of unequal pay, unequal promotion prospects and unequal opportunities generally are a continuing concern to everyone who would wish to see society benefiting – equally – from the talents of both men and women. Girls go out into the workplace, full of confidence and capability, and come up against a very different culture: at one extreme, they may be subjected to active prejudice or harassment: being excluded from the Friday afternoon game of football or being pursued by the older boss. But equally disturbing is that experience that some women describe of becoming invisible – their views going unheard or ignored. This was a new idea to me until comparatively recently; I experienced it for the first time myself when attending the conference of a traditionally male-dominated professional organisation. It was a very odd feeling standing in a circle at a drinks reception and feeling like a pane of glass – I could easily have disappeared without anyone noticing. Ah, so this is what they talk about, I thought.

Change is afoot in some quarters, stimulated by the more recent opening up of the question of gender identity. A case in point was the decision in summer 2017 by the then newly appointed (female) artistic director of the Globe Theatre, Michelle Terry, to commit to 'gender-blind' casting and a 50/50 split of male and female roles – presumably because, otherwise, men would be getting the lion's share of the great Shakespearean parts, as they always have done. This is great, but I reflected that in girls' schools, gender-sighted – rather than gender-blind – casting in drama productions has *always* ensured that women win not just half, but *all* the most significant roles, producing generations of practised Macbeths, Hamlets and Henry Vs. It was with some satisfaction that I thought how well prepared these girls' school-educated actors would be for the new and more empowering approach to casting at the Globe. That even-handedness and neutrality is of course emphasised further when we also see men playing female roles with great brilliance: who can forget Mark Rylance as Olivia in Shakespeare's *Twelfth Night*, for example. Twice as many actors to choose from, twice as many roles to audition for, and it becomes about talent and skill, not about the limitations of gender.

This is all very well, say the detractors of single-sex schools, but the real world is mixed – what's the point of pretending otherwise? Girls just have to get used to it (which usually means playing nicely to get what they want), so they might as well start at school. Of course education must prepare young people for reality, for society as it is. But it must and can do more: inform and drive the values by which that society is shaped. When all things are

equal – my former head girl and I agreed – there may be no
further need for single-gender schools. But it seems that despite
some excellent work going on to change things (spearheaded by
men as well as women) we are still very far from that point. Until
then, St Paul's and its fellow girls' schools have a vital and influential role to play in ensuring the continued disruption of social
norms, so long established that no one even thinks of them as
norms. The impetus towards genuine equality cannot be assumed
but must be actively led by the talented and confident young
women emerging from our gates. Whether girls are wired differently or not really does not matter in the end. Either way, what
we're dealing with is a society that has deep-rooted, often subcon-
scious expectations about women and structures which still limit
the contribution they can make. While this is so, we need to
educate girls themselves to change that. The case for girls' schools
is as much about preparation for what is to come, as it is about
the experience of the here and now.

So what do girls' schools do differently? Many things. By freeing
girls to be themselves so they don't feel the pressure to conform
to predetermined patterns of behaviour, girls' schools make them
more aware of how the media seeks to manipulate them. They
train a lens on the problem to make girls think critically. In doing
so, they give a framework to evaluate the image of girls in today's
media. Is that the image we want for ourselves? What is the image
of female attractiveness to which young women are taught to
aspire, for example? Who is shaping it? The insidious encouragement to conform to an absurd idea of beauty embodied by
emaciated fashion models has, for example, caused great damage
to many young women's self-esteem and health. We want them
to pay attention to this and develop the resilience to reject it,
because nobody else is going to in an industry that is making
money out of controlling them in this way. When the then editor
of *Vogue*, Alexandra Shulman (a Paulina herself) came to talk to
the girls at St Paul's about her career in fashion journalism, as part

of the weekly Friday lecture programme, this highly intelligent, unexpectedly normal-looking woman – chic in a reassuringly rumpled way – was asked by one of the girls what she was doing about the fact that *Vogue*'s models looked 'emaciated'. Her magazine was still implicitly promoting the idea that size zero should be every girl's dream. Her reply was that she saw the problem but this was down to the designers: with clothes being created for tiny figures, fashion editors could only provide tiny models to wear them. I looked at the faces of her difficult-to-impress audience and saw politeness warring with scepticism. Surely this was an issue on which a female-run magazine like *Vogue* should be making more of a stand? As so often, it was in the post-lecture informal conversations that the most interesting thinking emerged; here about the tension between principles and commercial imperatives – an example of how a girls' school can give time to foregrounding a subject of special significance for women and enable untrammelled discussion.

Girls' schools don't just concentrate on protecting their pupils: they also empower them, confidently promoting a positive 'can-do' philosophy. There are no barriers, real or perceived. In terms of academic life, for example, girls do not face unspoken prejudices about subject choices. No one is particularly amazed that you like physics. An enormous amount has been written about why physics is seen as a male subject: more boys take it at A level and beyond so it is seen as inhospitable to girls; it is associated with 'hard' skills, such as making circuits, which are typically perceived as isolated and not involved with other people, and hence also 'unfeminine'. Textbooks also tend to employ traditionally boy-friendly examples, such as car construction. All this is changing gradually, but physics is still a subject where girls are having to fit in. That said, and somewhat to my surprise, I was gratified to learn about a recent international initiative to encourage more young people into engineering through designing, 3D printing and racing Formula One-inspired cars. This scheme, F1 in Schools, has attracted girls in large numbers. Where the girls win out is in the leadership and organisation: the mixed teams have proved more successful in galvanising themselves to raise funds and see through the project than those with boys only, and guess what? The most successful teams of all are those who have a girl as the leader.

The great head start in a girls' school of course is that the whole curriculum is tailored to their interests. There is no subject area or activity in which girls do not excel or are seen as less apt or capable, or where their capability is seen as somehow surprising or counter-cultural. The scientists are all girls, as are all the mathematicians. The significance of this has been highlighted in a new way now that we are seeing so much more emphasis on capability in the STEM subjects (science, technology, engineering and maths) and their link to higher pay. In the summer of 2017, Emma Duncan wrote a very well-researched article for *The Times* ('Maths for girls is the way to close the pay gap') arguing that as the best-paid jobs are in technology and computing, and as boys tend to choose maths more often and do better at it than girls, the answer to closing the pay gap is to have more girls do maths. This recommendation is already long since in place in girls' schools, where maths and science are not, and never have been, seen as boys' subjects – where so-called 'maths anxiety' isn't a thing and where girls take up these subjects with all the enthusiasm and confidence you could wish. The Girls' Schools Association, for example, analyses the take-up of all A-level subjects in its schools against national data, revealing that a girl educated in a GSA school is twice as likely to take maths and two and a half times as likely to take physics as her peers in all other schools taken together. Unsurprisingly, therefore, the numbers applying to read physical sciences, medicine and dentistry at university from GSA schools far outstrip national figures.

As well as giving them unprejudiced access to the curriculum, training women to expect to lead is also a vital part of their education. A girls' school is fertile ground for the emerging leader as there are so many opportunities to take initiative and show responsibility. In most schools, you can aspire to be form captain – or library monitor, or playground helper, or lunch queue supervisor – from the age of eleven. Later you may graduate to being on the school council or being captain of a sports team. And eventually you may reach the heights of house captain or even prefect. I recently saw a magazine advertising the open day of a distinguished co-ed competitor of ours in London. The photograph showed two smartly dressed senior pupils: a dark-haired boy looking confidently out at the camera and a blonde-haired girl, a little shorter as shown in the picture, looking happily up at him. Here was an image of confident leadership, certainly, but what an unfortunate and presumably unconscious message about gender. In a girls' school, there is no question of being marginalised: girls hold all the senior leadership positions; all sports teams have a female captain, the first violin in the orchestra is always a girl and, as we've seen, girls get the chance to play the leading roles, whatever the school play.

Those youngest girls who joined a month or so ago are getting to know one another, gradually piecing together their independent world of school, letting their parents into it a little, inviting them to watch their netball matches, or describing their teachers perhaps – and all the time keenly observing the older girls and their ways. As they become more confident, they become bolder: the senior girls say to me (as they do every year): 'We were never as confident as that! I used to be terrified of the girls in the senior school! Yesterday I actually saw a MIV girl roll her eyes when I told her to go to the back of the lunch queue! What's happened?' So the new ones are settling in well, I'd think wryly . . . The desire to lead and the confidence for it is often there from an early age and will receive regular encouragement throughout the school.

Some of my most rewarding times as a head have been spent with these all-female student leadership teams. The moment of appointing the new head girl was always a particular high point, making up as it did for some of the less edifying exchanges that

...ook place in my office. The girl would arrive having
... see me. She must have had a good idea of the reason
... not be quite certain. The door would open and I'd
... ..er in. A cautious, slightly stilted exchange ensued:

'Juliet, with the strong support you have received from your
peers and from the staff, I'm delighted to invite you to become
the next head girl. Of course I mustn't assume you would want
this . . . What do you say?'

'Err . . . thank you very much . . . ?'

'I mean . . . you'd like to accept? You'll be happy to do it?'

'Totally . . . Yes!'

And as she struggled to contain her delight in an attempt to
convince as being entirely unflappable and mature, we would go
on to discuss the practicalities of the announcement, before inviting
in and appointing, together, the deputy head girl and team of
prefects. By the time they had all been sitting shifting uneasily on
my sofas stealing glances at each other with polite restraint for
ten minutes, I realised they were about to burst so would release
them into the school – hearing, once they thought themselves out
of earshot, an explosion of excited mutual congratulation and
pent-up laughter.

The novelty over, it was impressive to see how quickly these
teams would organise themselves without fuss, choosing the areas
to work on during the year and hatching plans: building relationships with the younger year groups to tackle friendship issues or
bullying; giving an assembly on phubbing (no, I didn't know what
it meant either: it's tapping away on your phone when someone
is trying to speak to you – a form of 'snubbing') or helping with
revision strategy for those taking GCSE. I loved to watch the
economical efficiency with which they would divide up a problem,
assign tasks, get things done. And of course I watched them learning
some of the lessons of leadership: the challenges of getting large
groups to work together, the difficulty of fronting something your
peers don't necessarily like ('Look, guys, we have to get to morning

registration on time . . . okay? Just get over it'); the difference between the people who talk and those who get things done. It was with both sympathy and amusement I watched them one year plan their summer ball in liaison with the boys' school prefect team, which obviously had more pressing things to think about:

'How's everything going with the ball?'

'Well . . . We met with them [the boys] last week and they hadn't really *done anything* since the previous meeting? They kind of just sat around wanting to know if they could bring their plus-ones . . . Why would we want girls from *other schools* at our ball? I mean . . . Then they were just arguing about the price. So we're going to see some venues this weekend. Do they actually even care if this gets organised?'

Those girls were important role models for the younger students. In a girls' school, there are also strong role models of female leadership amongst the staff. While there are of course female heads of mixed schools, and even of boys' schools, male head teachers still predominate, especially in the private sector. In girls' schools, girls learn that it's normal for a woman to be in charge and that just as girls aren't expected to prefer certain subjects, women don't have to be the ones fulfilling the more traditionally pastoral or caring roles, underlining gender expectations about their skills and preferences. A woman can be pastoral deputy head but she can also be finance director – or indeed take on any other responsibility that interests her without it seeming unusual.

Importantly, it isn't only girls who need to learn to accept and be at ease with the idea of female leadership – boys do too. Many of the boys growing up in today's schools will find themselves working for female bosses; if this seems awkward to them, they will be at a disadvantage. The key at school level is for the staff to model relationships of genuine equality and unforced mutual respect. To that end, schools should try to ensure they do not have a predominantly single gender common room but one where roles of responsibility and leadership are held by both men and women. Boys' schools might look to ensure that they have women in their senior leadership teams (and not only in pastoral posts, where they underscore the idea that women are best at looking after people) and girls' schools should welcome employing capable men, including in those posts. I found it hugely beneficial and enriching in both the schools I led to have a mixed staff team, adding to the diversity of perspective and demonstrating to the girls that talented men had no difficulty in working with a female leader; to work in a girls' school was to be a modern man, not to be emasculated and therefore commit career suicide. But perhaps the ultimate female role model was created when a much-admired and well-liked member of the senior leadership team at St Paul's became the first woman in the 700-year history of Eton College to be appointed as its 'lower master', the most senior education post after the headship itself. This was an immensely proud and exciting moment for both schools – proof if it were needed that girls can indeed aspire to do anything.

A girls' school then is where tomorrow's women can really flex their capability, expand into all areas of potential interest and revel in learning for its own sake. They can unselfconsciously display their intelligence and curiosity, regardless of those powerful age-determined notions of popularity, attractiveness or peer pressure. Even super-confident Paulinas report that they don't necessarily do this in a mixed group, where even bright girls can have a tendency to check themselves and to dumb themselves down, especially if hormones are coursing round the system and getting mixed up with the brainpower. Where girls are accustomed to being heard and being valued for who they are, irrespective of what they look like or what they wear (did we have to endure so many cartoons of Theresa May's animal-print shoes?), they are encouraged in their capacities as confident individuals, leaders and agents of change.

Every school has its own personality which is only partly a matter of whether it educates boys, girls, or both. As the head of

a girls' school with a brother school just across the river, I had
ample chance to think about the benefits and drawbacks of
single-sex education in relation to two specific institutions. I came
to know St Paul's boys' school in both a professional and personal
capacity, because my son Adam was a pupil there, thriving on the
academic stimulation and strong sense of tradition. As a mother
I liked the proudly masculine ethos, in which personal responsibility and brotherliness were encouraged through the vertical tutor
system, where boys of different ages were grouped together in a
form. I saw my son grow in confidence, forging respectful and
friendly relationships with his teachers, loving sport and then
loving acting even more, learning to look up to older boys and
look out for younger ones while building lasting friendships. The
'Paulines' I encountered hanging out in my kitchen were likeable,
well-grounded young men who knew how to speak to adults in
a natural way, neither gauche nor ingratiating. They teased each
other mercilessly but were essentially kind and I saw that there
was room for gentleness in this version of masculinity. The large
school site, the generous rolling pitches (unusual to have so much
green space in a London school) where rugby and cricket are
passionately played and which lead down to the river, underline
an expansive and confident sense of identity. Did I feel that my
son was missing out because there were no girls in the school?
No. True, he had a sister at home with all the independence of
mind a mother could wish, but there was no sense to me – or to
him – of something missing. He was busy, stimulated, committed:
growing up in a healthy environment that was thoroughly positive
and right for him.

The girls' school I came to know quite differently, both more
intimately and less objectively. I loved it as my home and my
all-consuming project for eleven years. As you look at the school
across Brook Green, it is a fine prospect. Gerald Horsley's elegant
main building of rose-coloured brick and white Portland stone is
set off nowadays by elegant green and white landscaping behind

the clipped hedges and curled ironwork. It has an orderly grace. As one of the first purpose-built schools for girls, this is where some of the most prominent intellectuals and thinkers of the twentieth century were schooled: former pupils, or Paulinas, as they are called (never *Old* Paulinas) include Rosalind Franklin, Kathleen Kenyon, Shirley Williams and Jessica Rawson, as well as those who have carved their original careers in other fields, such as actresses Celia Johnson and Rachel Weisz. Its smaller, compact and more urban site and buildings feel scholarly and focussed, the setting for a fierce sense of the pioneering spirit of women's education, marked by a secular foundation, a commitment to liberal learning and a confident emphasis on independence of mind – the policy of having no uniform is matched by having remarkably few rules. All this can make some of the Paulinas, these latter-day bluestockings with their steady gaze, ripped jeans and dyed hair, somewhat daunting. Known for their quick intellect and an uncompromising mental tenacity, their reputation for asking awkward questions can make eminent speakers quite nervous while waiting in the wings to deliver a lecture. They are unconventional, individualistic and confident. As one of my son's friends summed it up, while a sixth-former at the boys' school: 'We are just fairly normal guys, know what I mean? Your girls, well . . . they are just – you know – more *out there* . . .' Yes, more out there perhaps, but also wonderfully warm, informal, friendly and completely unstuffy. That pungent, irrepressible sense of intellectual curiosity is all-pervasive while, as my predecessor Elizabeth Diggory beautifully put it, the classrooms and corridors ring with laughter.

Schools develop their particular character according to location, tradition, culture, the built environment, the pupils and, perhaps most of all, the cast of characters that make up the staff. So, here we have two very different schools, each with its own distinctive qualities. Would we really want to combine them and have just one, large, vanilla sundae? The lively balance between mutual respect and competition always seemed to me a good thing and in no way impeded the continuing conversation about how we might work more closely together. We all enjoyed doing so. Despite the unignorable and inconvenient geographical fact of the River Thames dividing us, necessitating a brisk thirty-minute walk across green-and-gold Hammersmith Bridge, there had long been joint plays; shared university preparation classes in some subjects (notably in my time English and economics) were working well, joint musical concerts had seen a renaissance and by the time I left in 2017, a shared sixth-form conference was in the making. Rowing was another obvious area for collaboration. All this provided excellent opportunities for the students of both schools, who could learn from each other. I would hear about 'uni prep' in my Friday morning break-time meetings with the head girl and her team:

'How was uni prep this week?'

'The boys are so, like, confident! They just come out with stuff.'

'Actually I thought what Ben said was pretty rubbish . . .'

'Didn't you speak up and say you disagreed with him?'

'Oh, Angus was already saying something else . . .'

'True, he was talking a lot, but then when Sophie said that thing about the symbolism in the second text he obviously hadn't actually read it . . .'

The girls in this group could work on their proactivity and risk-taking in debate which would serve them well at a university interview, and the boys could consider doing the reading thoroughly in advance rather than winging it. The best of both worlds, perhaps, but there was a tacit understanding that neither they nor we would want to compromise and lose our prized independence.

Passionate though I am about girls' schools, necessary though I absolutely believe they are with the exhilarating experience they can give young women, it would be narrow-minded to say that all really good schools are single sex: excellence comes in many forms. When I look back at my time at Sha Tin College in Hong Kong, for example, where I taught English and Drama and had

huge fun directing plays and setting up the first sixth form, Sha
Tin was mixed, like most international schools, and I can't say
that the education of the girls was weakened by the presence of
the boys. The students there were mostly resilient, well-travelled
children used to their parents moving around the world and having
to adapt to new schools and make new friends quickly. It was a
school typical of its type: students and teachers on first-name
terms, no uniform, with a breezy, energetic and entrepreneurial
approach to life, much of which was lived outdoors. I remember
the students there as open, confident and well balanced. Perhaps
the more mature girls occasionally became frustrated with the
horsing around some of the boys did in play rehearsals, and how,
maddeningly, they didn't learn their lines until the last minute,
but there was much give and take. Since leaving headship and
working now in the international schools world, I have seen many
more examples of an empowering culture within mixed schools.

These schools thrive because, on the whole, they are populated
by modern, mobile families with wide horizons, amongst whom
it is not difficult to create pools of liberal and enlightened thinking.
A number have been founded by talented and bold female entrepreneurs, which in my post-headship life as an adviser, it has been
a wonderful privilege to get to know. But co-educational schools
at large are not changing the game in society for the next generation of women. In order to do that, and to ensure that young
women go out into the world ready and confident to take on the
challenges and inequities they still face, the case for girls having
the *opportunity* to be educated separately remains strong. Paulinas,
in those same formative years, are laying down foundations of
confidence about their intrinsic worth and ability which are not
being modulated or diluted, however unconsciously, by margin-
alising or stereotyped attitudes to women and girls, by being
photographed next to a boy who looks ahead as she looks at him,
by attitudes so deep-seated and long-standing that they soundlessly
permeate the very walls of the institution.

Taking a step back as an educator and looking at provision both nationally and internationally, I think the most important things of all are that there should be consistency of quality and diversity of choice for parents. No school deserves to continue just because it's a girls' school, if what it offers is not providing the best for the children. Schools that know what they are and what they do well, that are distinctive and coherent in their ethos and values, allow parents and children to make informed decisions for the future. That choice requires the schools to help by being very clear about what they are as well as what they are not, helping parents cut through any hearsay and mythology and see the school as clearly and truthfully as possible. As the October trees blew about on Brook Green, and with the elegant facade of the French school opposite becoming more visible as the brown leaves curled and fell, I would find myself looking out of the study window thinking through all this afresh, as I prepared to describe the culture of St Paul's to prospective parents. It was autumn and therefore the season when parents would be spending their Saturdays doing the rounds of the London schools: the first stage of the eleven-plus entry process that would take their children to new senior schools the following September.

Open days were very important to us, not simply because we needed to set out our stall and make sure there were going to be sufficient applicants of the right calibre for the hundred-plus places we would offer after the entrance exam in January (contrary to popular myth, St Paul's is by no means the most heavily oversubscribed school in London, perhaps partly as a result of its forbidding academic reputation) but also because with so much misinformation out there, we were on a mission to get the school properly understood.

Looking back, and perhaps ironically, I never felt it necessary to make a particular point about St Paul's being a girls' school. You surely felt the special power of confident but unparaded female capability the minute you stepped through the doors: the school in all its distinctive individuality largely spoke for itself, as all schools must do. At the same time I would try to explode some of the myths: we were not a hothouse where we were boiling up the girls to the highest temperature to pass exams – we were providing an exciting environment for learning, with teachers who were leaders in their field, still learning themselves; we were not negligent about the girls' happiness and well-being but put that at the heart of their education by getting to know them as individuals, encouraging independence while at the same time building a sense of community and mutual responsibility. Whatever your prejudices, I told them, leave those at the door and look at the school with fresh eyes so that you can make up your own mind.

Naturally enough, the school spoke most powerfully not through messages delivered by me, or by the senior staff, however carefully composed and genuinely meant, but simply through the personalities of the girls themselves: articulate, enthusiastic, confident, authentic and bubbling over with pride to show the visitors *their* school. Being a girls' school is simply one facet – albeit an important one – of the unique character of St Paul's and that is expressed most tellingly and persuasively through the individuals that shape and are shaped by it. I believe in parents and their children having choice and here, for the right girl, was one distinctive and compelling one, spread out to be looked at, to taste and wonder at, and if the affinity was really there, of which to become a part.

So, when parents asked me, as they often did, to help them weigh up the pros and cons of single-sex versus co-ed for their daughter, as if there was a right answer, I would encourage them to think not in binary terms but about the particular ethos of each of the schools they were considering. For any parent, choosing a school for your child feels a momentous decision. And although there will be many aspects which can be rationally assessed – academic standards, provision for sport or the creative arts, location, single sex or co-ed, size of school – the most important consideration of all is what I would call alignment of values. To put it simply, will you feel comfortable leaving your child in the care of those people all day (or all term, or for five to seven years?). Are their values your values? Does it *feel* right? Better sometimes to set aside the rational considerations, stop overthinking it and just listen to that simple gut instinct about whether you and the school to which you are thinking of entrusting your child see the world in the same way.

All that said, and while I believe that excellent education comes in many forms, there is still a vital, contemporary role for girls' schools. Caricaturing them in a sentimental way because they represent a certain tradition or because they evoke a kind of *Daisy Pulls It Off* nostalgia may be amusing but it obscures what they are there to achieve in today's world. They are important because they anticipate what we hope and believe will be the future for women: breathing the clear blue air of their capability without a thought to any limitation born of gender. So while the society into which young people emerge remains as unequal in its attitudes and opportunities as it still – sadly, shockingly – is, there will continue to be a role for girls' schools to *concentrate* on developing resilient, clever, capable young women to take on the pressure and change it. So far from their being an anachronism, in fact, it turns out that girls' schools are ahead of their time – the problem is that society isn't quite ready for the young women educated in them. There is an argument about adapting to the realities, and I am thoughtful when people say that girls need to get used to the 'real world' that is out there. But how long are we going to wait before the gender pay gap is closed, or the excellent work of the 30% Club is replaced by the achievements of the 50% Club? Schools are not there merely to prepare young people to conform to society: they are about the future. The role of schools is to shape change. I don't believe that learning to 'adapt' earlier – which all too often means learning how to play nicely, avoid appearing too clever, succeed by flirting and conform to male expectations of what you will be good at – is, in the long term, what girls should be doing.

Emerging from a culture as empowering for girls as St Paul's may be a shock. But I like it that Paulinas are shocked at what they find. They should be. If they are not being accorded equal treatment, taken advantage of as 'diligent' rather than brilliant by being given the dull but necessary work on which their male colleagues build their success (as one young alumna described her life at a well-known investment bank), balancing on their heels at the edge of the pub conversation about rugby and cars while the boys network their way to promotion, then I want them to be shocked. I want them not to be ready for that and I don't want them to adapt. I want their secure sense of self and their deep confidence in their own capability, developed brick-by-rose-coloured brick at school, to give them the courage and clarity to drive change.

But it's time to talk about the other 50 per cent of humanity – the men. I want to reassure the men reading this book (I hope you're out there still and haven't rushed off to do the online shop or finish the vacuuming) that the answer is certainly not to demonise the male sex and hold them generally responsible for all the inequalities that women face. I admit we indulged in some affectionate teasing behind closed doors at St Paul's – as I'm sure happened too at our expense across the river – but seriously, we have to guard against slipping into lazy caricature here. In our zeal to make society more equal, we women would do well to keep in mind that alienating men is not going to help us. There is a particular problem for the many enlightened men in the world who actually get all of this completely, because perhaps unavoidably they end up having to share responsibility for the legacy of prejudice and unfairness that women have faced for so long. But the result is that many of them, great modern sons, husbands and fathers who support and respect the women in their lives totally, need to feel they have a role and a voice. Why shut them out?

They can't help us if they are castigated for just being men. Driving the important changes must come through cooperation, with men and women acknowledging the issues and working together, not in opposition.

Which brings me to Dads4Daughters and why we launched an initiative at St Paul's to harness historic male advantage and make it work for us, and why the dads loved it.

A few years ago I became aware of the United Nation's campaign HeForShe through a powerful speech given by actress Emma Watson. HeForShe is a call to action for men and women and challenges one half of humanity – men – to get behind the inequalities of opportunity faced by women in society and unite with women to bring about change. This simple but crucial idea of unity rather than opposition struck me as having a very particular application in a girls' school where, often, young women are being endorsed and supported in their education by their fathers who have been part of the decision to send them there. Putting it simply, if you are the father of a clever daughter, you are certainly not going to choose St Paul's unless you believe in female empowerment. So snatching the term almost out of the air I chose my valedictory address to the leavers and their parents to launch our own version of the UN campaign, calling it Dads4Daughters.

We started by inviting fathers to write guest articles for our fortnightly newsletter about their view from the workplace and this produced an enthusiastic response. Through it we learned not just about the problems but about various very effective practices – for example reverse mentoring, where an older man is mentored by a less experienced, younger woman who is able to help him look critically at his behaviour towards female colleagues and call him out for evidence of bias that may be so ingrained that it's unconscious. She will check his use of language (grown-up women don't like being referred to as girls or being described as 'feisty'), his assumptions about gender roles (women are not automatically better at making tea or taking notes) and will help him see the world more clearly from the female perspective. The father who described this process called it 'the best professional development I have ever had'. Not because he was rampantly prejudiced – far from it – but because it made him so much more aware of his own behaviour.

The survey of our alumnae in the 25–35 age group produced the shocking finding that well over 75 per cent had encountered or been aware of workplace prejudice. At our launch event in school, we looked at the findings and heard the personal experiences of some of them as well as some fathers. It was wonderful to see how many fathers wanted to come into school for this event, with their daughters, and spend time talking about a matter of such importance to them both. This was a new alignment; fathers loved having a reason to spend time with their daughters, we found – we were tapping into something they really cared about.

Further, it was surprising to discover that many men who had become fathers had never been asked about it in their workplace and this cataclysmic event in a couple's life was seen as solely the experience – and the responsibility – of the mother. No one wondered if they had had enough sleep or needed some flexibility to assist with childcare. Becoming a dad just wasn't a thing. Dads4Daughters was morphing into Daughters4Dads – a new awareness of the role of the father in his daughter's life. By now we were also thinking much more broadly about parenthood and its value. It was listening to a talk by St Paul's alumna Annie Auerbach of the company Starling, who 'solve business problems through cultural insight', that I began to see how being a parent, far from undermining your ability to be a professional, could actually enhance it. Parents, Annie explained to the audience, leaning forward in her even, modern, graciously unassailable way, are not just resilient and adaptable; they have stamina, they are problem-solvers, they have patience, they are lateral-thinkers and they are expert in seeing things from someone else's point of view. Who wouldn't want these qualities in their boss or their subordinate? It's time we saw being a parent – whether father or mother – as something to be proud of, adding to our humanity and capability, adding to our professional value too, rather than something to apologise for or be silent about as if it had nothing to do with the people we are when we go to work.

The power of the intergenerational blood tie that Dads4Daughters unlocked is of course nothing new. I've since read a number of studies underlining the powerful effect that having daughters has on a man's decision-making at work. For example, Iris Bohnet in her book *What Works: Gender Equality by Design* cites a study showing that male CEOs with daughters are much more likely to promote women into higher levels of management. So there may still be a long way to go, but regardless of any formal initiative, fathers of daughters can lead the way in encouraging greater workplace equality. And what better place to start than the fathers of daughters at girls' schools? The answer has to be for men and women to work together on this: for men to use their influence to effect change and to make equality normal. It isn't a women's issue any more, it's an issue for society as a whole, and I feel very optimistic that the rising generation will get over the adversarial attitudes of the past and bring about real change.

Nothing stands still and the advent of new thinking about gender has made the debate more complex still: what about the future of girls' schools in a world where your gender is a matter of choice? Over a period of several months during 2017, as more and more articles appeared in the press telling the personal stories of individuals who had transitioned and giving accounts of students confronting nonplussed authorities about perceptions of gender, their right to adopt gender-neutral pronouns and their demand for gender-neutral bathrooms, it became clear that we had our own gender conversation emerging within the school. Although at that time the issue did not yet seem to be exercising schools all over the country (at the national conference for deputy head teachers the question was greeted with bewilderment by some colleagues), the London schools were seeing their own first cases of individuals either transitioning or requesting non-binary identities to be respected. This was an entirely new minefield for a school to navigate. Exploration of sexuality was one thing, and in a thoughtful, tolerant and liberal school, something which had long been acknowledged as a life issue and did not normally cause great difficulty if it needed to be discussed. The St Paul's students had their own (then) LGBT society whose meetings were advertised in morning assembly. But the concept of gender identity was something quite new. How to harness the natural appetite of bright students to discuss and debate the issue, to care for the needs of individuals with a genuine personal quest or dilemma and all that went with that in terms of family attitudes, how to steer a steady course within the realism of the law as it affected our status as a gender-specific school and how not to be derailed by a potential 'trans-trender' element who might see this as a new and exciting way to create turbulence and challenge the conservatism of an older generation? It was an interesting management challenge.

As with any emerging issue the most important thing was to get onto the front foot by initiating discussion with the students myself before the topic was brought to me. In consultation with the senior leadership team, we therefore identified a small group of senior students for whom this was a personal issue and with whom I was confident I could have a conversation that would not just be about them as individuals, but also about how we might shape wider policy on gender identity within the school. Staff too were beginning to express the need for guidance about how they should manage students who were asking to use a different name or pronoun, and nobody wanted to get this wrong. We needed a strategy. As so often, I was impressed at once by the thoughtfulness and maturity of this group of seventeen-year-olds and with the help of some legal advice to give clarity, over two or three meetings we drew up a gender identity protocol. The aim was to provide a framework for discussion where an individual expressed a desire to adopt a different gender identity, setting out the responsibilities of the school to respect the welfare and needs of the individual, while managing expectations in terms of what was formally possible: exam entries, for example, would be made in the registered name of the student rather than the adopted name. The key provision, however, was that a student over sixteen who was deemed to have sufficient self-knowledge and maturity and for whom the request could be shown to have some endurance could, after consultation (including with parents, though the students were initially reluctant about this), be recognised as having a different or non-binary gender within the school.

I was aware at the time that we were dealing with a topic of public significance where policy would move quickly as case law developed, and we would need to revisit our protocol before long to keep in step. This was only a starting point. It was also apparent that this issue had the potential to give rise to another beautiful and unique St Paul's fudge: just as we had a secular foundation while much enjoying singing hymns, so we would be a girls' school while accommodating some senior students who would never dream of changing school (perish the thought!) but who no longer wanted to be thought of as girls. At the time our protocol was published, we were hailed as having done something revolutionary in bringing gender identity to the surface and allowing gender choice. But it was much simpler than that: we had just enlisted the support of the students to tackle a new issue on which they were well informed and thus, with the contemporary perspective and longer experience combined, created a policy. There is no knowing what my own headmistress would have thought about gender identity, though I remembered how over a much less significant issue some forty years earlier, she had taught me the importance of listening to your students, taking them seriously and giving real value to their opinions. Of course, the possibility of this highly personal and sensitive subject being raised and discussed in a mature way depended on trust and respect. I firmly believe that it was our particular character of openness as a girls' school that made this potentially difficult conversation possible.

Half a millennium has passed since John Colet founded his school. Now his descendants, the Paulines and Paulinas, are preparing to go out into a world he could not have imagined. But the confidence and love of learning they take with them, their determination to fulfil their potential whatever the challenges, are qualities he would surely have wanted to encourage. His legacy lives on in them. Throughout the school, as I've been writing, the autumn term has been unfolding. Six or seven weeks have taken us well into the syllabuses for each academic subject, homework has been rolling in, society meetings have been happening accompanied by quantities of tea and cake, plays and concerts are in rehearsal and the results from hard-fought netball and lacrosse matches are being heralded. Probably there has been the odd behavioural incident and it is already clear which pupil (or parent) files are going to finish up on the bulky side by the end of the year. In a London school, the sense of the seasons is less strong, but it is still there – the evenings drawing in a little and the afternoon air smoky, even if from the remembered bonfires of childhood. Bowling along at full tilt, everyone is glad to reach the two-week October half term. What's the difference between a two-week half term and a three-week school holiday, for example at Christmas? Answer: one week. And in this way, we have effectively by stealth introduced the four-term year, with the result that having had a proper break, there are fewer coughs and colds in November and December and we can normally get through the Christmas musical events without a mass epidemic of throat infections. I spend one week catching up, and the second away getting some country air with my family in Somerset, where there might even be an apple or two left to pick up.

With the best leaders
When the work is done
The task accomplishe
The people will say,
We have done this ours

– Lau Tsu, 8th centur
  Chinese poet

Our research suggests that if a le
is not 'in flow' he or she – like an
else – will not be able to make se
the ambiguities, interconnection:
unpredictabilities of their role, so
struggle to make robust decisions
– this is a key leadership element
or she will be far less able to prov
the conditions in which others ca
use their judgement wisely to sus
the resilience of the organization

Gillian Stamp, BIOSS, 'The Four
Journeys of the Leader'

The head's role according to children in
some GSA junior departments:

The head is someone who

– Writes letters and looks after everybody
– Arranges the food at harvest festival
– Gives people stickers
– Is very busy having meetings
– Drinks a lot of coffee and eats
  chocolate biscuits with visitors
– Picks up litter

A leader is a person who has an unusual
degree of power to project onto other
people his or her shadow or his or her
light ... A leader is a person who must
take special responsibility for what
is going on inside him or herself

– Parker J Palmer

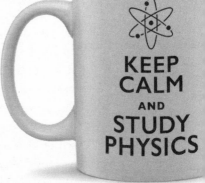

CHAPTER 3

November

Headship – opening up the path on which the next generation will travel

The second half of the autumn term began for me with the annual residential conference for head teachers. Roller cases packed, determined headmistresses would set off to different parts of the country: I have compared the Bayliss & Harding bathroom products in Buxton and Brighton, Bristol and Birmingham. Imagine 200 headmistresses confined for three days to an air-conditioned hotel – the brisk competence, the curbing of instincts to say 'shush!' and take control, the sidelong glances at each other's outfits. And what was going on in the schools they were supposed to be running? I wished my senior management team an enjoyable few days and caught the train, knowing they would appreciate the freedom – after all, why develop people's leadership skills if you're not going to trust them? I just had to promise not to come back with too many bright ideas for them to listen to patiently – a sudden whim to do away with bells, perhaps, or a scheme to buy a field-study centre in north Wales . . .

As I picture myself on that train journey, slanting November rain spattering the windows, the image of a certain familiar and bespectacled headmistress from the 1970s reappears, smiling quizzically before me. She is the headmistress of Sunny Hill, the romantically and improbably named Desirée Fawcus Cumberlege, *my* headmistress: Dizzy. Born in India in 1919, a cross between Maggie Smith and Joyce Grenfell, she would tiptoe along the polished parquet corridors of Sunny Hill in fully fashioned stockings and kitten heels, dizzily occupying some higher realm, her academic gown, worn over pastel tweeds, floating out behind her like sails. Her hair was always disciplined into a silvery permanent wave and her winged glasses, sitting at a slight tilt, gave her a faintly surprised look. Like many of her generation she appeared to live entirely for her work: there was no Mr Cumberlege, though we invented for her a tragic past and a dark, dashing officer fiancé, who had (ah! poor Dizzy!) been lost over the Channel in the war. He may even have existed – we embellished him regardless and the lonely life we supposed her to have led since. A distant figure, Dizzy rarely spoke to us except to address her pupils in assembly: 'Let me make it clear, girls: there are to be no more non-regulation shoes seen, otherwise we will all wear sensible, lace-up "Rosamund"!' But I do remember one thrilling afternoon when my friend Avril and I were invited to go with her to tea at the house of an elderly former pupil. It was for me an unconscious lesson in leadership that I would remember years later.

The invitation arose because of my bossiness. It was the summer term and we had been asked as pupils to make recommendations for the award of the Radford Award, bestowed annually on a pupil in our form who had shown the most public-spirited attitude during the school year. A benefactor nowadays would know better than to lay themselves open to the risks of litigation inherent in this gesture, but in those days it was genuinely thought that the girls could simply exercise their good judgement and choose appropriately – such simple times we lived in then. When success fell on the most popular girl in our class, admired for her smooth brown hair, permanent golden tan and exotic elephant-hair bracelets bought at home in Kenya, I felt it right to make a democratic stand and insist that, the next year, proper criteria were drawn up to ensure that this was not merely a popularity vote. No doubt I was motivated largely by envy at not being chosen myself, but Miss Cumberlege (she had met girls before who wanted to advise her on how to run the school) brightly suggested we should put this idea to Miss Radford, our benefactor, who duly invited us to tea in her garden.

Accompanied by Avril, a compact, hockey-playing girl with a straight black fringe sitting above an equally straight nose, I waited on the appointed afternoon outside a dark wooden hut we knew to be Miss Cumberlege's garage. Neither of us had ever seen what was inside the garage, suspecting it to contain agile spiders and perhaps a broken-down lawnmower, but when the headmistress arrived, dressed for the occasion in a silk headscarf and looking very slightly like a primmer Grace Kelly, the doors opened to reveal the back of a very clean, pale blue Ford Anglia. This remark-ably slim car with its upturned tail lights reminiscent of its owner's glasses was clearly Miss Cumberlege's prized possession, neatly parked in the tiny garage like a model in its matchwood box.

Avril and I waited. Miss Cumberlege squeezed herself behind the wheel and backed expertly out. We climbed in and were soon bowling down the Somerset lanes, the huge cow parsley stems in the summer hedgerows parting as we passed, like the palm trees on Thunderbirds Tracy Island. We felt free as air. I have no recol-lection now of the outcome of our conversation with Miss Radford, though the old lady seemed delighted at this impromptu tea party with young visitors from her dimly remembered school. Sitting in the wild country garden with its gnarled apple trees, where lazy wasps knocked against our glasses of homemade lemonade, she served us large slices of seed cake, and ever since I have associated the taste of caraway with grandmotherly baking and with being on your best behaviour with older people. For us, the adventure lay in the fact that, contrary to our belief, Miss Cumberlege was actually a real person: she did *not* cease to exist when outside the school gates. Perhaps when the term ended, she got into the Ford

Anglia and went far away from Sunny Hill to a home somewhere, where there was another small garage and a mantelpiece with a silver-framed photograph of a darkly handsome man. Who knew? It was from this afternoon adventure that I understood long afterwards the importance of taking the challenges and opinions of young people seriously, being seen to do so, and giving them time. I was satisfied aged twelve that I had been listened to and my point considered carefully. I don't remember what happened subsequently about the awarding of the cup – somehow it didn't seem to matter anymore.

A creature far removed from us in age, dress sense and attitudes, Dizzy was not a figure who had a major impact on our lives at the time; besides, we saw too little of her. How I should love to be able to sit over teacups and ask her about her job, and her life, now that I've spent over twenty years treading in her unlikely footsteps. How much of her world and mine would be similar? How much has irrevocably changed?

A little light was shed on this question while I was casting around one Friday afternoon for assembly material. I opened a slim book of essays left on a shelf by my predecessor, called, with studied decorum, *The Headmistress Speaks*. Originally published in 1937, with contributors as redoubtable as Mary G. Clarke, head of Manchester High School, and Edith Ironside, head of Sunderland High, the words called up for me the spirit and tone of Dizzy herself. But some sounded strangely modern. It was a shock that Ethel Strudwick, for example, appointed High Mistress of St Paul's in 1927, could write with candour and empathy: 'School has come to mean something very much warmer, closer and more home-like than it was in earlier days, and the relation between teacher and taught is friendlier, freer and more natural.'[1] I don't know whether Miss Strudwick embodied this freedom or warmth herself: her portrait hanging in the Great Hall rather suggests not. The aspiration is striking, however, in its informality and recognition of the importance of relationships based not entirely on authority. And Miss Clarke of Manchester, writing about the life of a head, says simply: 'For the headmistress herself, there is also the personal problem of reconciling the claims of an exacting and unleisured profession, with her own functions and development as a woman.'[2]

Headship still is exacting and unleisured – some might say remorseless. But these two women acknowledge that for all that, the quality of humanity is absolutely central: both in being able to create a sense of community for those within the school, as well as at the same time paying attention to your own identity and growth as a person, so that you bring to the job, and preserve within it, an authentic humanity of your own – expressed in your distinct character and personality. Their words remind me that inside every headmistress – and headmaster – under the sometimes heavy mantle of authority, there is a living person following a unique path of development, separate from, yet inextricably connected to, that professional persona.

There are a thousand ways to think about headship and as many ways of doing it well as there are heads. The wisest know they are not good at everything and gather around themselves colleagues who complement, rather than replicate, their particular skills. It is this human dimension which I have found the most rewarding and the most challenging aspect of the job, and which made the prescient words of Miss Clark and Miss Strudwick resonate with me.

When you join a new school as the head, it's a bit like boarding a moving train. Nothing stops for you: clambering on, you haul up your suitcase, steady your balance and, moving up through the carriages as best you can, find your way to the driver's seat. Meanwhile the life of the school and its journey into the future continue and you must learn about them and how you want to steer the train while it hurtles along. You may be the one steering, but you can't achieve much unless you bring everyone along with you – and that means building effective relationships.

Settling in involves watching and listening. Especially you have to understand the mood and climate of the staff and to find out what they are used to. It takes time to work out the exact shape of the hole your predecessor left. In my first week at St Paul's, I would wander into the staff common room at morning break – usually a rather pressured fifteen minutes where everyone is jostling to get a quick coffee or catch a colleague before going off to teach their next lesson. One particular morning, as I was spooning instant coffee into a mug emblazoned with the slogan 'Keep Calm and Carry On', the head of science came up to me and said, 'Nice to see you in here. We don't normally see the high mistress in the staffroom.' A small point perhaps, but this gave me a hint about the relationship my predecessor had had with her colleagues and therefore what they might be expecting. My style would be more informal – they were sensing that – and while they didn't altogether mind, they might take time to get used to it. Similarly, when it came to my first heads of department meeting, the director of studies explained that normally those attending the meeting would assemble and then the high mistress would be collected from her office and escorted to join them. Grateful for the heads-up, I suggested a less ceremonial approach, choosing to be in the room first rather than last, so I could catch one or two people before the meeting and help things begin with the idea that we were coming together to think and confer, rather than that I was arriving to preside. So, by gradual steps, I established my own way of doing things and we adapted to one another in a natural and unforced way.

Small details like this accumulate and are the start of making relationships, winning the trust and confidence of the staff. They are a group, so you engage with them both en masse and also as a collection of individuals. Before taking up my post, I took the advice of a wise former head and learned the names of everyone on the staff from a set of photographs. So much more reassuring to be able to address people by name at once and start forging a working alliance from day one, minimising the sense that because you are a newcomer everyone has to start at the beginning for you. Then there is navigating the uncharted waters of the staffroom. There, a unique dynamic prevails, with professional and friendship groupings a new head needs to assimilate and read, listening, observing, absorbing. Here will be laid out the lines of loyalty and tension that may come to the surface at times of crisis or controversy: the more you know and understand of people's personalities, priorities and preferences, the more you are able to anticipate and manage reactions in the moment. And because the staffroom or common room is where people relax, it's not just words but also body language that can be revealing: the small group who always sit together lounging on a particular sofa, swiftly dispatching the *Times* crossword and sharing familiar humour; the science teacher who checks his pigeonhole meticulously but never sits down and rarely speaks to anyone; those two modern linguists sympathising with one another over mugs of tea in the far corner . . . If you have an interest in people, reading all of this is not only fascinating but an absolutely necessary part of forging a team: the staff gradually get to see, know and accept you, and you develop a fuller understanding of them.

Getting to know people and recognising their talents are amongst the most important and underrated aspects of good leadership, laying the foundation for those around you to feel happy in their work. To enjoy what they do, people need to be in balance: with their capability stretched enough to feel stimulated but not so overstretched that they are always stressed. When we talk to young people about their future careers, we often encourage them to 'look for the hobby in the job' – to find the thing that is so natural to them, that they enjoy so much, it doesn't feel like work at all. As workplaces, schools are highly reliant on achieving this because so much is done within the now old-fashioned-sounding concept of 'goodwill' – doing things that you are not strictly being paid for because you are well disposed towards the institution, feel well rewarded and are willing to give your time without counting it too closely. You might be taking a group of students to the theatre in the evening, or accompanying a camping expedition over a weekend, or even taking a school party to Rome in the Easter holidays; it's all part of the job and you give up your own time to do it normally without extra pay. Most teachers' contracts still enshrine this idea, referring to 'any other duties that the head teacher may deem reasonable', leaving open the exact number of hours you will actually work or the exact nature of your duties during those hours. Anathema no doubt to professionals who charge their time in six-minute units, this is all about the traditional give and take of schools, and what helps them feel more like communities than corporations. While it's one thing to contract people to work in this way, it's another thing to cause them to do it with genuine willingness and enjoyment. For this to happen, the overall culture of the community has to be a happy positive one where teachers feel valued and appreciated and where there is a high degree of job satisfaction. But with life in a school so very busy, with always a sense of urgency and more to do than there is strictly time for, how do you bring this about? There is no quick, obvious solution here because ethos and culture have to be worked at constantly, but part of the answer lies in getting the balance right between treating people as individuals while building a sense of corporate spirit.

Because I can now hear her words echoing through mine, I must now introduce Gillian Stamp. Gillian has been easily the most important influence in my development as a leader; she is now a dear friend and was, for the second half of my headship at St Paul's, my revered and trusted mentor. Without Gillian, with her long experience of working with leaders in many sectors across the world through BIOSS, the foundation of which she is a director, few of the ways I now think about leadership would have become so clear to me. The philosophy behind BIOSS (the Brunel Institute of Organisation and Social Studies) is simply that for long-term sustainability, all organisations, whatever their nature, need to design themselves to make the most of what is best in human character while minimising those impulses which are destructive. And this is not just so that we contribute to human happiness and flourishing, but so that organisations can succeed. Where there is a lack of motivation because people feel anxious, frustrated or undervalued, an organisation may be profitable in the short term, but over time, cannot achieve its purpose. In a nutshell, to quote BIOSS: 'In an organisation that induces confidence and respect, people work together in ways that strengthen bonds of mutual trust and fairness, enhance imagination and innovation, and ensure competence; thus the organisation achieves its purposes and contributes to the wider society.'[3]

I would often arrive at Gillian's quiet house having rushed from meetings, feeling overwhelmed by the multiplicity of challenges and unsure how to seek her help. Our conversations, which invariably clarified my thinking, would almost always revolve around some aspect of developing human capability – making the most of the constructive aspects of human nature – as the key to achieving success in whatever matter it was I was facing at the time. When we talked about working with individual colleagues, she would remind me of the adage: 'How can I know what I think until I see what I say,' helping me see that people often don't need advice so much as space to bring what they already know to the surface of their minds. This is what I often found myself doing while sitting in Gillian's peaceful sitting room, with its seascapes on the walls and with her still, serene presence framed against the light from her garden, offering encouraging prompts.

Unsurprisingly, given that focus on developing human capability, one of the great pleasures of headship for me has been derived from time spent with individual colleagues, helping them think through their work, their aptitudes and their ambitions. I wasn't so much advising them, more just actively listening, perhaps offering a few prompts of my own, as the person thought aloud about what they enjoyed and what they wanted to do – talking about the obstacles and then talking them away. Often much was tangentially revealed about what drove that individual, what made them happy, what bothered them. Sometimes the person would leave my room with newly focussed ambition; sometimes it was a matter of giving themselves permission not to chase the conventional promotion route that they thought they ought to want, and instead think about a lateral route that was much more suited to them: the head of department, for instance, who recognised that they did not enjoy management and wanted to devote themselves instead to teaching and research. Over time, I came to know many colleagues well in this way.

Building a happy, collegiate staff team also means speaking with the staff as a group, painting in words a picture of the school that you are making together using the more expansive, public voice rather than the understated private one. This is when the leader is out in front, casting their light, creating unity and a clear sense of shared purpose. Those leaders called 'inspirational' are at their best at these moments, though not all occasions for leading one-on-many have to be formal. For example, we would hold a short staff briefing each Friday morning, which became something of a ritual marking the end of the week. It had a practical purpose: the timely sharing of information and the all-important thanking of individuals, but it was also an opportunity to bring the working week to a close together with everyone in Friday mood.

There was something of the comic serial about these briefings which left people feeling well disposed having enjoyed the repartee. Visitors would often be surprised by the relaxed friendliness and shared dry amusement or mutual teasing that was the norm. Much can be achieved through humour, if it comes naturally; every common room has its own style – another thing to listen for and become a part of as the community moulds itself to you. And as well as the capacity for ready laughter, modelling simple good manners and a considerate attitude is a vital habit heads must develop. Thanking people for what they do genuinely and often is always appreciated and while the private word is important, public acknowledgement matters too. It's hard to overstate the importance of catching people doing things right and showing appreciation – a much better use of time than catching people doing things wrong because, quite often, it leads to the things which are not so good going away or solving themselves. Of course there are sometimes difficult, even shocking messages to convey. But regardless of the circumstances, the leader must herself exude a relentless positivity and optimism, to carry the community in hope and confidence into the future, whatever the challenges. Everyone looks to that person to paint a picture of how things will be, to tell the story, and for each person to know their role in that. This is how you build commitment and enthusiasm for what the team will do together, energising everyone to throw themselves into it wholeheartedly. Fortunately, in a school full of young people looking to the future, optimism normally comes easily.

But there is more to leadership than just keeping everyone happy, though that is absorbing enough. However collegiate, listening and consultative a culture you have, a leader must be able to make decisions, sometimes difficult ones: a strong community is one that feels energised but also secure. A vacillating leader makes people nervous and is not respected, however good they are at consulting and listening to all sides. However flat the management structure, there will be times when, standing alone on the mountain top, visible to others sheltering below, the leader chooses the path forward out of the difficult terrain. How can you both be decisive and at the same time take people with you? Consultation is important, even if people tend only to value (even remember) that they were consulted when they get the outcome they want. When the decision goes against them, they tend to forget that they were asked what they thought and 'senior management stitch-up' mutters its way around the building.

Achieving good decisions through consultation means knowing not just who to ask (which constituencies will be affected?) but what exactly to ask them (frame it as an open question or as a choice between alternatives?), how long to take (when do we need to achieve a decision?), and how to manage expectations (when will a decision be taken and an outcome communicated?). I was involved in a complex consultation recently as adviser to an international school, revisiting its accreditation with the Council of International Schools. In revising the guiding statements on vision, mission and values, a selected group of about thirty staff, parents and pupils spent a whole day taking apart and recreating these statements. There was much use of chunky marker pens and flipchart paper before the hard-working headmaster and his dedicated colleague took it all away to distil. The newly minted statements would then go to the wider community, eventually emerging for board approval. At first this seemed to me an unnecessarily convoluted way to reach decisions which a group of four people could have arrived at in half an hour. But there was another purpose in it. Grouped around tables, we thought together about the school as a subject of shared interest and by the end, felt that our words actually counted, even if in the final translation, they had been superseded by others. The benefit was building community engagement, which was valuable in itself regardless of the outcome.

In a thinking, listening school where pupils and staff are used to being encouraged to voice opinions, as the head you are much less likely to misjudge the mood when it counts because you will be tuning into it on a daily basis. It's a constant process because you make it a habit. By going into the staffroom, I would pick up on conversation and sense the things that were bothering people. Similarly, by walking about the school and talking with groups of girls in corridors or classrooms, I could do the same. The members of the head-girl team with an ear to the ground were always frank when I wanted to know how the school felt about – for example – a slight change to the timing of the end of the school day. (Not happy! They would miss the 4.20 tube at Hammersmith and have to wait half an hour), or changing the school logo (very unhappy indeed – but more on that later). And there are always certain subjects on which you would never achieve agreement, however many people you asked. How to decide whether school exams are better the week before the summer half term, allowing the girls to get a proper break, or the week after, giving them time to revise? We could never agree and tended to seesaw between the two. As for the school lunch menus, especially pudding – fruit for better health, or crumble and custard for greater satisfaction – if you don't want to spend all term talking about it, offer both.

The requirement to be decisive first came home to me at Queenswood. In my first weeks of headship I was asked one morning whether we could spend £1,300 on some gym mats that the PE department suddenly wanted. That's a lot of money, I thought. What if someone else wants £1,300 for something more important? How on earth do I decide that *right now*? Surely they should have budgeted for that at the start of the year? Then the rain had got in and soaked the old ones, and there was a display for parents the following week . . . my mind raced over the issues. I'll ring up the bursar, I thought. But he was away at a conference all day. It dawned on me that I'd have to decide myself. The head of department was soundlessly sighing in the doorway. With a sense of reckless astonishment at my own temerity, I agreed it. There. She went off down the corridor, no doubt already thinking about something else. I would go on to make many, many decisions about matters much more significant than gym mats – whether to move to the International Baccalaureate and give up offering A levels, whether to require all girls to take three sciences for GCSE, whether to buy a building that came up for sale nearby, whether to extend the school day, whether to create an exchange with a school in Argentina, whether to cancel the contract with the catering company, whether to close the school early because of the threat of snow – and so on, endlessly every day. In each case, just like that first one, there might have been discussion or research first, but in the end, while I knew some of the pros and cons, could foresee some of the consequences, I didn't – couldn't – know everything. I just had to use my judgement and decide.

Fortunately, decision-making is like public speaking in that the more you have to do it, the calmer and clearer you get. Today all organisations are operating in times of increasing uncertainty – geopolitically, environmentally, economically, technologically. What will the school of 2060 look like? We can speculate about how remote learning, the potential of artificial intelligence or the changing nature of cities and patterns of work will change the way schools work, or even perhaps lead to their extinction, but in practice we have little idea, except that it will be radically different. As a leader having to take decisions means having to be comfortable with some degree of uncertainty yourself, as well as providing reassurance and clarity about the direction of travel for others. It's a fine balance plotting the short and mid-term steps an organisation will take – next year, the next five years – while keeping in mind that longer and largely unknowable trajectory. Leaders who listen, who constantly ground their decisions in the core values and purpose of the organisation, who talk about 'we' not 'I', who are authentic and truthful, are more likely to win trust and confidence to weather the difficult times and manage the unknown than those who adopt a blinkered optimism or seek to shield their colleagues by keeping them in the dark.

And then there is the question of timing: judging not just whether to do something, but when to do it and when to tell people. Managing information flow in a school involves thinking about the different audiences – the pupils, the trustees or governors, the staff, the parents. Controlling it is also a great deal harder now that almost everyone has their own hand-held device and can inform whoever else they like (or be informed) instantly. I remember sitting at my desk one day and receiving a panicked call from a mother, saying that after speaking to her daughter she thought the girls away on the Spanish exchange might be at risk from a terrorist attack. It turned out that some of the exchange pupils had a room facing a wall in the town square where a group supporting ETA had pinned up a small poster. The accompanying teacher who patiently explained matters over the phone to me had just pacified a different mother, who had called him complaining about the food the girls were eating. Her daughter had apparently rung home to report a slug in her lettuce. Major news that affects the whole community, the departure or arrival of a new head for example, is particularly sensitive. There was recently a change of leadership in a school I've been advising where, despite good planning, we had to deal with angry parents who had picked up an hour too soon on social media that the much-loved head was departing. This had happened because his arrival in the school where he was taking over as head had been announced fractionally earlier. The ubiquity of technology often means that we may rush to communicate too quickly because of the fear of information escaping in the wrong way. But there is still judgement to be exercised about the readiness of people to hear something, or the manner of it. And let's not forget pitching the timing of good news to have maximum impact: I can still hear the Great Hall reverberating with the assembly announcement at the end of a gruelling term that the forthcoming musical would be . . . *The Sound of Music*! Yes! Sometimes you are dropping a stone into a pool of water, choosing your moment to minimise the ripples. But sometimes you want to make a great, big, glorious splash.

Leadership involves shaping community but can also be lonely. The head must not depend on constant feedback or encouragement – at the annual conference we all agreed on that – but equally, no one could do it without the support of a strong leadership team. And if there is to be a supply of people who want to be heads in the future, it's doubly important to develop the leadership ability of others. Most schools, just like other organisations, are run with flatter structures, more emphasis on shared responsibility and empowerment with less left solely in the hands of the head. The nature of delegation has changed. When I became Principal of Queenswood over twenty years ago, I remember being advised by an elderly and much-revered predecessor where I should sit in the chapel. As I was about to sit down at the end of the well-worn wooden pew, shiny as a conker, I recalled her words: 'No, not there. You sit in the second seat in, with your deputy next to you on the outside, so that she can do any running around.' This was my first tutorial in delegation: you had a deputy, and she ran around, while I did – what? Sat and surveyed the scene, conveying dignified authority? Prayed? Wrote a speech in my head? No, I kept still. This was what was expected of the Principal and this is what she would do. While working with the leadership team came to mean for me something rather more interactive, keeping still, I came to learn, is one of the hardest and most underrated skills of the leader.

A particular reward of headship has been working with outstanding colleagues in the senior teams I have either inherited or developed, and I feel lasting gratitude to all of them. We worked very hard, but we learned a lot together and had some great times. I learned early that as a leader you should always appoint people whose talents are different from yours (as well as often superior) and who may challenge you. I therefore feel doubly privileged to have known the stimulation and equilibrium of a talented, well-balanced team, working together and somehow producing results which are more than the sum of the parts.

What might such a team look like? It has to be diverse yet aligned. It's dangerous to appoint in your own image because this tends to promote an introspective groupthink that comes from people approaching things too similarly – many traditional schools fall into this trap. Best to gather together individuals whose talents and personalities are different but complementary, who share respect for each other's abilities without jealousy of each other's responsibilities and who are committed to the mission of the school.

First, that means knowing what you are like yourself and what your own strengths and limitations are. For example, while I like public speaking, no one would accuse me of being good at spotting errors in documents – amongst other things, I need people with an eye for detail. It isn't the work of a moment to put such a team together. As a head you are never starting from a blank sheet (unless building a school from scratch). So it's a matter of identifying where the gaps lie in expertise or temperament, grafting each new person onto your team as carefully as you can, recognising what they bring that is fresh, and gradually coaching them in the culture and values of your existing team which, for the most part, the others in the team, their peers, will do for you. Every team needs its completer-finishers, its creative minds, those with the kind of Exocet brains that love data and detail, those who are gregarious and skilled with people, the listeners, the enforcers and so on. Most talented people have a constellation of strengths and anyone destined for headship knows that they will need to work on being versatile; doing what comes naturally (in my case sitting in the study thinking and writing or talking to one person) and practising what is more effortful (for me, working the room at a large social event).

The resulting strong axes within the team, the mutual recognition of talent and the respect that comes from it, not forgetting the value of the occasional maverick prepared to be the challenging grit in the oyster, are what leads to effective collaborative work. If you believe in genuine delegation where people are working independently much of the time, the team isn't necessarily physically together all that much, except in formal meetings: you have to work at the collegiality with the staff as a whole. I have never been one for those raft-building exercises, or days spent swinging through the forest canopy with imaginary crocodiles snapping their jaws below, any more than I am one for sitting cross-legged together in low lighting listening to whale song. There have to be more grown-up ways of building team cohesion. There is every reason to relax together (usually we would do this by going out to a good lunch) but there are no shortcuts to developing true team spirit and in my experience, coming together to manage something really difficult – and real – is far more effective than any fashionable and expensive leadership course. My teams grew closer in times of crisis. Essential too in any team but much underrated is a highly developed sense of humour: so much can be navigated and kept in perspective where there is a humane but sharp sense of the absurd and in the intense atmosphere of a high-achieving school – this can be a vital safety valve.

Somewhat allied to my earlier point about timing is the question of pace within the team – the personal pace you set yourself and the natural pace of those around you. Judging and combining varying habits of pace is one of the skills of working together successfully. There will be some in your team who are extremely cautious about implementing an idea – they want to check it for every possible glitch first, they want to avoid any difficult conversations and well, if it isn't broken maybe we don't need to fix it. These people tend to speak more slowly and will literally slow things down, which may be an excellent way of avoiding disaster or may create frustration. Then there are the 'no time like the present' people, who want to rush out of the room and implement their idea at once. They may get bored and lose interest if their idea does not win instant approval. But never mind, because they will soon have another one. Modulating the preferred pace of a diverse team is the job of the head and an interesting challenge in meetings, where it's important to keep everyone focussed and get an outcome that all can support. You might hear a conversation like this:

A: I think the tutor sets are too large – tutors can't get to know every girl. Let's cut each group in half in September – that way they'll get more individual attention – cut them down to twelve.

B: Err . . . I'm thinking that will mean all heads of department will have to become tutors, or we won't have enough.

A: Fine! Time they took an interest in pastoral care. And we can take one teaching period off each of them to make up for it. Easy.

B: Right. I'll need to work out what the cumulative cost of that will be. Let's see . . . Possibly another half a teacher . . .

A: Sounds manageable. Shall I put it in next week's bulletin then?

B: I think perhaps we should do some consultation amongst the staff first. You know, good to keep everyone on board . . . And we need to watch the staffing budget . . .

A: Oh come on . . . Don't contracts say we can expect teachers to do anything 'within reason'? This is within reason isn't it?

(Sound of bell)

B: Ah. there's the bell. Look, this is a really interesting idea. Let's come back to it at the next meeting – and maybe share any thoughts we all have over email in the meantime?

You may have a wonderful sense of team spirit, but able and creative people with an appetite for leadership also want to exercise their abilities with relative freedom. The modern deputy head is not satisfied with 'running around' but expects – needs – to have a sphere of action which is independent. How does the head provide for this while still offering guidance and support?

This is another subject Gillian Stamp and I would discuss at length, as I tried to find this balance and as new colleagues arrived to join my team and I thought about how best to integrate them. With her natural predilection for horticultural metaphors, Gillian would talk about the triple process of tasking, trusting and tending. So first, you must task: this means to make clear what it is you wish a person to do, or the areas of responsibility you are delegating to them. This is the task. Within the senior team of a school, as well as encouraging collaborating on the overall strategy, each individual will have a special sphere of influence and responsibility of their own. This must be defined so that there is no doubt about where they should place their energies: who leads on the curriculum, pastoral care, finance, buildings and premises, marketing, the sixth form etc. Once the tasking is established, you bestow trust – perhaps the most difficult of the three stages. This means stepping back and waiting – allowing them to get on with the matter in hand in their own way and at their own pace. You'd be surprised how difficult many leaders find this. Still secretly thinking they could do a thing better, or quicker, themselves, they immediately start interfering or doubling up so that the newly tasked colleague is frustrated, loses belief in their own abilities and their own growth and confidence are slowed down. You may remember my apparent negligence when leaving for the heads' annual conference. There was method in it: this was trusting. When you have delegated something you must *leave it alone*. Leave it alone, even if this means the thing is done less well, less quickly, or in a different way from that which you originally intended or would have done it yourself. You may well learn something: on many occasions, I've helped a colleague think through how to respond to a complaint from a parent, for example, and on following up, found they have achieved a resolution in a manner that I would not have thought of.

Then comes the tending, which means the gentle, not invasive but steady continuation of interest and guidance, to augment, challenge, quicken, soften, focus, make more spare or more detailed, which helps consolidate the other's confidence and leads them on to satisfaction in being able to exercise judgement and make independent decisions. In this way, through being tasked, trusted and tended, new leaders develop their own capability. You are not imposing your style (though they will learn from watching each other and you) but each person develops their own ways of working. Then as a team, you are stronger through the diversity of approaches and everyone is able to hone their own unique contribution. The modern head surrounds herself with a trusted team so that she can truly empower others, freeing herself to give as much personal time as possible to individuals while also paying attention to strategy and the big picture.

Where strategy is concerned, ultimate responsibility sits with the non-executive directors or governors, most of whom will not be specialists in education but who bring other skills and experience to the table. Especially they bring their commitment to and belief in the success of the school. This is another key group with whom the head must forge an effective relationship, just as the CEO must do with the board of a company. In the commercial world, the spotlight has been trained frequently in recent years on the shortcomings of corporate governance, citing poor decision-making, lack of foresight and groupthink leading to some catastrophic outcomes. Board leadership and board dynamics are, rightly, now under keener scrutiny. The governors of a modern school who are also charity trustees (the case in the majority of independent schools) carry responsibilities no less weighty. They are held to exacting standards of legal compliance and expected to be increasingly vigilant in all matters of policy, in particular the safeguarding of children. In a world of obsessive anxiety and well-intentioned but increasingly nervous legislation about such matters as child protection, internet safety and religious radicalisation, being a governor is no longer a matter of turning up three times a year to a meeting and a special lunch. As well as planning strategy in uncertain times, governors must be visible in the school, watching classes, looking into corners, checking that policy is being followed. The demands are greater and the long-accepted distinction that governors should be 'eyes on, hands off' – appointing an executive team and holding them to account while not doing the job for them – is becoming blurred.

All this provides new challenges for the head, as CEO, who must contribute to strategy and provide the governors with the right kind of information, while helping them discharge their burgeoning duties as efficiently as possible without encroaching on the smooth running of the school. Where there is mutual respect and relationships are good, the leadership of a school can be enormously enriched by the collective wisdom of a governing body which brings together expertise from other sectors. Extracting the benefit of this, while making sure that governors feel their time has been well spent and appreciated, is something for the head and the chair of the board to work at together. With governance taking up more and more time and imposing more exacting demands, how long will anyone actually want to go on doing this and, in rapidly changing times, can the stately pace of decision-making enshrined in the formal termly meeting cycle actually work? And with the educational landscape evolving, technology playing a larger part, will a governing board not need much more age diversity as well and diversity in other forms than is typically the case? As we look to the schools of the future, the best model for agile, challenging and effective governance needs to be part of our thinking.

But of all those for whom the head must be the leader, the relationships with pupils are the most central. In times past, when headship involved much less administration, PR, marketing and general outward-facing activity, heads had more time to teach and spend with pupils. Perhaps heads have always worried about how to be strategic while remaining accessible; how to be approachable to staff and especially students without losing that necessary distance and authority – mystique one head called it – which are essential for people to feel secure and grounded. I was crestfallen when during one formal appraisal, a parent had apparently said, 'The headmistress is very remote. She has never spoken to my daughter.' This new mother was perhaps more used to a primary school headmistress who stood each day at the school gates seeing the children onto the bus, but still the words rumbled round my head like a bad school report until a friend and fellow head said to me: 'For goodness sake! Someone's got to be remote – how would any decisions get taken otherwise?' She had a point, but I realise now there is something to be said for standing at the school gate, even in a senior school. In my final year, we divided up this duty amongst the leadership team so as to trial placing a greater security presence at the front of the school. I had thought I knew how to keep in touch with the grass roots: this was another good way. I enjoyed some happy and illuminating conversations with parents and girls while standing there on the driveway and wished I had done so sooner.

Being accessible and approachable to the pupils is of course vital, not just when they are tripping out of the door, and you have to work at finding the best ways to do it. I would teach the youngest girls English, rotating round all the classes in the first year; by giving regular assemblies, by having small groups of girls in to my room for chocolate biscuits and chat, by walking the school regularly and informally, by supporting their myriad activities, whether reading the magazines they produced, watching them in a drama showcase, or buying their baking to raise money for charity, and by working with the student leadership team. What did they think about homework? How was the IT working? Were they getting the right kind of help with university applications? Was sport something they enjoyed and should it be compulsory for them or not? What were we going to do about exam anxiety? We discussed whatever the matter of the moment might be and I encouraged them to bring anything to me that was on their minds. It was through this group, for example, that I first had an inkling we needed to think more deliberately about gender identity in the school. With an easy, unforced atmosphere of mutual respect and trust, we were able to think together about real issues of importance and I gained an invaluable insight into the mindset of the students. Headship may be lonely at times, but I never felt that when talking with any one of my succession of twenty-one head girls and their peers.

It's a truism of our profession that while we get older, our pupils don't. What changes is the world around them: the opportunities, the challenges – what they have to contend with and be prepared for outside the school gates. More than ever, leadership in schools must be about listening to young people, not imposing outdated ways of looking at the world but trying always to see it through their eyes. This is not to say there is no value in the wisdom derived from experience, and it doesn't mean making unsuccessful attempts to occupy the realms of popular culture (I sense my own children cringing with embarrassment at this point), but it does mean being prepared to question long-held assumptions and not falling into the catastrophising, instantly ageing trap of thinking the world is going to hell in a handcart. Our tomorrow will soon be their today. Buoyed by their optimism, with school and home working together, we must ready them for it.

Bringing together all these thoughts about how the leader works with the different constituencies within a school, understanding individuals and building corporate spirit, I am reminded that while schools occupy a particular niche in society, the value of creating successful alliances in any organisation is universal, even if not always recognised. Now that I have come to work in the world of international education, outside the charity sector, where decision-making is more fast moving, the drive for results always pressing and there is constantly the need to create bridges across different jurisdictions, the value of developing human capital in schools, in the manner enshrined by BIOSS, has become newly evident to me. Because while you may secure short-term business success without it, no long-term or sustainable growth is possible unless you pay attention in a serious and systematic way to the people.

This idea is powerfully captured in one of the excellent research reports produced by the global management consultants Hay Group, in association with *Fortune* magazine, *Lighting the Path to Success*. This reputational study, designed to identify the 'World's

Most Admired Companies' (WMACs) focuses on Fortune 1000
companies, along with the largest Global 500 and top companies
operating in the US. To establish a ranking, 10,000 senior executives are asked to rate companies against nine performance
dimensions: innovation, quality of management, long-term investment value, social responsibility to the community and the
environment, ability to attract, develop and retain talented people,
quality of products and services, financial soundness, wise use of
corporate assets, and effectiveness in doing business globally. The
headline findings I found fascinating. In this highly commercial
arena, even though the study included fifteen years' worth of data
during a period of phenomenal change (1997–2012), many of
the WMACs remain constant and, moreover, the best practices
that make them most admired have direct financial consequences.
Not only is it the case that even in periods of uncertainty the
most admired companies have the courage to innovate and break
new ground, they are most notable for achieving success through
their people. To quote: 'It's perhaps the most consistent theme in
our fifteen years of work with the World's Most Admired
Companies. Recognising that their employees are the key driver
of their success, these top performing organisations go to great
lengths to create the right conditions for people to thrive.'[4] An
important element of this is of course attracting and developing
the right talent, and growing the leaders of the future. This and
other studies like it may concentrate on the commercial world,
but they underline the important point that developing human
capital is not a 'nice to have' which you can do if you have time
and there is nothing more important to address, it is absolutely
fundamental to the long-term success of any organisation.
Ultimately, no metric has yet been designed to measure the enjoyment people feel in doing something they care about and the
exhilaration of feeling part of an inspiring mission for its own
sake. But there is no doubt that to neglect to look after your team
is to be taking a nosedive on the productivity graph and no

non-executive director wants to be looking at *that* sort of picture
in the board document pack.

I can see Miss Strudwick and Miss Clark looking somewhat askance
at this headmistress of the twenty-first century drawing analogies
with business. A school is a school: we shouldn't sully it with
commercial thinking. It's not so long ago that a distinguished
former governor pulled me up for mentioning the word 'marketing'
– a vulgar commercial term surely, that could have nothing to do
with St Paul's? Let's not forget that the world's 'most admired
companies' innovate: they don't stay stuck in the past or rest
complacently on their success. You often hear leaders now say
proudly that theirs is a 'people business'. It seems to me that a
school is the best possible example of one. People are its lifeblood
and its reason for being.

Looking after all these relationships is demanding and can be
draining, so for the head, as Miss Clark so presciently points out,
there is a need to pay attention to your own need to keep challenge
and capability in balance and give time to your development as
a person. Not every day feeds the spirit and even experienced
leaders may feel vulnerable and exposed sometimes, although they
train themselves not to show it. A well-known and, as I thought,
tough-minded fellow head once confided to me that she had felt
personally upset by the rudeness and aggressiveness with which a
particular parent had treated her. At the same time, she felt it was
a weakness in her to be wounded by the words that had been said
in anger and which had stayed with her, keeping her awake at
night and making her doubt herself. We agreed, however, that
while self-protection is important, if we lost all capacity to feel
things personally we would lose with it the empathy which is so
essential to our jobs. And then I told her about the visualisation
technique I was once taught for such occasions by the wonderfully
wise Elizabeth Nicholson – which involves me zipping myself into
an invisible inflatable transparent suit in which the insults just

bounce off and fall on the floor somewhere and disappear, so that once the diatribe is over I'm able to resume speaking with perfect calm and no flesh wounds. Despite the very positive relationships I had with most parents, I admit that life in an academic London day school caused me to deploy this invaluable technique more than once.

Heads tend to be by nature highly conscientious, idealistic people with a strong sense of public service and duty. I'm making us sound slightly nauseating, but it's true that if you carry responsibility for others, especially other people's children, it's often a problem taking proper time off or achieving anything like a work–life balance (as it's called, by people who presumably think your work and your life are two different things). All the more reason for us to take ourselves to that conference each year. Far away from our desks, pens poised and iPads balanced in a cavernous conference hall, we are absolved for a few short days from our regular duties. Here we can take a step back, think about the future of our schools more deeply, hear from experts the latest thinking on educational prac- tice and leadership, present papers, lead workshops, brainstorm, plan. Best of all, we're able to talk with others and discover that we face the same issues: a way to gain vital perspective. We'd all met the parent who simply would not let go of their outrage at their child's 'catastrophic' A grade in GCSE biology (much nodding); the head of IT who had yet *again* put forward an astro- nomical budget proposal without any clear cost–benefit analysis from last year (sympathetically raised eyes); the director of music who had to be smoothed down because no, we really *could not* hire a West End theatre to put on *Grease* as the Christmas show (knowing glances). This was the stuff of every head's life. And then some light relief: at Manchester one year, a hardy headmistress stood up to say that, with the help of the outward-bound organ- isation World Challenge, who were exhibiting at the conference, tackle was going to be set up across the ceiling of the fifth floor of the grand Midland Hotel, enabling anyone who wished to to show her commitment to the wider curriculum by abseiling down the five floors of the central stairwell. Some young ambitious types volunteered eagerly to take part, others offering to form a human cushion to soften the landing. To my disappointment, it was decided that the strain on the building would be too much, but this was undoubtedly the most exciting item ever to be raised at an AGM under any other business.

Any account of a group of responsible women coming together, headmistresses especially, has the potential to spill into caricature and even though I don't personally dress like Dizzy or wander round the school in an academic gown singing snatches of hymns, I can still find myself slipping into that mode as I recall the conference – perhaps it's conditioning. Given that headship is as complex a modern leadership role as any, with so much exposure to risk and so many different constituencies to keep happy, it's curious that the image of the old-fashioned, sexless, harridan headmistress persists and is so regularly reinforced in the media. Look no further than the portrayal of Prime Minister Theresa May when, in 2016, hardly one cycle of the academic timetable into her premiership, she announced her intention to bring back grammar schools. Newspapers rushed to print cartoons of a hawk-nosed, hectoring monster with big shoulder pads and Cruella de Vil hair, terrorising pupils and staff. A figure savagely stripped of womanhood. Even though at least one glamorous headmistress of my acquaintance has been known to wear full-body leathers and ride a motorbike, the dated caricature seems to be too hard to resist when you want to poke fun at the hilarious and unnatural idea of a woman wielding authority, particularly over vacillating men. Angela Merkel has fared hardly better. We saw it all before with Mrs Thatcher, but why is this image so persistent? There must linger something about overt female authority that is abhorrent and that we can't quite cope with unless we make fun of it. We are not very far here from the world of pantomime, where traditional cross-casting has a male actor playing the stock character

of the pantomime dame – ugly, old, loud and vulgar, a figure of
fun – while the romantic figure of the principal boy is played by
a young and attractive girl showing plenty of leg in her swash-
buckling boots. The female can assume the male role only in a
bland, restrained, decorative way. Which makes me think there is
something here too about appearance. In the real world, unlike
men, women it would seem have to be both understated and
beautiful – in other words not challenge conventional ideas of
womanhood – to be acceptable as leaders or influencers and escape
being lampooned. We don't see cartoons of Sheryl Sandberg or
Helena Morrissey in the newspapers, but then with all their formi-
dable brilliance, they don't lead by raising their voices.

Now, back at school after the conference, I'm reminded afresh of
someone else critical to my school life – Lindy Hayward. The
embodiment of elegant minimalism, Lindy occupied the office
adjacent to mine and there, with the connecting door rarely closed,
we ran St Paul's together. As my assistant (or was I hers?) unflappable, all-seeing Lindy organised the front-facing side of the school
with perfect equanimity and economy. Mistress of the one-word
response, her 'whatever' and slight flick of the silvery bob meant:
think again, you've got this wrong. On the other hand: 'cool'
signalled unqualified approval. And that approval we all sought.
When less than a term after my departure she died of cancer,
leaving us, as one colleague put it, entirely without fuss, many
felt lost. I realised how pivotal a figure she had been emotionally
in the lives of staff and students. If Lindy was there at her desk
– patient, discerning, wryly teasing – all was well with the world.
    Back then, with my return from conference, it was business as
usual. I see that emails are off the bottom of the screen (even
though Lindy had been assiduously filing and deleting) and there
is a line of people wanting to tell me something, ask me something
or lobby me about something. There is so much to do as a head,
and even if you have someone like Lindy working alongside, you

can't do it all. You work long hours and you delegate. Every leader must make deliberate choices each day about how to spend their personal time. There is no truer cliché than 'there are only so many hours in the day' and as a leader with the privilege of directing your own time, it behoves you to spend those hours as productively as possible. A wise predecessor of mine advised me always to do the thing I was least looking forward to first. (Parents on the warpath with a complaint will now know that it wasn't just respect for coinciding with the school run that made me suggest we met at 8 a.m.) To choose between the multiplicity of possibilities for action my job offered every day, I had a very simple rule. This was, as far as possible, to do myself only those things which could *not* be done by anyone else. This rule of thumb led me to the realisation that the thing only I could do was equally simple: it was to give people my personal time.

In our fast-moving and febrile world, we complain constantly of not having enough time. Time-poor parents bring up their children with a combination of mobile phone and nanny; time-poor students rely on online shortcuts rather than reading whole books; time-poor professionals live on microwave meals. Constantly under pressure, we have come readily to accept that quick communication, quick cooking, quick answers, quick tyre repairs, quick shopping etc. – doing everything as fast as possible – is a virtue in itself. It follows that doing several things at once is even better: the ability to multitask is what we are all aiming for and – thrillingly – women are thought to be better at it than men! Like a circus trick that shouldn't really be possible, it's called juggling: we've all seen those telling birthday cards celebrating the successful modern woman, her baby flying up in the air alongside her iPad and washing-up gloves. In fact, very few of us are more efficient if we try to do too much at once and I've had enough overcooked, stressed and exhausted people in my office at the end of term to know that speed and efficiency, never mind good health, are not always correlated.

In this world of crazily whirring clock hands and relentless metronomes ticking in our brains, where time to get everything done is never enough, what does it mean to *give* your time, and what kind of time is worth having? When I say I gave colleagues my personal time I don't mean my half-presence while checking emails under the table and with an eye straying to the clock so as not to be late for the next meeting. And I don't just mean the fact of my beating heart in the same room as someone else's while my foot taps uncontrollably and my mind runs on the myriad other things I have to do before I miss lunch because I'm too busy. I mean my full, still, patient and undivided attention. We use the phrase paying attention, but I'm not paying anyone when I'm doing this, I'm giving them my attention freely and not in return for anything.

This act might take many forms and, like the building of relationships and corporate spirit itself, can involve working with large gatherings, with smaller groups or with individuals. Giving a speech is an example of when one person gives time to many. Here, there's not just the attention required at the time, but, implicitly, also the time required in preparation. The late-night, lamplight hour writing the speech or the report – that too is being given, and is felt to be given. In making a speech too there is an important element of listening – it isn't just one-way communication – so the attention is about that too, as you adapt and modulate what you are saying to respond to the mood or atmosphere in the room. You pause. You engage. You empathise. Perhaps you make people laugh. Or there is the formal meeting. There are many good books on chairing meetings, but most of them are actually describing this same simple act. Your job is to ensure that business gets covered and decisions taken (never put anything to the vote in a meeting by the way, unless you don't care about the outcome); but most of all, it's to ensure that everyone has the opportunity to speak, that you say only as much as is required to lightly steer the conversation and summarise the conclusions, and that throughout, everyone in the room knows that you are listening to them with your full mind. This can be quite difficult if you have already privately decided what outcomes you want to achieve before the meeting starts, but if you are genuinely giving attention, your mind is open to the possibility of being changed or influenced unexpectedly by the views you will hear. Many times I've been surprised to have my view altered, not necessarily by the wise words of an experienced colleague, but by a much younger member of staff who has made me see something with fresh eyes. Attention then is not judgemental or fixed; it is open to possibilities; it is always a kind of listening.

There is a special role in leadership for the public address when a little like the lone figure in Caspar David Friedrich's painting *Wanderer Above the Sea of Fog*, the leader must be fearless, clear-sighted and visible on the lofty peak, working with the emotive power of language. These moments happen naturally at the start of the year and the start of each term, where a page turns and there are new beginnings. Like the first assembly of the year, these are important milestones and vital opportunities to shape and reinforce values and ethos. That spirit needs to extend not just to the staff but throughout the community. I looked back recently on the file of twenty-one valedictory addresses I have made to parents at the end of the academic year, when their daughters were leaving, and noted their increasing frankness. At first, these were little more that fact-filled reports about the activities of the year. Latterly, I used these opportunities as my predecessor at Queenswood, Audrey Butler, had advised me, to 'get anything across to the parents you want them to hear', which became more often a way of developing wider thoughts about the purpose of education and the role of St Paul's in developing the minds and aspirations of the next generation. One Christmas, the girls gave me a book called *Speeches that Changed the World.* Napoleon, Stalin, Hitler and Nixon rub shoulders with Jefferson, Churchill, Nelson Mandela and Indira Gandhi (yes – only one woman in that list, which reflects the proportions in the book). Great speech-making has been a talent of tyrants as well as great leaders. And the ability to move with words is a powerful skill for any leader to have. I cannot read Lincoln's Gettysburg Address – that shortest of emotive speeches – without a lump forming in my throat. His realism about the world and gracious honouring of the dead (there were 51,000 casualties at Gettysburg). 'The world will little note nor long remember what we say here, but it can never forget what they did here.' I imagine myself as a bereaved mother standing in that crowd. It's unbearable. And talking of great American orators, who doesn't recall the thrill of being part of changing history when Barack Obama made his acceptance speech in Chicago in 2008:

> This is our time, to put our people back to work and open doors of opportunity for our kids; to restore prosperity and promote the cause of peace; to reclaim the American dream and reaffirm that fundamental truth, that, out of many, we are one; that while we breathe, we hope. And where we are met with cynicism and doubts and those who tell us that we can't, we will respond with that timeless creed that sums up the spirit of a people: Yes we can.

Being swept up in the emotive beauty of oratory is a powerful thing – speeches are a vital part of effective leadership. But it doesn't follow that great speeches always have to go hand in hand with an ebullient, obviously extroverted leadership style. Indeed, many leaders are by nature introverts, and their ability to be effective 'one-on-many' – as a sole figure addressing a large number of people – simply one facet of the way they communicate best. As Susan Cain confirms in her marvellous book *Quiet: The Power of Introverts in a World That Can't Stop Talking*, not all great leaders, those whose gift is to bring people together behind a vision, are chatty, outgoing and spellbinding. Those who are by nature quiet and more introverted, drawing their own strength from within rather than from the endless flow of people, words and action around them, have something different to offer a leadership role. Speeches have their important place, but I always felt the most valuable kind of time and attention was deployed in the small, unscripted, sometimes even impromptu interactions with individuals or small groups. The kind of conversations that might range from a difficult meeting with a parent about their daughter (at 8 a.m.) to a conversation with a colleague about a promotion opportunity, to a tête-à-tête with a final-year student about her university plans. These are the small personal scenes that bubble up constantly with pupils, teachers or parents. Whether occasioned by a success, a request, a sadness, or a crisis, whether scheduled or unplanned, my days were filled with them. One way or another, the whole substance of my leadership, I came to realise, rested to a large extent on this simple thing that only I could do: the giving of my personal attention in the living moment. Sometimes, it would be a simple matter of giving permission – yes, you can leave early on Thursday to see your daughter in her nativity play (here I was remembering the tender experience of seeing my own daughter, Isobel, as Mary, the microphone attached to her cheek with Elastoplast, eyes wide and a small but steady voice singing: 'How can it be? Why has he chosen me?'). Sometimes though, the value would be more obscure. A colleague or pupil who wanted to talk about a difficulty they had – thinking they wanted advice. Actually, they often just needed time in the calm of my room, for the answer that was there to float to the surface and show itself. Going along with this recognition about the importance of giving time, I therefore found, was also a growing awareness of the value of economy and restraint. The success of an exchange rested often not on what I said, or did, but on what I refrained from saying or doing, allowing the other person to come to the conclusion themselves.

And here, still thinking about the importance of the head giving time, and the need sometimes to keep very still as the emotions whirl about, it's worth distinguishing between two different kinds

of attention and the role and effectiveness of each. Always generous
and imaginative in her reading recommendations, Gillian Stamp
introduced me to the work of the English psychoanalyst and
educationalist Marion Milner. In her book *A Life of One's Own*,
Milner makes the distinction between 'narrow' and 'wide' attention.
The former is when we are, as she puts it, head down, following
the scent – that urgent, focussed attention which is conscious of
time and seeking a solution or conclusion, excluding other influences or distractions from outside. Wide attention in contrast is
when we allow a subject to make itself felt to us with much more
patience and openness, when we refrain from effortful seeking
after answers and wait patiently for our responses to form. A
lifelong wanderer in art galleries, and as a parent, having become
adept at the forty-minute rule (you can get your children interested
in anything as long as it doesn't last more than forty minutes), I
now deliberately practise that wide attention when I am in a
gallery, which often means spending an hour or so looking at just
one or two pictures. (I noted recently that the Tate has begun
promoting this practice as 'slow looking'. The average time anyone
spends in front of a picture in a gallery is apparently a mere
twenty-eight seconds . . .) The difference is quite extraordinary,
as the design, colour palette, subject matter and technique begin
to suggest themselves and gradually cohere into the whole. But
you can't hurry it, this deeper looking and thinking, and the same
is true with the kind of attention that's needed as a leader when
listening to people. If you offer wide attention, you help the person
relax enough to bring the whole of what is on their minds to the
surface. Often, the real issue may not be what they thought they
had come to talk about – this comes out only later, if you are
patient and if your attention is wide, undemanding and not
insisting on its own way.

The practising of wide attention and the quality of stillness that
attends it is particularly important in a high-achieving, fast-moving
environment like St Paul's. I think now that I unconsciously

developed this style in response to the school, as a way of creating balance, of hallowing and sometimes gently directing the creativity and enthusiasms, while also sometimes slowing down the pace to give more time for the right solution to present itself. To be in such an environment, with extremely talented pupils and staff, all engaged in the pursuit of learning, bringing them joy and struggle and frustration and triumph every day, to be in a community where the air is constantly filled with fast-flowing debate and conversation and wit, where all of us were challenging ourselves and learning new things every day, from pupils as well as colleagues: that is an extraordinary experience. Sometimes within the school though, we might forget just how brightly everything was burning – bright enough to burn us all up, if we weren't careful. One wise and reflective colleague spoke about what it was like to go home at the weekend or the end of term, to a family who were not part of the school and had been doing other things. She said: 'Sometimes at the end of term it takes time . . . I realise I need to dip my headlights – the glare is hurting their eyes.' What I now see is that while the expectations of any leader will vary enormously and may change without warning, you develop your style and emphasis to complement the prevailing tempo and character of the organisation.

Above all, leadership requires an instinct for flexibility. And the ability to adapt. Sometimes you are leading publicly, out in front; sometimes you are stepping back and giving others space to take the limelight and grow in their own confidence and unique style, and sometimes you are somewhere in the middle. And this leading from the middle, from the centre where there is stillness, seems to me the most important and appropriate, not just for a particular school but for our times, when life is full of turbulence, stress and unreliable public role models. Of course the pupils, staff and parents will look to the head for inspiration, for vision and for courageous, energetic clarity of purpose, but they will also look to them for stability, for generosity and the ability to give scope and confidence to others. Imagine yourself walking along a favourite country road or city street – in my mind I am in Paris, the Seine on my left and the Eiffel Tower in the distance – holding onto many strings, at the end of each of which is a brightly coloured balloon. The blue, the yellow, the pink, the purple, the green all jostle about one another dancing as the breeze catches them; the balloons are all connected by their strings, but lightly, moving together, sitting higher or lower in the air as they move. And as you walk along holding them you look up and out, confident that the balloons are not going to fly off into the blue yonder, but seeing that they have a life of their own. They are connected, but not too tightly; you have them held, but not too obviously.

To me, this is the greater part of how to lead a school – giving others freedom of action and creativity while making sure they feel secure and supported. And with this structure there is much more fruitful creative thinking amongst the team: people are confident to develop their own ideas and appreciate their respective differences and strengths as well as the many synergies. In writing this, rising into my field of vision too are the mentors who helped me along the path to headship, showing belief in my abilities and encouraging me to take responsibility.

Another of those former headmistresses writing in the 1930s, L. E. Savill, head of Lincoln High School, refers in her essay to another Chinese saying: 'One generation opens up the road on which the next generation travels.' She was talking about the role of teachers in relation to their pupils, but for me this equally applies to the way new leaders emerge for our schools. I came into headship at the age of thirty-seven as the youngest person in the senior team, owing much to those who had encouraged and supported me in a former generation. Some twenty years later, the day I decided to step down from St Paul's, I realised that the tables had turned, and that it was therefore time for me to find a new field where I could continue to learn and challenge myself in a different way.

At the heart of the leadership role, behind the charismatic speeches and visionary pronouncements, there is the quiet, patient stitching together and repairing of relationships, of encouraging people's sense of themselves and of their role within the wider fabric of the whole school. An endless weaving of meaning that goes on often in those small-scale, personal interactions with individuals and which spins out to shape the ethos of the school as a whole. The dissident writer Pavel Hollar in Tom Stoppard's play *Professional Foul* sums it up: 'The ethics of the state can only be the ethics of the individual writ large. One man's dealings with another.'[5] This is the heart of headship – leading from the still and private centre outwards – making those individual dealings as positive as they can be, and seeing a confident sense of the whole gradually emerging.

And looking up from my desk at this point, I see the afternoon has grown dark. My cup of tea placed silently at my elbow by Lindy some time ago has gone cold, and there's a knock at the door. It's the deputy head. Not 'running around' but, November being almost over, coming to discuss the details of the end-of-term Christmas concert.

A dummy run...for a giggle

SHOPPERS in Kensington today stopped in their tracks as a couple of shop window mannequins suddenly got fits of the giggles.

Schoolgirls Candida Whiteleuge (left) and Saskia Whitfield were given the chance to be window models after a request to Barkars in Kensington.

It was a special treat for the youngsters, on the last day of the Christmas holidays from St. Paul's Girls' Schools Brook Green.

When they arrved the window in Derry Street was specially prepared for them and after being made up by the shop experts they braved the public.

Candida, ... of Aubrey Road, Kensington: "I got the idea after watching Jim'll Fix it, but I decided to fix it for myself.

"I rang the shop and the ... ... great at them ..."

'What life have you, if you have not life together?
There is not life that is not in community'

From Choruses from *The Rock*, T.S. Eliot

May 3rd, 1973.

...day dinner until 6 p.m. unless ...

b) To Frome by train at 1.37 p.m. returning ...

To Yeovil by train 1.03 p.m. to return 5.?? p.m.

Cyclists may go to Wells, Sherborne, Shepton Mallet, Wincanton with packed lunches after 11.20 a.m.

c) Not to Yeovil on Football Match Saturdays.

d) The book must be signed in and out by each gi...

e) There must be no fewer than three in any ...

f) The excursion must be arranged person... ...ps with their own Housemistress.

g) Not more than 2 excursions per ...

2   Lower V1th Cycle Rides on a Satur... ...l parental permiss...

a) Only in the Country

b) The group **must** consis...

c) State your route to y...

d) You may take packed l...

e) You must report to yo...

f) This may take place t...

- Please stand if you played a shepherd
- Please stand if you played Mary
- Please stand if you played Joseph
- Please stand if you played one of the three wise men
- Please stand if you played the angel Ga...
- Please stand if you played either the front or back, or the whole, of the ox or the ass, or a sheep or a camel, or if you played a palm tree

3   Shopping for Upper V at ...

a) Tuesday – Old House ...
   Wednesday – Highcrof...
   Thursday – Wayside ...
   Friday – Old Vicarag...

b) Mufti must be worn f...

4   Shopping at Mrs. Stockley's, Pitcombe

CHAPTER 4

December

Living in community – the love of tradition and the role of co-curricular life

December is a short month. Only three weeks in school before the Christmas holidays during which time, at St Paul's, breath is held as final-year students set off to Oxford and Cambridge university interviews and excited anticipation rises as rehearsals intensify for the play and concert. In the staffroom, heads are down: hundreds of school reports must be crafted and fingers are crossed the IT doesn't crash. The teachers don't yet admit they are longing for a break – and best not to as Christmas is rarely that, if you pack up at school and go home to lay on wall-to-wall festivities for a family. For some reason at this time of year, there is always just one more event squeezed into the calendar, of the overambitious *Ben-Hur-on-Ice* kind, than is really practical; it seemed a good idea back in the summer but now threatens to send everyone over the edge. Like the mince pies, people will be getting decidedly crispy round the edges, but with any luck they will not crumble just yet. In my room I keep a fresh box of tissues handy. We just have to keep everyone calm and concentrate on enjoying doing things together: the school play or concert; the various Christmas traditions: music, carol services and end-of-year celebrations.

A school is not just where you go to acquire a body of knowledge and pass exams. It's a living, breathing community. To me, this is more than a happy accident – it's a central purpose of schools and one that is ever more important in the contemporary world. The sense of belonging a school provides is essential now that young people are growing up often without a grounded sense of community in their local area, especially in cities. In London, knife crime is escalating sharply and city streets can seem threatening and hostile. A few years ago a very talented student (who has gone on to become a doctor) found herself first on the scene after a knifing incident not half a mile from the school in respectable Brook Green. Few children walk to school and fewer play in the street at home with friends living nearby, as my brother and I once did – dragging an old table and chairs out onto the pavement along with the dressing-up clothes. Today's children are more likely to be alone in their rooms, connected by technology to social media but with only the blue screen-light for company. School is beneficial as a contrast to this, because it's where you spend time with real people – throughout your day, whereas technology is socially isolating. Many people now work alone at home because they can and we must all have walked past offices where there is similar isolation: rows of employees sit at screens wearing headphones, close enough to touch one another but rarely making eye contact, much less speaking. Schools are often criticised for being old-fashioned; behind the curve. But perhaps we're actually ahead of it. If we know what's good for us as human beings, school can be the place where the fundamental need for human contact, with all its joys, difficulties, frustrations and complexities, will be freshly recognised and valued. Who knows, perhaps a school will be the seed from which multi-generational twenty-first-century communities will grow. In the past, I never thought of school in itself as therapeutic. I do now.

As social entities schools are also endlessly fascinating. Each has its own personality, sensed as soon as you enter the front doors, and embodied in the collective memory of traditions, events, habits and spaces. Stable, touchable, solid places where within familiar walls and outside them patterns repeat themselves and traditions flourish, schools feel permanent. At the same time they have an essential transience: the students are constantly progressing along a path which will end in their departure. They come together during that 'frail/ Travelling coincidence'[1] of Larkin's train journey from Hull to London in 'The Whitsun Weddings', sharing experiences before scattering across the world when they leave. Retaining what? Some values, some memories, perhaps some knowledge and, if they have had enough time in one school, strong friendships that endure. We all have a connection with our contemporaries from our school days, even if we have not kept in touch. You only have to listen to school friends meeting after long separation – they quickly fall into a litany of 'oh you remembers' recalling with nostalgia (or dread, as equally uniting) those experiences they shared during the formative years of childhood and adolescence. Whether these were happy days or not, they stay with us and become part of who we are.

The things we remember about school may be the teachers we loved or loathed, perhaps even some of what we were taught, but very often our most vivid memories are of other experiences altogether. I wonder what memories are coming back to you now, from those times. As a small child, I was often cast as the angel in the nativity play (never Mary, an honour saved for my daughter Isobel). It was certainly not because of my character but simply that I had the most hair, of the kind which tended to grow outwards, forming a convenient halo. I can see now my costume made from an old flannel sheet, long since sides-to-middled by my mother, with gold braid carefully sewed around the bell sleeves. 'Sew in your thoughts, dear,' my grandmother would say, as she worked at her dressmaking. And in her turn my mother sewed in her own thoughts, for me. Later, as a sixth-former, the role of brooding, revolutionary Dora in Camus's *Les Justes*, performed with the local boys' school (hair up this time), was much more my natural persona. My parents, both keen amateur actors, made us theatre-goers from an early age: I remember the thrill of being out at night for the first time, the frosty cold and watching the stars through the car window as we sped towards the Yeovil Assembly Rooms. There, settled on canvas chairs, the music striking up, we would watch the red velvet curtains swing apart to reveal another world. The theatre was always magical to me – still is – and many experiences at school, as well as some formative lessons as a teacher, have sprung from either acting in or directing plays.

My first production was of modest scale: John Burrows's *The Golden Pathway Annual*, a series of twenty-four sketches which tell the story of an ordinary boy, Michael Peters, growing up in the period from the end of the Second World War to the late 1960s. Not the most sophisticated material but as a new teacher at a sixth-form college, where the students were hardly younger than me, I was thrilled to be given the responsibility of directing and set about blocking and making a model of the simple set, poring over my plan until late at night. There was a salutary lesson over the casting of parts. I'd chosen a very charismatic, flame-haired girl to play the mother, while her quieter friend came to the auditions and looked on. Only after my female lead had been late or failed to turn up to the first week of rehearsals, eventually dropping out pleading too many commitments (most of them social), did I notice the friend who had come along to prompt. I gave her the role with a heavy heart – this was not the leading lady I had envisaged – and then watched her learn her lines over-night, lift the whole cast with the example of commitment she set, and make the show a resounding shared success. I hope some of them can remember it now. Ever since, when casting a play, or actually getting a team together to do anything, I look for those whose motivation is greatest before those with the most immediately obvious talent. Learning generosity of spirit and enjoying doing things together, focussing on teamwork rather than personal glory and making the shared aim the thing: these are amongst the life-lessons of living in a school community.

Over the last four decades I've seen many occasions where being in a play has had a formative role in the lives of students. Studio productions done on a shoestring, such as my Sha Tin College's *Macbeth* – involving a small cast clad in black rubber gloves and bin liners with a mop head guesting as Banquo's ghost – live on. As do the more ambitious musicals. I doubt the joint St Paul's schools' *Les Misérables* will ever be forgotten. Even with budget overshot, set design hugely ambitious, seats overbooked, the music and drama staff just short of breaking point as the electrics threatened to fail at the final technical run on a dark Sunday afternoon – 'Okay, everyone, we'll just have to run that one more time!' – the cast barely hanging on through throat infections and colds, rehearsals threadbare because of clashing university interviews – somehow, under the direction of teachers whose stamina was equal to their talent, the most extraordinary, unforgettable thing was created. Nothing illustrates better how working with young people, a project becomes greater than the sum of its parts. They drive you mad in rehearsals but on the night, young actors seem to produce some sort of genius. Time and again I've watched students find capability they did not know they had, their parents watching proudly from the darkened auditorium. How important that as a student, as well as taking away a sheaf of qualifications as your passport to the next stage of life, you take the memory of what it is to create something unique and satisfying through working with others. I doubt many of the corporate away-weekends they experience in future will be as formative, come even close in enjoyment or be so warmly remembered.

Music also unites, in its powerful and unique way. Some of my most thrilling memories of St Paul's are of watching the orchestra in action under the baton of the director of music. I'm there now in the December dark. There's that hush: in the school's Great Hall an electrifying sense of expectation as the concert is about to begin. The conductor raises his arms; in the stillness, his head slightly tilted as he scans to see all instruments are poised, all eyes on him. And then, with a split-second intake of breath, the flame ignites, sending a lightning flash shooting down every spine as we're launched on the vast ocean of the music, held spellbound and in thrall until the very last note. Conducting is a fascinating example of charismatic leadership from the front: personal, brilliant, daring. Those young musicians would have done anything for him, and he made them believe they could – willing them to risk everything, to achieve that exhilaration in performance, when you are playing not just at your full capability but even beyond it. In the orchestra, the rapt concentration and absolute will to rise to this expectation. Then at rest and receiving their applause at the end, their violins held aside, the girls tap a free hand against a leg to applaud one another, thrilled and astonished at what has taken place. I often think that if music were all we taught them, our children's lives would be rich indeed.

The third great plinth of the co-curricular life of many schools is sport. Here we have to distinguish between sport – usually competitive team games – and physical education – the promotion of physical health as an end in itself. Both are important to both boys and girls. Much is said about the value of sport in boys' schools, channelling aggression and so forth, but if you've seen a girls' lacrosse team in full cry you wouldn't associate this only with the playing fields of Eton: many girls play competitive sport just as keenly. Perhaps because I paid very little attention to physical education myself before the age of thirty, largely as a result of my own laziness and a fear of aggressive PE teachers, I find myself, like many late converts, keen to encourage girls to enjoy physical exercise, whether in team sports or simply for their individual health, because this is a habit that can then last for life. (The number of women well into their seventies who attend my local gym is a source of great satisfaction – their granddaughters could follow their example.)

With concerns about sugar consumption leading to obesity and diabetes so much in the news, there has been a big media push to get girls active through advertising campaigns, which have done much to dispel the image of sport as punishment. Women of all shapes, sizes and ages can enjoy exercise and it doesn't have to mean going to the kind of gym where you feel inadequate next to impossibly toned and Lycra-clad Amazons. Or in fact going to the gym at all, if that isn't your thing. I have never been exactly a role model in this respect, though I did lead (or usually follow) a small running group of senior girls on Wednesday afternoons at one point. We could take that forty-minute run along the Thames towpath and feel all the more energetic afterwards. Having arrived at St Paul's to find that most of the senior girls spent the PE afternoon sleeping on the common-room sofas, we agreed that girls at all levels should do some sort of regular exercise up until the Christmas of their final year. In the top two years this might be rock climbing or Zumba; it didn't have to mean running out onto the lacrosse pitch waving and twisting something looking like a string vest on a curtain pole, though those of a competitive turn of mind were encouraged to do so. Having had no feeling for team games at school myself I was keen to offer choice. There is a world of difference between practising health-related fitness, which you can then do independently, and promoting competitive team games. A good school will provide for both and there need be no girl who can say this is not for me, because everyone can enjoy something (as I am living proof) whether on an individual or team basis. Just do it!

Of course, team sports fulfil a very important and much more complex role in the lives of lacrosse and netball players than merely providing a healthy dose of fresh air and exercise. The psychology of working as a team, showing dedication by turning out to practise early in the morning, taking your team to victory or picking each other up after a defeat – all this provides invaluable life-learning that underscores the commitment to community. I was told that the way to stop the girls being lured away to the sixth form at Westminster was to get them involved in lacrosse. Nobody who cared about her team would dream of committing an act of such gross disloyalty as to apply to another school, especially with some frail excuse about wanting different A-level options, when everyone knew it was just about being with those scruffy, farting boys. There were matches to be won. It was unthinkable. In our rowers, out on the river in the early morning winter dark, I saw this in its most extreme form because of the sheer physical demands and the hours of training that competitive rowing requires. It was a proud and thrilling moment for the school's rowing community when Oxford won the Newton Women's Boat Race in 2014 with a Paulina as president of the crew; they had been training for that moment for three years.

The girls' love of unusual role models was a gift: a favourite assembly was about Fanny Blankers-Koen, the Dutch sprinter known as the flying housewife (you can tell this was some time ago) who was voted the greatest female athlete of the twentieth century. Born in 1918, she took up athletics only at sixteen, but loved running everywhere, hurdling effortlessly over the garden gate on her way to school. At eighteen she went to her first Olympics in Berlin and from there, rose rapidly, despite the problems of pursuing an athletic career as a young mother and even competing while pregnant. At the London Games in 1948 she took four gold medals. The robustly athletic form of Blankers-Koen in the grainy black and white picture I showed as she breasted the finishing line might not be the aspiration of girls today, used to the tanned and glamorous female athletes of their own generation, but she certainly won the prize for grit in their eyes.

Drama, music and sport do not necessarily add to a student's formal qualifications but they provide intrinsic enjoyment, invaluable life-learning and memorable experiences that endure. All very well you say, but not all children attend schools with elaborate state-of-the-art theatres and concert halls or pristine AstroTurf pitches. That's true, but while specialist facilities may be desirable, they are not the most important thing. You can make theatre almost anywhere: as the great director Peter Brook taught us in his 1968 book, *The Empty Space*: 'I can take any empty space and call it a bare stage. A man walks across this empty space whilst someone else is watching him, and this is all that is needed for an act of theatre to be engaged.'

What should and can be available to all children, wherever they are at school, is the time and expertise of teachers to mentor, coach, guide and encourage so that students can come together to make remarkable things happen. Of course we can only be sure of having those teachers and for them to be given the time if governments have the foresight to acknowledge the important role in personal development played by these subjects and support the training of teachers who specialise in them. They are not frills around the edges – nice-to-haves which we use to fill in the gaps or stretch those with special talent. The creative arts are essential to human flourishing and I will come to the reasons why in the next chapter.

With adequate time, there are so many other activities to be pursued: if music and drama or sport are not your thing, a rich co-curricular programme can offer many other experiences to harness the existing interests of students and inspire new ones: clubs and societies can be formed for debating, public speaking, chess, film, classics, literature, or even dissection ('don't diss diss soc' was the girls' jingle when they gave notices in assembly about society meetings). Children love competitions and there are national leagues and competitions for debating and public-speaking, activities which teach such essential, transferable skills of confidence and concentration, available to all. Apart from the opportunities created by clubs and societies, organising them and running them is valuable learning. I was referred to a skin consultant a few years ago who mentioned that he had once been invited to give a talk at St Paul's by Med[ical] Soc[iety]. 'The girls invited me, met me, introduced and listened to me and asking some pretty searching questions, then gave me tea and cake, saw me off and wrote to thank me. I didn't see an adult the whole time I was at the school – I was most impressed.' Having a silent nightmare about the safeguarding implications that would have in jumpier times today, I felt inwardly gratified at the independence and sheer efficiency of the girls.

The co-curricular life of the school is not only integral to the educational experience; in bringing students together, it helps children learn to collaborate and strengthens the bonds of friendship. During the autumn term I would have a dedicated conversation with each girl in her final year, to look back at her education and to think ahead both for her and for the school. These encounters gave me intriguing insight into what they had most valued and what they would miss. Eager in most cases for all that lay ahead, but with the hurdle of A levels still to come, they were nostalgic about the heedless days of the 'MIV', when they were still eleven, not seventeen, and it was all before them. One gregarious girl who loved lacrosse was reluctant to let go of her teachers and fellow teammates: where would she ever feel so much at home and at one with the world? Another, self-possessed, said what she liked was that she had felt free – not too much fussed over. They each had their own view of school, liked especially that they had been allowed to develop their individual interests and explore new realms, that they were not pressed into a mould. All of them valued their strong friendships and having grown up together through those adolescent years ('Do you remember what we were like in the Lower Fifth? OMG . . .'). Was the school pressurised? Yes, they thought . . . sometimes. 'But we put the pressure on ourselves because we want to do well,' they said. 'It's not the teachers! Everyone thinks that. It's us – it's the way we are. Most of us actually like doing lots of stuff'. . . 'And the lunches of course – they're amazing' . . . 'I actually always look up what's for lunch in period 2 – while following the lesson of course!'

What had been the best part? For most, being in the top two years, when they came back together as a year group, had their own common room to make toast, drink coffee, find a quiet place for a sleep (the teenage body clock does not necessarily align to the school day), to be themselves and just to be together. They would come in, books spilling to right and left and sit on the end of one of my peacock-blue sofas, a little warily at first (finding yourself in the high mistress's office isn't necessarily a good thing) but soon relaxing when they saw I wanted to listen. And when we got onto suggestions for the future there was no stopping them. Should we be admitting boys for example? No! Certainly not! (They took revenge on me one year for suggesting this by producing and distributing around the school multiple copies of an impressively convincing letter to parents, on the school letterhead, signed by me and purporting to announce the introduction of co-education from the following September. It was clever and amusing – luckily I don't think any of the copies actually left the building.) I loved these times, seeing in them the appealing mixture of radical ambition and conservative loyalty. You can run all the detailed satisfaction surveys you like, but few things give a truer reading of the atmosphere and happiness levels in a school than listening to the students who know it best.

Of course, this being St Paul's, not all the conversations flowed so smoothly. There would be the occasional girl who made it clear from her body language and clipped answers, eyes roving over the room, that the others might have sold out to convention but *she* wasn't going to sit there telling the high mistress what she wanted to hear in this . . . *bastion of privilege*. But that was all right. A good reminder that we really did encourage individuality and intellectual freedom. We were not turning out nice girls – though many of them were – we were growing strong-minded young women.

Strong-minded young women expect a lot from their teachers. What are good teacher–student relationships and how can these be fostered to build community in a school? A simple point often overlooked is that students are good judges of teaching and the primary requirement of any teacher who wishes to win respect is to be effective in the classroom. Without this you will not be able to form the mutually respectful relationships on which effective learning is based. Students are not impressed with teachers who wear Father Christmas ties that play jingle bells and tell good jokes unless they also know their subject and can teach it well. That means helping students widen their understanding, giving them confidence to express themselves, providing challenge to hone argument, making it safe to say when they don't understand and having the patience and the pace to move at the right speed for all – whatever their needs. This is why student evaluations are such a vital part of teacher appraisal: nobody knows better where the best work in the school is being done. Given that foundation of professional respect, healthy student–teacher relationships can be key to the whole experience of education and, time and again, when former students come back to visit their school, it's their teachers who are most vivid in their memory as formative and influential presences. Boundaries between teacher and pupil have to be observed of course, and we hear all too much about mistakes and their consequences when these get crossed. Setting those boundaries isn't always easy. There must be the right level of professional distance, but there needs also to be warmth and genuine, appropriate personal interest. In a world where there are new child protection and safeguarding cases in the press almost daily, this has become more difficult – responsible teachers are afraid of being thought too close to their students. This is a great shame. In the best schools, there is an entirely appropriate habit of deep individual interest in the needs, aptitudes and character of each student. Their particular needs will be carefully discussed, just as they might be by their parents at home. While she may not be aware of all these conversations, the student herself feels secure – known and understood by her teachers. This confidence and trust forms the bedrock upon which not only a happy school life is built, but academic achievement too.

The student–teacher relationship is set within a context of cultural norms and expectations, special to each school. As we've seen, every school is wrought with structure and pattern, which provide security and reassurance. At the same time, relationships thrive when there is a sense of relaxed good order and normality, with the minimum of visible rules. Those thoughtful final-year girls commented on how they had appreciated not being constrained by a lot of petty do-nots, but had instead been allowed to find their own path, pursue their interests, make their own mistakes and grow up at their own pace. Rather than have a long list of school rules, we developed with the girls a positive code of conduct – some simple statements about tolerance, respect and personal responsibility – emphasising the fact that a person's behaviour and its consequences are their own to manage, whatever their age or level in the school. Independent, questioning self-regulation was what we were aiming for. I knew better than to think that Paulinas would dwindle into compliant, biddable yes-women (even though that would occasionally have been welcome) but I almost invariably found that if you treated the girls as responsible individuals worthy of respect, that was how they would behave.

If you can achieve that balance between structure and freedom, and between formality and spontaneity, then you have a happy equilibrium in which individuality can thrive and lasting friendships form. Gillian Stamp often uses the image of the vine growing over a trellis. The school is the trellis, providing a framework of support and clear structure, clearly but not too obtrusively. On it, the vine of each person can grow, guided and encouraged upward, but free enough to give plenty of room for individual expression and personality. This was how St Paul's seemed to me: the important thing was to make sure the trellis was there, but not to remind everyone of it too often. Meanwhile the girls naturally enjoyed learning together because they were interested in many things. While each set herself high standards (too high, sometimes) the girls did not on the whole seek to outdo each other. They aspired to do their best against their own standards and were happy for one another's successes. One memory stands out as illustration. One morning when Oxford and Cambridge were announcing their offers, and tensions were running high, the head girl heard she had not been successful. Minutes later, she was due to be arriving for her weekly meeting with me and the rest of the student leadership team, a number of whom had just received the offers they were hoping for. This was the prize they had been working towards for two years – it was impossible to disguise the fact that it mattered a great deal. Without missing a beat, she congratulated all of them and we fell to eating biscuits and chatting animatedly about the year ahead. That remarkably generous-spirited girl had a gap year working and travelling, before reapplying successfully to Cambridge rather than Oxford. The self-control and generosity she showed on that day of disappointment would take her far in life, I remember thinking, and be just as important as her academic success.

Mutual affirmation and support was one of the cornerstones of the strong bonds of friendship the girls formed and the resilience they were able to build. No wonder that the school has such a strong alumnae association and that Paulinas remain in touch with one another, long after they have left school. 'Once a Paulina, always a Paulina' may have many connotations – not always positive in the minds of some past students. But in relation to friendship, it rings true.

No discussion of community could be complete without a mention of humour: I keep coming back to it, but how to talk about it? So difficult to analyse something which just has to be lived to be understood. There is no truer saying than that laughter is the shortest distance between two people and it follows that if you have to keep explaining to another person why you find something funny, the two of you are never going to be really close.

Paulinas with their quick wits are highly susceptible to laughter, and especially enjoy surprising juxtapositions, the absurd or the ironic. John Colet's bust adorned with sunglasses. The hilarious lampoonability of the school prospectus. They also have a taste for the stagily outrageous: I heard about a couple of girls (before my time, thank goodness) offering themselves as live models for a window display at the very proper London department store of Derry & Tom's. They were taken on at once and standing in the window, began to draw quite a crowd. This is no doubt funnier in the recollection than it was at the time for their exasperated parents, but gives a flavour of their daring and originality.

Occasionally, exuberance got the better of Paulinas and humour would be unrestrainedly bawdy, their 'muck-up days' (which I never quite managed to ban) sometimes teetering on the edge of acceptability (or tipping over it, in the eyes of some teachers). One year I was welcoming two distinguished academic visitors to the science department. As I walked them across the Great Hall, we looked up at Horsley's elegant ceiling where a string of some thirty or so brightly coloured bras had been hung, washing-line style, from one side of the balcony to the other. Ah, the girls . . . I murmured, attempting to distract them by pointing out a portrait of former high mistress, Heather Brigstocke. But they were unperturbed. They had brought up teenage daughters and had seen it all before. These moments of ritual misrule we weathered, but it was in the daily life of the school that humour was constantly felt – often quick verbal wit that was gone as soon as it had arrived – bringing people together across barriers of age and status, defusing tension, helping keep things in proportion – a vital safety valve.

What makes a Paulina a Paulina? Who were the members of this highly intelligent, original tribe? I was often asked what sort of girl would thrive at St Paul's. What did you need to be *like* to enjoy being there? Were they all incredibly articulate extroverts, sashaying down the corridors in ripped jeans, flicking their hair and quoting Virgil? I can hear myself now, reassuring the parents at open morning: 'There is no absolute Paulina type. Yes, the girls enjoy learning and tend to have strong opinions. But personalities vary enormously and both the extrovert and introvert can find her place here.' It was true we had both: the girl who dyed her hair a different colour each week and tried everything from electric blue to grey was surely wanting to be noticed; and her friend who preferred to remain in the library or sequester herself in a remote corner of the Religious Studies Department at lunchtimes perhaps just wanted to think her own thoughts and be left to do so. It was a matter of respecting personal preferences.

In my experience, almost all children want to feel that they belong at school, but individuals need to adapt in their own way. At the end of the first year, one school report would say: 'Alya fitted in and made new friends at once', while another might read 'Henna is still finding her feet'. There were lots of girls who for one reason or another felt they didn't immediately fit right in, taking longer to be comfortable in the bigger environment of senior school. I wanted the girls to feel they *could* be different and apart, and from the school's point of view, that was respected. Not everyone is a joiner-in. As teacher Jonathan Smith observes in his book *The Learning Game*, many of the most interesting pupils are angular, not easy or naturally sociable.[2] And quite a few of the most thoughtful and sensitive like to be left alone. For some Paulinas, it didn't mean they didn't want to be included – they just had trouble sending the right signals. According to the leadership course I took at the suggestion of my far-sighted chairman of governors when first I became a head, these are people who have 'low expressed inclusion'. I often recognise this because I have it myself: yes, I want to be accepted by others, but I don't always give the right verbal cues, expecting others to realise this without my sending out any include-me signals. If you are like me, you'll also be used to being described as aloof and remote and finding that rather extraordinary. Why can't everyone see you want to be a part of things? Children like this simply take more time to find their circle of friends and be happy and secure members of the community.

However much the school embraces its pupils, you can't win them all over. Just like the final-year girl I saw narrowing her eyes at me, a small number would prefer to be detached and not to engage, remaining always at that slight angle to things. I would watch them pass through the school in their own world, taking the benefits of a great education but not really engaging with the wider life of the school and somehow not ever 'joining'. They were observers, on the outside. One I remember even withdrew from the much-anticipated leavers' ceremony, pleading that her post-A-level holiday job wouldn't allow her time off: a signal that even after seven years she didn't recognise herself as a part of this clan. I felt sorry for her – because of what she had missed of collegiality and the fund of shared experiences. But such cases were few. On the whole, the school found a way to reach and embrace the many individuals it sheltered, who, unforced, all found their place in the complex web of relationships in their own time and in their own way.

A community is the weaving together of people and they are held in place by habits and shared traditions. Just like the people who live and work in them, schools have personalities, expressed through the continuing rhythm of daily life: the shared language, the uniform/lack of uniform, the school magazine, the crest – the small, eccentric ways of doing things that often defy logic and seem to have evolved of their own accord. Take, for instance, the gloriously illogical way St Paul's labels its different year groups. The eleven-year-olds are known as the Middle IV, or 'MIVs', who then become UIV, progressing to Lower V, V and finally VI, VII and VIII. Where were the Lower IV? Or the Middle V? Nobody knew. This system regularly defeated busy parents who had enough trouble getting a handle on the term dates. But change to standardised national curriculum years 7–13? You must be joking. Then there were the names for locations: everyone at St Paul's knew the Marble, not a sculpture but a long stretch of gleaming black and white chequered corridor in the main building – a meeting point and starting point for all. At Queenswood, we had a similarly iconic location in the Monstros, a particularly ugly (monstrous?) raised flower bed around which it was notoriously difficult to drive a four-by-four, even on full lock. The older the school, the richer its unique vocabulary: I still struggle to understand a conversation between two Wykehamists (as the pupils of Winchester College, founded in the fourteenth century, are called) despite having been a fellow (governor) there for several years. Whatever type of school you attended yourself, the world of school to the young being so private and unique, you will probably be summoning up fragments or memories of your own, of the nicknames you had for certain places or the games you played and the lore and rituals you invented. These were your 'traditions' and they were what made school . . . school.

My memories of being a boarder at Bruton in the 1970s and of the habits of our lives are still vivid. Small privileges loomed large. Apart from the weekly excitement of *Z-Cars*, watched in our dressing gowns while sipping hot mugs of lurid orange squash (we were easy to please in those days), the highlight was our end-of-term midnight feasts. These involved consuming (while drugged with sleep) copious quantities of crisps, twiglets and those chocolate-covered marshmallow biscuits wrapped in foil. For some reason, our clandestine feasts were always held in the confined quarters of the school airing cupboard. I don't think this was entirely due to the fact that our dormitories were so cold – although they were, so much so that even putting our green gabardine raincoats on top of our blankets didn't stop us waking with numb feet every morning. It was more because a degree of imposed inconvenience and discomfort (as one of the smaller girls, I had to sit folded up like a contortionist on the shelf where the under-sheets were stored without getting chocolate on them) somehow made the whole thing more exciting. Which is probably why we delighted in daring each other to sleep in the 'Judy Box' (as we called the wardrobe, with charming Ladybird Book innocence); and why, at the end of term, we ceremonially took out all the drawers in which we stored our clothes and slept curled up like hamsters in those. I recall these antics now with bemused nostalgia and occasionally wonder whether the boarding-house staff knew all the time what we were doing and, after a long day, just put their feet up and turned up the television, hoping to drown out the scuffling and giggling.

Although the Paulinas of today are a world away in sophistication from the habits of my Somerset childhood, pupils have in common that they are greatly attached to traditions of all kinds, regularly invent new ones and will defend them to the death, whether or not they have any intrinsic merit of purpose. I found this out to my cost when in my early days as high mistress at St Paul's I rashly hired a consultant to review the oddly weak and amateurish (as I thought) school badge and logo. (I can already feel the bristling hackles at the adjectives I've used here as waves of Paulinas mass afresh in affronted rage at my temerity.) I almost laugh now at my own naivety in thinking I would be able to implement this 'simple marketing exercise' successfully. Categorically not. Despite engaging a professional designer (a Paulina herself, I might add) to come up with something more effective, I became aware that the new emblem we chose was the the focus of an unbridled loathing. After an interesting period where opinions were expressed with increasing clarity and vehemence, as only a displeased Paulina can, we reverted to the traditional wreath (properly drawn this time, in a small victory for aesthetics) with new lettering. I saw then the sheer intensity of the affection in which this emblem of the school – whether well drawn or not – was held. It was *their* logo, *their* tradition, and who was this jumped-up arriviste of a high mistress who thought she could come in and change it?

Events, language, traditions – all play their part as does singing. I was at a wedding recently and the man next to me said after the service: 'I really enjoyed singing those hymns. I haven't done that since I was at school.' There was nostalgia in his voice. As is now much more widely understood, to sing together in a large group is beneficial both to mental as well as physical health. Some of the big corporates should try it first thing in the morning, instead of vaguely hoping to create togetherness by having people balancing cups of coffee and pastries on tiny high tables while listening to a TED Talk. Singing is good for your health because it's aerobic exercise and, when done with others, builds a sense of closeness to those around you – ask anyone who has ever been in a choir. Our head of singing at St Paul's, a brilliant teacher whose hymn practice assemblies were a therapeutic and enjoyable end in themselves, told me that when people sing together, their hearts start beating in unison. Whether scientifically true or not, it certainly describes well the feeling of connection you have when your inhibitions fall away and you find yourself singing your heart out surrounded by others doing the same. Try it as soon as you can. It was one of the strange miracles of life at St Paul's that although the girls were proud of their school having a secular foundation, they were equally fond of singing hymns in assembly and did so for the most part lustily and well. Of course there were always the girls who for their own reasons were making a point and would not sing, standing arms folded daring me to look at them. But I think, secretly, they may have felt rather left out and wished they could find a dignified way to drop their silent protest and be a part of it.

The spontaneous rising of the descant from members of the choir, soaring up into the roof space of the Great Hall when we sang carols in December assemblies, still makes the hairs on the back of my neck stand up just remembering it. And it reminds me that at the Christmas concert, a thoroughly secular event, the twin highlights were singing the impossibly difficult carol composed by the former director of music, John Gardner, 'Tomorrow Shall Be My Dancing Day', together with 'The Holly and the Ivy' sung as a complicated round with special actions. This will long be identified by Paulinas as among the most-loved and remembered events of the year.

The school song itself is a tradition you had also better not tamper with. The girls regard as exclusively their own the English hymn 'I Vow to Thee My Country': sung to the tune 'Thaxted', by the school's first director of music Gustav Holst, the melody is taken from the 'Jupiter, the Bringer of Jollity' movement of his orchestral suite *The Planets*, and has words by Sir Cecil Spring-Rice whose daughter was a pupil. Written in 1920, the words are not ones you would immediately associate with a community of liberal-minded female intellectuals:

> I vow to thee, my country, all earthly things above,
> Entire and whole and perfect, the service of my love:
> The love that asks no question, the love that stands the test,
> That lays upon the altar the dearest and the best;
> The love that never falters, the love that pays the price,
> The love that makes undaunted the final sacrifice . . .[3]

Yet Paulinas sing this with passion and on the final day of their school careers, when they sing it for the last time, it is often with tears rolling down their cheeks.

So finally, as we hurtle towards the end of term, to Christmas and the end of the calendar year, I return to bells and think about their significance in the soundscape of the school. Memories of early school life are for many of us accompanied by the sound of bells, whether tolling at the start and end of the day or more shrilly punctuating our lessons and break times. We've seen how the rhythm of the school year and its undulations of terms and holidays gives shape to our lives, how school days follow a regular pattern and are another facet of the framework within which we get used to living and working. The school bell is a reminder of that framework and its familiar sound echoes down the intervening years, linking us to childhood and that ordered world.

The school bell itself is a lofty and visible symbol of that order and community. Lovers of Iris Murdoch's novels might recall the mysterious tale of the huge, ancient bell at Imber Court (*The Bell*, 1958), eventually fetched up out of the dark depths of the lake, its newly cast successor mysteriously plunging after it into the dark waters, as passions break through the apparently tranquil life of the enclosed order of Benedictine nuns. Richly resonant emblems of both permanence and the passing of time, all bells have a distinctive 'voice'. Take for example the single tolling of Big Ben described beautifully by Virginia Woolf in *Mrs Dalloway*, whose heroine Clarissa goes out in the London morning, hearing how 'the leaden circles dissolved in the air'.[4] Church bells too have their own particular associations, as A. N. Wilson writes:

It would no doubt be very sentimental to argue – but I would argue it nevertheless – that the peculiar combination of joy and sadness in bell music – both of clock chimes, and of change-ringing – is very typical of England. It is of a piece with the irony in which English people habitually address one another.

Try it out on yourself, the next time bell-ringing catches you by surprise. You are driving through a town or village and suddenly the air is awash with that music. You roll down the car window and listen. Yes, your heart will lift up, unless you are the noise nuisance officer of North Somerset. But it will also sense paradise lost, something gone. The German word *Sehnsucht* – yearning – does not have an exact equivalent in English. Maybe we have the bells instead.[5]

It was with some of this in mind that I decided a few years ago to restore and bring back into use the school bell at St Paul's, which sits atop the main building and had fallen silent after the

Second World War. History tells how architect Gerald Horsley included a belfry in the original 1904 building and an order was placed for a bell during construction. The bell itself, cast in 1902, was made by the distinguished firm of J. Warner & Sons, Cripplegate, whose foundry dated from 1739 and remained in operation until 1949. At the beginning of each school day, the bell at St Paul's was rung manually by means of a stout cord accessible from the Marble. An elegant clock, made by the London watchmakers J. W. Benson, was installed in 1908, enhancing the appearance of the belfry turret. The full refurbishment of the belfry was duly carried out in 2009 by which time the supports were so badly worn that rehanging was a tremendous task. One of my more exciting afternoons was spent climbing the scaffolding – touching with my very own hand the iron bell itself, while teetering precariously on a ladder and looking out, Quasimodo-like, over the rooftops of Brook Green.

The bell, now electronically operated, tolls at 8.20 each weekday morning for exactly forty seconds, this being the maximum amount of time a bell can be sounded in a built-up area without being classified as 'noise pollution'. When one reflects on some of the forms of noise our ears are assailed with in modern city life without the advantage of a forty-second limit there is a small irony in this, but despite some initial complaints from the neighbours (an actress who, after a late night treading the boards, did not want to be reminded it was 8.20 in the morning: not unreasonable) our bell has become part of the daily soundscape of Brook Green and a timely reminder to those lingering in Starbucks that they had better scurry along to school. During the day of course, we sound other, much less appealing and entirely functional, electronic bells, marking off each thirty-five-minute lesson and the various breaks. Some schools have experimented with running the day without any bells, thinking they add to the stress and general urgency of life. But I would always argue for retaining them: good teachers work brilliantly to the arc of this time division, and for the students it's the audio guide to where you should be and when: constant, reassuring, the coordinates of the day in your ears.

A school life and career is to be summoned by bells, of one kind or another, and eventually to be set free by them. For us all, perhaps, the sound of bells is a reminder of the measurement of our lives through time and space, childhood and school time, of church bells tolling joy and sadness, and the inexorable moving of all our days into the realm of memory.

Final assembly draws to a close. The singing has been particularly hearty, unfettered and joyous. The holidays are coming. I stand on the Marble saying goodbye to girls, clattering downstairs in pairs and groups laden with bags and lacrosse sticks, then out into the winter light of Brook Green. The living school disperses as the building settles itself and at last, falls quiet – they've all gone. And now . . . the staff lunch. In the dining room a glass of wine is pressed into my hand. Tired but cheerful colleagues gather and our chef, Fred, has surpassed himself again. How he can produce perfect roast beef for us all, after wall-to-wall Christmas lunches for a thousand over the last few days, is a mystery. We bring the kitchen staff out to say thank you for the wonderful lunches during the term, and everyone gets to their feet.

Half past two, and I'm back at my desk. I need to finish my reports but something about bells has been eluding me. That was it. Those lines from T. S. Eliot's 'The Dry Salvages':

And under the oppression of the silent fog
The tolling bell
Measures time not our time, rung by the unhurried
Ground swell, a time
Older than the time of chronometers, older
Than time counted by anxious worried women
Lying awake, calculating the future,
Trying to unweave, unwind, unravel

And piece together the past and the future,
Between midnight and dawn, when the past is all deception,
The future futureless, before the morning watch
When time stops and time is never ending;
And the ground swell, that is and was from the beginning,
Clangs
The bell.[6]

But now the school bell – our bell – falls silent, for a few weeks.
With Lindy still 'just finishing off a few things', I close the study
door soundlessly.

Dean Colet's Orders for St. Paul's School

1. If your child can read and write latin and english sufficiently, so that he shall be able to read and write lessons, then he shall be admitted into this School for a scholar.

2. If your child, after a reasonable time proved here, be found unapt or unable to learn, then you, warned thereof, shall take him away, that he possess not his room in vain.

3. If your child be apt to learn, you shall be content that he continue here till he hath competent literature.

4. You shall find him

5. You shall find him ing.

6. He shall continue forenoon and fro winter and summ

7. If he be absent six show not cause re ness) then his ro this school, unless ~~he be~~ again admitted by the Master.

8. If he falls several times into absence he shall be admitted no more.

9. If your child, after he is received into our school, go to any other school, to learn there after the manner of that school, I will, for no man's suit, that such a lad be received again into our school, but go where he list, or his friends think there is better learning.

Children must be taught how to think, not what to think
— *Margaret Meade*

TO DO

- Get Adam to explain to me how to drag images into a document
- Check results of Chinese poetry competition
- Buy 70% chocolate for entrance exam marking team
- Listen to French news

CHAPTER 5

January

Competition and cooperation – what kind of education do we want for our children?

The Christmas holidays are over and my assembly on new year's resolutions is almost ready. Woody Allen once announced on 1 January that he was going to give up using grape scissors. I would try to come up with something more educationally significant. But before that we have the annual eleven-plus entrance exam. Picture a raw January morning: the trees on Brook Green are blasted and bare, their branches a sinister fretwork against the steely grey sky. The surrounding roads are chock-full of impatient cars, as ten-year-old daughters arrive for the long-awaited day of tests. I stand on the stone steps observing the tense moments of parting and watch as solicitous parents turn reluctantly away.

Inside the school building, a well-tuned machine is humming. Wide-eyed examinees are checked in and swept along by the smiles of older girls who have come to help, glorying quietly in the memory of their own entrance exam day, now thankfully over. The first paper is English – a carefully chosen passage from a novel with questions followed by a piece of creative writing. With a rustle of turned papers in a multitude of classrooms, the day begins, with maths to follow before a break for lunch and the final exam of the day, in which the candidates are given a set of

challenges on a theme – the discovery of Richard III's body in
that Leicester car park, one year – testing a variety of skills including
code-breaking and deduction. By 3.30 p.m. we're finished and the
parents are hovering, arms reaching and heads inclining to encircle
their daughters as they spill out into the winter sunlight. 'How
was it . . . ?' In times gone by these exams were shrouded in
mystery; now past papers can be sampled on the school's website,
making the process less daunting and more accessible to candidates
from a wide variety of schools. Not all the girls who are right for
St Paul's are sitting in privileged prep schools where preparation
for entrance exams is down to a fine art; we want to see through
the immaculately drilled answers to find the exceptional girls who
might only be beginning to show glimmers of what they are
capable of.

In a few days, after intense hours of marking, we invite the
most promising candidates back for an interview. Mythology is
rife about what these entail: will you be asked to do fiendish maths
problems in your head, a fat stopwatch ticking? Extemporise in
Latin? Recite a Shakespeare sonnet from memory? Above all,
everyone knows, you will be asked your future dreams and hopes.
The fashion amongst well-drilled candidates varies: one year, there
are several hundred would-be astronauts. Another, we contemplate
a world filled with marine biologists moonlighting as fashion
designers. In reality, the interview is a chance to understand a
little more about personality and gauge the genuine appetite and
aptitude for learning behind all that exam preparation. I can recall
some memorable exchanges with self-possessed, upright young
interviewees, their badges pinned like rows of military buttons to
their felt blazers, as well as with more eccentric little characters
who hadn't seen a hairbrush that morning but were eager to tell
me about their interest in pond life and how they loved baking
cakes with their younger brothers at the weekend. One once asked
me artlessly, a ginger pigtail tucked behind each ear: 'What's it
like being High Priestess?' And there were always the amusing

glimpses into parental strategy: 'I want to come here because my mother thinks it will make it easier for me to get into Westminster for the sixth form. She just *loves* the headmaster . . .'

Eventually, with all the information gathered in – exam marks, interview notes and confidential reports from the current school – we meet to make our offers of places: a solemn process, as we sit around the heavy library tables, considering each candidate. We feel the weight of the responsibility: a decision which will set the life course of a girl and send her on her way to become a Paulina. Or not. So much resting on this decision and all the similar ones being made in London schools at roughly the same time. What was it all about and why did it matter so much?

Parents naturally want the best for their children. The trouble is, that 'best' in education terms is too often narrowly defined by the annual competition of published league tables, ranking schools by examination results, giving the subliminal message that exam success is the main goal of education. Despite well-meaning protestations from national educational leaders to the contrary, it isn't surprising that these bald measurable outcomes are how parents will assess the quality of a school, making competition for places fierce. More concerning is the pressure such comparisons place on schools to privilege exam results over learning and even to massage results. For example, students may be encouraged to take easier courses in which higher results are more likely or, as is common, the process of learning is degraded, so that rather than offering an exploratory experience where there is room to ask questions and debate, more and more teachers feel under pressure to cut out material not directly related to the eventual exam, resorting to 'teaching to the test'. I am not against exams in themselves, but they have to be kept in their place. I watched a dispiriting A-level English class recently where in the very first lesson of the course, rather than introducing the small group to the delights that were in store for them in studying *The Great Gatsby*, the well-intentioned teacher was instead laying out the assessment objectives that the class would need to know so as to hit the right buttons in exams that would not be written for another year. Where was the spark to ignite their love of English literature? Today it seems to me we are in danger of losing sight of what education should be about. Driven by the fear of our children not getting a place at the right university, or failing in some way to enter the competitive race that is adult life, we have become swept up in an impoverished, narrow idea of school where the only thing we are sure we know how to value is exam success.

In this climate, parents are intent on a certain perceived hierarchy of schools and with getting their children's feet firmly on a rung as far up that league table ladder as they can. In the race to attract the 'best' students, fee-paying schools have become spellbound by the same academic goals and are increasingly monofocal in their approach. They see oversubscription (the great aim to be a selecting rather than a recruiting school) as a reason to select on ever more limited grounds, squeezing out the life from the vision of education that they might have had when they started. While what I know best may be the small bubble of the London independent school world, it is symptomatic. This narrowing of focus is a reflection of a deep-seated way of looking at education and what we value – something traditional and peculiarly British. Whatever lip service we pay to other more practical skills, academic learning and intellectual achievement remain the capabilities that confer most status – no surprise then that these are therefore regarded as the most important ways to excel at school. Other kinds of talent – practical or technical ability – are nice to have, but less impressive. We have two of the world's great universities in Oxford and Cambridge, which remain the goal of many of the most academic students and themselves enshrine that realm of aspiration, but we have made little progress in bringing about a broader, complementary and diverse understanding of what excellence might look like, how to recognise it, provide for it and reward it.

This stubborn adherence to one way of measuring talent contributed to the binary model of state education, in which some children were chosen for the academic route in grammar schools while others were forever rejected as less clever. Why this isolated way of measuring talent? The non-selective comprehensive model was an attempt to efface that false division and give equal access to all, but my own experience of teaching all-ability classes has showed me that the counter-proposition – that in order to be fair all children should be taught together and receive the same education – is also very far from ideal. A brilliant teacher can do it, but for most of us, trying to stretch the most able (in conventional terms) at the same time as giving attention to those who need very different support is extremely challenging. The brightest tend to be left to teach themselves because they make less fuss and just get on with it. Our persistent adulation of academic success and snobbery about other intelligences has served to encourage a divided society and entrench an over-simplistic view of what constitutes a good school. A negative attitude to the private sector, envied for its freedom to innovate and at the same time resented for its perceived divisiveness, has also meant that genuine collaborative working has taken much longer to develop effectively than it might, hindered rather than helped by unrealistic and clumsily applied compulsion from government and the Charity Commission. And while national standards in basic skills such as numeracy continue to cause concern, reaching desperately for bits of old policy – bringing back grammar schools, for example – is no answer either. We need to think much more carefully about what education consists of, and what will serve all our children best as they move into a twenty-first-century adulthood.

We've thought about schools as living communities, about the myriad activities and traditions which provide the glue binding the community together, and about the reassuring rhythm of the school year with its structured opportunities for fresh beginnings. But what about the formal curriculum? What goes on in lessons and what are children being taught?

What are all those subjects on your child's timetable in the back of the school diary – and are they the right ones? How did a subject become a subject? Stepping out of the classroom for a moment, if you make your way to the British Museum in Bloomsbury and wander along the length of Gallery 1, built to house the library of King George III (easy to find as it opens directly off the central Great Court) you're reminded of how we have developed the habit of sorting and classifying knowledge about the world into neat, labelled subject packages. The Enlightenment Gallery is divided into sections that explore the major new disciplines of that age: religion and ritual, trade and discovery, the birth of archaeology, art history, classification, the decipherment of ancient scripts and natural history. It's said that the behaviour of the general public in this gallery is the most quiet and respectful anywhere in the museum: there's something about the orderly setting out of information that calls up the obedient school child in us all. Wandering the book-lined gallery, peering into meticulously labelled display cases, the array of curious objects, from stuffed animals to ancient pottery, shows us how collectors, antiquaries and travellers categorised and understood the world around them.

And such categorisations have lasted: it isn't all that difficult to unearth a domain of the modern school curriculum within these same disciplines. The idea of the boundaries between subjects is another form of order and pattern that provides a frame for our learning and subject distinctions alter only very slowly. Most people enjoy and can answer the question: what was your favourite subject? Mine was English. Bringing a literary text to life is still at the heart of it, even if technology has made research quicker and reduced our stamina for the 900 pages of an eighteenth-century novel. And Shakespeare is still Shakespeare, where the whole of human experience is surely contained: love, loss, grief, anger, jealousy, hope, disappointment, absurdity, regret, joy. Because his themes are timeless and universal, he is as relevant now as he ever was. New areas of knowledge that can be given the status of being a subject are emerging, most recently the more sophisticated realms of technology where understanding is growing so rapidly, and some subjects are dwindling, such as classical languages. Some, such as religious education, are gaining new significance and importance in the light of wider global developments.

Most subjects today, in the English curriculum at least, are similar to those we as adults recall from school. What was your favourite? Perhaps you were a scientist or a mathematician. In these curriculum areas where new knowledge is emerging all the time, there has been rather more change. I have dismal memories of science education in my girls' school of the 1970s. Many of my generation, including me, also grew up with a mental block about maths. I can see now the sea of figures on square, solid Miss Lawson's too-shiny roller blackboard, as she paced in sensible shoes, her glasses glinting, willing us to complete our exercises before the bell. Occasionally I would have that glimpse of beauty as the equation cascading down the page worked itself out. But for much of the time I floated in a tepid sea of half-understanding. I gave it up as soon as I could. Little did I think I would eventually become the head of a girls' school where maths was the most popular A-level subject.

As if to make up for past neglect, we now hear constantly about the importance of STEM subjects. The approaches to teaching and the emphasis on science, technology, engineering and maths have changed dramatically: science, for instance, is no longer about the acquisition of dry theory or performing experiments unconnected to the world around us, but is linked to everyday life and the solving of the world's pressing contemporary problems. We are training scientists in our schools who have skills of analysis and deduction that they can apply in the real world, not filling up buckets with rote-learned knowledge that will soon be superseded. It's accepted we need capable scientists and mathematicians in an increasingly technological society and, as we've seen, it's often the jobs in these fields that attract the highest financial rewards. A subject is still a subject, but the headlong rush towards a world dominated by STEM seems unstoppable.

I'm delighted that in girls' schools we are now teaching science and maths to such a high standard and the girls are doing so well in them, with no sense that these are really the preserve of boys. But if education is about preparation for life and not just employment, we cannot overvalue these subjects at the expense of others which are just as important, both to being effective in a work context as well as being a responsible citizen in the modern age.

The imbalance of skills in the workplace has had catastrophic consequences in the recent past. In the wake of the financial crash of 2008, some of those from within the banking world I have listened to, including former students, are all too mindful of what went wrong: they point to a failure to measure and manage risk, an over-reliance on economic theories and ultimately on a chronic failure to communicate and explain. Bad strategic decisions, weak people management, questionable practices and fortress mentalities, they say, all played their part. Where, we might now ask, were the practical, clear and critical thinkers who should have been demanding common sense and human values?

In banking, certainly, but in many other fields where we face factors that are unknown, we need more breadth. This must mean moving from a highly technical, data-driven approach to one that includes the ability to be more intuitive and qualitative. We need to encourage and value artistic intuition, lateral thinking, creativity, foreign language proficiency or literary critical thought. Diversity is vital: the critical mind, the probing, searching, restless questioning that comes with arts subjects complements that of the scientific mind's more linear progression.

Put simply, in today's complex world intuition and creativity are as necessary in making good business decisions as the more logical, scientific mindset. We therefore need people trained in the arts, languages and humanities to give that diversity and avoid the groupthink which has led to so much poor decision-making in business in recent years. And the arts/science divide is a false one anyway – scientists need imagination, just as literary scholars need a rigorous eye for detail.

The arts and humanities are intrinsically important to a healthy society for even more fundamental reasons, as explained by Martha Nussbaum in her brilliant book *Not for Profit: Why Democracy Needs the Humanities*. Political scientist Professor Ruth O'Brien, writing the preface, highlights the danger of undervaluing subjects that are essential not just to the world of work but to creating balanced and democratic societies: 'The humanities and the arts play a central role in the history of democracy, and yet today many parents are ashamed of children who study literature or art. Literature and philosophy have changed the world, but parents all over the world are more likely to fret if their children are financially illiterate than if their training in the humanities is deficient.'[1]

Nussbaum's thesis is that our view of education has become – rather like the competitive eleven-plus exam process – unduly instrumental. We worry about our children being equipped to compete and see education as valuable only insofar as it contributes to national profitability. It's one thing to encourage more girls to take maths so that they can have access to the higher paid jobs that are dominated by men; it's a laudable aim as far as it goes. No wonder the STEM subjects hold sway, if they are seen as more immediately useful and also more likely to lead to greater financial recognition. But if we care about more than pecuniary profit, about having stable societies in the future, if we care about fairness and democracy, we cannot afford to continue downgrading the subjects that teach us how such societies are shaped.

The humanities, by which in a school context we normally mean geography, history and religious education, teach us about our planet, about how mankind has lived in the past and how religion and worship have become integrated into our lives. The substance is in the name: these subjects are the study of humanity. And, like art and literature, they help us imagine the lives of others and through that, teach us empathy. For example, take former British Museum director Neil MacGregor's *History of the World in 100 Objects* and, within that, his description of the Clovis spear point, a small handmade arrowhead found in modern-day Arizona and dropped there over 13,000 years ago. Taking us back in time, he asks that we imagine ourselves to be hunters in the scrubland, stalking a herd of mammoth. You throw your spear, with its painstakingly sharpened point designed to cause the maximum amount of bleeding and disable the huge animal quickly. But the wooden shaft breaks and the spearhead drops to the ground, where you discard and replace it with another as the tribe moves on. 'You leave behind you something that's not just a killing tool that failed, but a thing that's going to become a message across time.'[2]

The message is that there is an ineradicable connection between us and those early ancestors seeking their own survival and using their ingenuity to solve problems, just as we do now. The ability to develop a sense of where we have come from helps us situate ourselves in the history of humanity and, as the poet Mary Oliver puts it, 'find our place in the family of things'.[3] However difficult it is to find order and security in a world spinning apart through the infinite possibilities of the internet, however easy it might be to become untethered from our communities and lost in cyberspace, history and its artefacts can connect us with those who have gone before, and provide a rootedness which we absolutely need in order to find our place in the world. A rootedness that in other ways is now much more elusive. From that more grounded sense of self comes then the crucial ability to empathise and to imagine the lives of others. Only by studying human behaviour and analysing motivation can we hope to follow the advice of Atticus Finch who says to his daughter, Scout, in Harper Lee's famous novel *To Kill a Mockingbird*: 'You never really understand a person until you consider things from his point of view . . . until you climb in his skin and walk around in it.'

For similar reasons, we have also to think about protecting the arts (as is newly acknowledged with the adaptation of STEM to STEAM). A good school takes art – and the creative arts – seriously. The arts may not be equated with financial reward but they unlock other riches. In an interesting counterweight to the current emphasis on teaching resilience and grit, the arts encourage personal discovery, leading us, as Nussbaum says, to experience vulnerability and surprise as states to be explored – as positives – rather than making us fearful of not having total control or of anything that could result in failure. What is delicate or uncertain is not always to be guarded against and avoided. No worthwhile art, our former head of department used to say, was ever accomplished without struggle. Creating is hard work. With that in mind, it's frustrating to see this most demanding of subjects marginalised as 'relaxation' – a kind of therapy after the rigours of more serious academic work. Art requires bravery, a willingness to be exposed. I was always struck, when the girls put on their annual art exhibition, how trusting they were; how they were prepared to reveal such a personal and private side of themselves through the work they had made. References to relationships, family, success and failure – the internal workings of their minds and hearts. In a world so focussed on helping us toughen up, important though this is, we should not lose sight of the fact that there is something in people that remains, as Nussbaum identifies it, essentially fragile. Our openness to others, our capacity for empathy and compassion depend on that not being entirely trained out of us. In her words: 'To be a good human being is to have a kind of openness to the world, an ability to trust uncertain things beyond your own control, that can lead you to be shattered in very extreme circumstances for which you were not to blame. That says something very important about the condition of the ethical life: that it is based on a trust in the uncertain and on a willingness to be exposed; it's based on being more like a plant than like a jewel, something rather fragile, but whose very particular beauty is inseparable from that fragility.'[4]

If art helps us understand and express ourselves, helps us lead an ethical life through respecting and recognising the essential fragility of human nature, its exploratory nature also allows us to accept and live with the fact that some aspects of life are unknowable. In a world dominated by STEM, we are less comfortable with that which cannot be predicted and measured, yet so many aspects of our lives are set about with uncertainty. The poet Rainer Maria Rilke recognises this state of mind and what it requires when he counsels patience in his *Letters to a Young Poet*: 'Be patient with all that is unresolved in your heart and try to love the questions themselves, like locked rooms, like books written in a foreign tongue . . . Live the questions for now. Perhaps you will then, gradually, without noticing it, live your way into the answer, one distant day in the future.'[5]

Finally, growing from that naturally there is the question of what we would call internationalism, of promoting global understanding through sharing ideas and communication. My work earlier in my career in Hong Kong and more recently advising in the international schools world, has been an important reminder of taking account of the perspectives of other cultures and societies. I'll always remember Ruth Gledhill, then religious affairs correspondent for *The Times*, saying at a talk to head teachers that before 9/11, many Americans would have struggled even to place Afghanistan on a map. And not just Americans. Ignorance is dangerous. Children educated today in a school which is part of an international group are provided with many opportunities for collaboration across boundaries and find themselves exposed to different ways of thinking as a normal part of their education. This doesn't mean that local traditions and ways of doing things are less valuable or respected, simply that they are set within a wider context – hence the coining of the term 'glocal': local character within a global setting. I was in discussion recently at a school in Bahrain about the practicalities of the period of Ramadan. How does a school manage when many children are fasting during daylight hours, staying up late for the iftar meal and rising well before dawn to eat, when they are also taking public examinations and trying to cope with a normal school day? This is just one of the questions that arises as different cultural patterns and the living of daily life are woven together. To broaden cultural respect and understanding must surely be an important dimension for all children in the future, wherever they find themselves at school.

Cultural understanding is one thing, but internationalism can only go so far without addressing foreign language acquisition. In Britain language-learning has been shamefully neglected. This being another field in which I failed to distinguish myself at school (my return to the study of French in my late fifties has been brain-bending indeed) and having felt that disadvantage, I am doubly determined that we promote and protect the study of languages in our schools, which is currently under significant threat. Since 2004 it has not been compulsory to teach children a modern foreign language up to GCSE. So, at age fourteen, you can opt out of ever studying a language other than English again. What is this saying about the importance we attach to preparing the next generation for a global society? The reason for the decision was that there was a dearth of language teachers and GCSE was felt to be too difficult for many pupils. Unsurprisingly, languages have declined further, the supply of trainee languages teachers diminishing and recruitment difficult, especially in challenging schools. There are examples of excellent provision, but in general the divide between the public and private sector is widening as private schools choose to protect these subjects. The same applies more acutely in classical languages: in 2017 there were over twice as many applicants from the private sector to read classics at Oxford even though those applicants come from a mere 7 per cent of the country's children. Fashions and tastes in the study of modern foreign languages change: Mandarin Chinese is gradually gaining ground (though the flurry of interest a few years ago in expanding the provision across all schools dissipated as ministers came to grips with just how difficult it really was) while German continues to be less popular than Spanish and French. Schools with real strength in languages, are more and more a rarity and, as I write, I see that this year, numbers taking A-level French have fallen yet again. This must change if we are to wake up from our increasingly myopic view of our place in the world and show a greater awareness of the importance of understanding other cultures. Governments need to be less afraid of poor exam results reflecting badly on them.

Equally, future educators need to think of the curriculum not in unrelated subject-by-subject silos – those carefully labelled museum display cases – but rather, by exploring further the connections between the disciplines. Primary education has long favoured project- or theme-based learning, where children collaborate on a shared objective – planning an event or making a model – and bring to bear their skills and knowledge from a range of different subjects. In other words, taking that important step of consolidating their knowledge by applying it. (Next time you hold a children's party, divide them into small groups, give each a packet of spaghetti and some jelly babies and see who can make the tallest, most stable tower. Then step back and watch physics, maths, art and design and language ability all being tested alongside those all-important skills of leadership, collaboration and teamwork.) The pressure of exam syllabi in senior schools has largely driven this kind of approach out but innovative schools in the future, mindful of the skills children need to acquire for twenty-first-century life, will give more emphasis to collaborative learning. Opportunities are sometimes serendipitous: I was delighted to see girls at St Paul's turn the interior of their derelict sports pavilion before its final demolition into a magical art installation, each room expressing a particular mood or emotion and festooned with the branches of pruned trees amongst the builders' discarded materials.

A chance visit to an exhibition in Cambridge in May 2008 gave me a fresh insight into the possible links between the arts and sciences and maths. Called 'Beyond Measure' and held at the small, out-of-the way gallery Kettle's Yard, it invited the viewer to 'explore how geometry is used by artists and astronomers, biochemists, engineers, surgeons, architects, physicists, mathematicians . . . as a means to understand, explain and order the world around us'. I was struck first by the reference to that human need for order, an echo of our containment within the structured academic year and also by some of the artworks that had geometry as their inspiration. Latvian mathematician Daina Taimina's *Hyperbolic Area*, for example, appeared a knitted jellyfish at first sight, but had in fact been made to an intricate geometric formula – one of many such experiments. She had a barrier reef full of work that you could look at: craft, maths and a playful sense of the world coming together. At St Paul's, some of the most illuminating learning I saw came about when the students explored independently a subject link that interested them – one bringing physics to bear on the experience of hearing music, for example, and another where art and maths came together to create a structure visualising four dimensions. The chemistry of a lemon meringue pie, with worked example, was another memorable experience. Not only is there a glory in the sheer discovery of these connections – the 'useless learning' prized by one scholarly headmaster I know – but surely this is also the way to open up the new insights that the future world of work will draw upon?

Like most things, designing the curriculum is a matter of balance. The traditional subject classifications remain important, because they ensure that value is still attached to discrete bodies of knowledge. Knowledge is not static but still you cannot be an historian unless you know some facts, a scientist unless you know some formulae or a linguist unless you know some grammar. There is no sidestepping the fundamentals of knowledge acquisition and memorisation – a most unfashionable but necessary skill. Policymakers focussed on achieving flattering exam statistics have been too ready to approve draining the curriculum of tough and substantial content – hard to acquire because you just have to learn the stuff – and in the focus on skills, privileging the how of education over the what. Worthwhile and lasting education means rich content, promoting a breadth and depth of knowledge complemented by the honing of skills through imaginative exploration. We need to look at what is needed by the next generation not just in a narrow instrumental way but in a broader, human sense to promote long-term sustainability in a world where, if we are to survive, mutual understanding and sharing has to trump competing and taking.

In considering the curriculum itself, its boundaries and connections, it is impossible to move on without emphasising the importance of reading. Reading, like drawing, is a fundamental skill on which so much else depends. Sustained reading requires stamina in the same way that it takes staying power to acquire knowledge. As we will see, the ubiquity of technology has largely undermined both the appetite and the capacity for reading material of any length, as there is the assumption that the quick and short always trumps the slower and more considered; it is no longer necessary to concentrate on written sources for long periods of time in the course of research. The role of reading is changing. There is still a place – arguably an ever more important one – for reading as a source of contemplative resto-ration and solace: a way of withdrawing into the self as respite from the endlessly ticking world. It's no surprise that amongst adults, reading groups are springing up that don't involve meeting to talk about a book, but meeting to actually sit together and read. How many of us would not feel guilty picking up a work of fiction before lunchtime? Or even any time much before bedtime? Surely there must be something more pressing that should be getting our attention. We see reading as a leisure activity rather than as an important facet of lifelong learning and a necessary solitary activity which restores our well-being and calm. Helping children develop the habit of reading for enjoyment from an early age must remain an important priority for schools and, given the profound comfort often felt in the physical presence of books, their smell, their promise of patiently waiting interest for the mind and the imagination, libraries themselves are places we would be wise to protect. What's more they are loved by young people: I was delighted recently to hear that the chief advocate of the threatened library service in Northamptonshire was not a pensioner but a schoolgirl.

So to the underlying curriculum. Once you begin to look specifically at the importance of empathy, an understanding of human behaviour and human nature, of why people do as they do, a sense of our place in the world and, in the flux of time, a willingness to explore what is within ourselves and the patience to live with what is unknown and uncertain – it's hard to conceive of an education without opportunities to develop these qualities. So much of this in the past has been left to chance, however. Part of the process of rebalancing is already evident in the growing recognition that we have to pay deliberate attention to the education of character. It can no longer be seen as a beneficial extra if children happen to pick up some skills of personal organisation, the ability to motivate themselves and the capacity to bounce back from disappointment. We now teach these things deliberately. Much of this character education essentially emphasises independence: how to stand up for yourself and cope in difficult circumstances. The popularity of television shows which teach survival skills is evidence that we think there is appeal in this. But at the same time, it's important to remember that an openness to the world and the protection of that fragility described by Nussbaum is equally important to our understanding and to our development as human beings.

Resilience feels like a solitary virtue but equally important is the ability to collaborate and work together. We're told that the resourcing problems of the world are not so much to do with a lack of what people need to flourish, as with their reluctance to share those resources equitably: food, water, energy. The encouragement of competition has led to a selfish drive for acquisition rather than a sense of responsibility for others. Thus the gap between rich and poor widens, societies fracture along social and religious lines and conflict results. Certain subjects in the curriculum promote empathy and greater understanding of other people, but students must learn in practical ways how to work together towards shared objectives. In a school with such a strong emphasis on individuality as St Paul's, both in the form of individual achievement and individual expression, the building of shared value is arguably even more important, though not without its particular challenges. How do you, for instance, encourage a spirit of collaboration and teamwork amongst those who are driven to achieve at a very high level as individuals? The girls grow up strong, determined and focussed – they will need to be – so how can that be tempered with an understanding of the value of working with others?

I had an early glimpse of what a really driven, competitive spirit looks like in my previous headship at Queenswood. At a house tennis tournament – a friendly affair played on a Saturday summer's afternoon – one girl suddenly threw down her racquet and shouted to the assembled crowd watching in the stands: 'This girl is not good enough to play with me! We are never going to win! You have to match me with somebody else!' Tina, sixteen, had come to the school with her twin sister, not at the behest of kind and supportive parents living in the home counties, but on her own initiative. Dissatisfied with her education at home in Hungary, she had been determined to come to an English boarding school, and had written to the headmistress asking for scholarships for herself and her sister. Impressed by her resolve and intelligence, my predecessor had signed her up. Tina's outburst on the tennis court broke all the rules of British decorum but it was this single-mindedness that had brought her to England and changed her life chances. Why would we be surprised that her ambition trumped her generosity in a sports match?

On the whole, at St Paul's, where academic motivation and engagement is a given, the girls seemed to be able to find the balance between striving for their own best without becoming destructively competitive with each other. More than that, they were generously curious about each other's learning and gained a great deal from that curiosity. Competitiveness isn't necessarily a bad thing and the ability to withstand a degree of it necessary: the girls entered external essay and other competitions all the time, entirely on their own, I can only assume because they liked trying to win – and often did. But within the school, setting yourself stretching targets seemed to be enough without having to do better than everyone else.

The education of the future then should continue to pay proper attention to the traditional domains of learning, but there needs to be more formal acknowledgement that character education matters, and more attention paid to developing it, lest we breed a generation unfit to thrive and succeed in the world they are inheriting from us. In previous generations, the idea of a career path was more linear. Look back at what you have done yourself.

Unless you are quite unusual, you have probably done one kind of job for most of your working life or, if you have changed, only made the leap once. My own career has been predictable by modern standards in that I have always been a teacher: apart from one daring spell working overseas in Hong Kong, I have moved from one job in education to another, gradually climbing the greasy pole of management and leadership to become a headmistress. A single trajectory. Only now, after many years doing that, have I decided to take a leap into the unknown and see what the world is like outside of the teaching profession.

The current generation do not necessarily expect their working lives to evolve in this way. The reassuring predictability of a forty-year career has gone. They see – and are unafraid by – both greater opportunity and less security. They are not impressed with the power of great institutions which previous generations took as bywords for stability and permanence. Instead, they are self-starters, seeing their lives and decisions in more immediate terms. Who could have imagined, a generation ago, listening to a panel of young entrepreneurs all under twenty-five, as I did at a conference recently, talking about their emerging businesses and expressing the intention to be 'financially free' (that is, having earned enough never to do paid work again) by twenty-seven? What struck me most about these young people was their sheer self-belief and confidence: they did not look to an older generation to show them the way; in charge of their own destiny, if one idea didn't work out or they tired of it, they would try another. The working pattern they looked forward to was not linear but a series of branches, with the capacity for many fresh starts. And with the possibility of financial freedom – for some at least – coming young, the opportunity to make creative use of your life without the pressure to earn money is also there. This outlook and pattern of working must draw on reserves of self-reliance and inner confidence that are of a different order from what was required a generation ago. Schools need to give time to teaching entrepreneurship; how to be your own publicist; how to have the self-reliance and resilience in order to be a career self-starter. And to understand that, far from being passive recipients of the education of the future, they will be shaping it too.

The secondary school and university students of today have grown up in extraordinary times. The financial crash of 2008 has banished the unquestioning respect for institutions when those who held the keys of the kingdom were shown capable of reckless irresponsibility. The harsh financial realities of the property market mean that house purchase is never likely to be a real possibility for many young people, more and more of whom are returning home from university not to lead the life of independence they are ready for but to live with their parents. Sofa-surfing and other temporary ways of living have become more common and, inevitably, if you live like this you have a more transient view of life; you are travelling lighter.

This generation is often criticised for being less engaged in party politics than their parents were at the same age (18–25-year-olds did not turn out to vote to prevent Brexit) but instead the internet has made them more aware of pan-global phenomena such as the inequitable distribution of natural resources across the world and of climate change. They certainly are passionately interested in these issues and see themselves as global rather than local citizens. While I believe the rise in problems of mental health amongst their generation can be linked to the darker side of technology overuse, by the same means young people today are well informed about wider issues and have a great desire to make a difference. Many are involved in community action and charity work which they take up through their own initiative. This is true in schools and equally so at the university level. And the same spirit informs their career aspirations. In 2016, accountancy giants KPMG sponsored the *Think Future Study* which surveyed 25,000 undergraduates about their career aspirations. Sure enough, 93 per cent of them responded that they wanted a career which 'made a difference' to

society, bearing out the much greater drive towards social responsibility. A mere 12 per cent wanted a career in financial services
and while being well paid was naturally a priority for many, the
top factors informing choice of career were enjoying what you do
and having time for a life in which work and family could be
successfully combined.

And today's students also have different study habits. Used to
being able to access information at the touch of a key, speed is
often valued over depth and students today will gather information
very rapidly from multiple sources. Anyone who has teenage children will also know that they seem to be able to do many things
at once: listen to music, check their social media channels and
complete an essay all at the same time. Whether or not this is
really efficient, it is what they do. The result is that concentration
spans are shorter and courses have adapted to reflect that. In my
subject, the much reduced stamina to read lengthy works of prose
fiction means fewer such works are set. Instead students read
extracts, shorter, less demanding works and abridged versions. The
question now is not whether you can glean enough information
on a subject, but whether what you have unearthed is any good.
In the school library you could be pretty sure everything was worth
reading – otherwise it wouldn't be there. Research on the internet
offers no such reassurance, so the ability to discriminate and sort
quality information from the unreliable is another skill particularly
relevant to the post-millennial student.

What does all this mean for schools, and the kind of education we should be designing for the future? There is a place, and
will continue to be a place, for the conventional school curriculum and for content, for bodies of knowledge which bring
together the best that has been thought and written in the past,
while also adapting to include new knowledge and modes of
thinking. We should continue to encourage the exploration of
links between disciplines without watering down what is distinctive and difficult. Alongside this, the education of character needs

careful and deliberate consideration. This must include education for living in an uncertain world where resilience, team-working and leadership will be ever more important, and where empathy and an acknowledgement that vulnerability is a part of our humanity also finds its place. More time and more seriousness needs to be devoted to developing people, in the fullest sense, not merely well-qualified technocrats.

I remind myself that schools are there not just to prepare young people for the world as it is, but also to help shape that world. Rather than just thinking of education as a process visited on the young, we need to involve them more actively in the designing of it. They are the influencers of the future and will be making decisions about our lives, very soon. They will also be parents of the generation that will follow. It takes twenty-first-century thinking to shape twenty-first-century education. I have talked to a number of bright and ambitious young people recently for whom the university experience has felt disappointing or irrelevant: one gave up his English degree after two years to work for an interior design firm and hasn't looked back. With the prospect of longer lives and more leisure, there is a special value in inculcating a love of learning for its own sake – a modern notion of scholarship – but perhaps the so-called third age is where it will come to be most valued and appreciated.

Living my own advice to the girls that they should widen their interests, I attended a sculpture class one year. This resulted in several clay heads which I ranged companionably on my office mantelpiece: I hoped they didn't look to unsuspecting visitors like the shrivelled totems in a Conrad novel. As I look up from the page, one of them appears to be looking back at me quizzically. I've been burning too much late oil. The school is silent: it's dark outside and I can hear our careful, patient caretaker locking up. Stepping out into the corridor with a sudden shock I see a long row of small, terracotta feet without any legs attached to them. The MIVs have been recreating their feet in clay and, with a

Pauline sense of humour, the head of art has carefully placed them padding silently up to my door. I pick my way carefully past them and, smiling to myself, make my way down the long echoing corridor towards home.

TO DO

- Compile English interview questions
- Distribute student survey
- Design teacher evaluation form
- Email Isobel's art teacher
- Buy marmite!

Schools We Can Envy

Because entry into teaching is difficult and the training is rigorous, teaching is a respected and prestigious profession in Finland ... the only reason (Finnish teachers) might leave would be 'if they were to lose their professional autonomy'
— Pasi Sahlberg

Every lesson shapes a li

Subject Trigonometry	Period Ending	19

Month Sept.	Sept	Oct	Tests
Date	28 22 26	2	
NAMES	M T W T F	M T W T F	M T W T F	M T W T F	M T W T F
Cunkle, James	1	✓ 5 5 8 4 7	2 5 9 32 2 17 11 25	9	
Currens, Galen	2	✓ 5 5 3 4 7	2 5 9 32 2 17 11 25	15	
Green, Harold	3 ✓	✓ 5 5 3 4 7	2 7 9 32 14 11 12 5	24	
Grove, William	4	✓ 3 4 3 7	5 24 2d 17 11 25	19	
Haralefood, Jack	5 ✓	✓ 5 5 9 4 7	2 5 9 26 2 11 11 6	17	
Rohr, Jerry	6	✓ 5 5 3 4 7	2 7 9 32 2 17 11 25	19	
Stauer, Thad	7	✓ 5 5 3	7 2 5 4 32 2 17 11 25	18	
Coffey, Jean	8	5 5 9 4 7	2 6 9 33 2 17 11 12 5	14	
Davidson, Mary	9 ✓	✓ 5 5 8 4 7	2 6 9 32 2 17 11 25	14	
Diehl, Elizabeth	10 ✓	✓ 5 5 8 4 7	2 6 9 32 2 17 11 25	14	

CHAPTER 6

February

Be a teacher – be the one you are

It's February. In the flower beds below my office window a few bulbs are beginning to push their way through and it's a bright, cold morning. We are well into the second half of the school year, spring is coming: a time of change. In the staffroom, the ambitious or restless are scanning the thick classified sections of the *Times Educational Supplement* looking for promotion opportunities for September. A face appears round my door: 'Clarissa – sorry to interrupt. A head of department job has come up . . . Of course, I'm incredibly happy here but just thought I'd take a look at it. You know, nothing ventured and so forth. Can I put you down as a referee?' The door closes and I see another excellent colleague on their way to higher things.

Continuity being much prized, the departure of a teacher does not normally go down well with students or their parents: far from being proud that we have nurtured a leader who will go on to make an impact elsewhere, feeding into the common strength of education, there is a sense of loss and betrayal. How could Miss Plant be *so selfish* as to leave Emily when she is halfway through her GCSE Science course? Has she no sense of responsibility? Why have you let her go, Ms Farr? *Why actually is she leaving anyway?* Was she being bullied/underpaid/ overworked? Mumsnet is alive with the many possibilities. And Lettice Plant herself is anxious: 'I'm not going to tell my classes until after half term. And my tutor group . . . well . . . I just don't know how I'm going to break it to them. I wanted them to know first but it's Claudia's birthday today . . . I just can't do it to them.' Thankfully, after the initial 'Nooooo . . . !', with the natural forgetfulness of youth the students soon channel their energies into making special cards, filming themselves recalling hilarious classroom moments and baking cakes in the shape of plant cells or the digestive system in order to thank their beloved teacher as she leaves. The waters will close over and she will be replaced by someone else of whom they will grow equally fond.

But today, it's *my* subject and we are appointing a new English teacher. Three candidates stand in a formal semi-circle on the chequered Marble: Muriel, in her late fifties from a sixth-form college in Cambridge who has been caring for her sick mother for some years and is now free to move. She loves Hardy and has lots of A-level experience. Then there is Luke, in his late twenties, who has been teaching for five years in a huge split-site school in east London. He has written a play which is due to be performed shortly by an all-female theatre company. And finally we have Jenny who is at Cambridge, where she has spent her whole student career, and is currently putting the finishing touches to her PhD thesis on the eighteenth-century novel. She has never taught a lesson before.

I greet them using first names and try to put them at their ease. We want today to be as enjoyable as possible so that they go away feeling they have had a positive, worthwhile experience, whatever the outcome. Attending an interview is great for professional development, I tell them; think of it that way and there is plenty to learn and take away, even if you don't end up working here. I see them looking round. So this is St Paul's: where are all the exhausted, stressed, anorexic girls with dark circles under their eyes? A gaggle of younger girls tumble and giggle their way past, suddenly quiet as they melt into the Great Hall for assembly. Welcoming, dark-haired Francesca from HR arrives, lists in hand, and the candidates are ushered away to start their day.

Having since participated in teacher and headship recruitment procedures in the international schools world, conducted with quick dispatch over little more than a half-hour skype interview, our methods for choosing teachers in the independent sector have come to seem somewhat stately. At St Paul's an entire day is given over to watching the candidates teach, putting them through a series of interviews, sending them on a tour of the school with a pair of students, and sitting them down to lunch with a group of colleagues from the relevant department. By the end of the day, I would have sought views from all these sources (as well as from the staff on the front desk and in the offices who had met them), which would feed into the final decision, to be taken many hours later in my office at the end of the day.

My role today is to interview alongside the head of English. We enjoy doing this together and I'm looking forward to his questions. Because we're 'people people', we think carefully about the layout of the room: a full-height table in the small meeting room for formality and chairs arranged around one long end so as to give the candidate space without seeming adversarial. The conditions, we hope, for encouraging a real conversation about English teaching, rather than a contest.

We begin with Muriel and, as we settle ourselves, pouring water, I open with something simple: 'Tell us what attracts you to working at St Paul's and why you think you are suited to this job?' Muriel considers: she's an experienced teacher and talks easily about her wide-ranging career, life in Cambridge and why she wants to work with us. The family context emerges, filling out our picture of this capable, disciplined person at last free to make some choices for herself. Jonny asks her to evaluate the A-level lesson he has just watched her teach, for which she selected the Ted Hughes poem 'Thistles'. She is self-critical, analytical – had the measure of the girls and how rapidly they can move intellectually, developing and connecting ideas. If not an entirely electrifying experience, it was thoroughly sound and, most importantly, stretched them. Later, we will hear about it more directly from the students themselves.

Now we are into our stride and, leaning back in his chair, glasses on top of his head, Jonny is asking Muriel about her literary interests: 'You have a completely free hand in the first term of the Pre-U [Pre-University] course. What are you going to teach?' And now we see Muriel light up, as she gets on to her favourite subject: the novels of Thomas Hardy. At these moments, I simply listen while the two subject specialists talk. With such able students, we need teachers who have a substantial intellectual hinterland – it's no good appointing people who only know the syllabus to be delivered and who aren't able to answer questions that go beyond it (as they quickly would have to do) or who cannot spontaneously draw in examples and references from a wider subject knowledge. The girls would see through them at once. Ideally, we want people who are not coming down from a great height but still learning themselves: writing, researching, reading, creating, thinking; alive in the moment and able to communicate that excitement about learning to their students.

Eventually, looking at my watch carefully positioned on the table (I can see these two could carry on all day) I murmur, 'Mindful of time . . .' and we move on to one of Jonny's favourites: 'You are teaching *The Merchant of Venice* to a GCSE class and you have a complaint from a parent who accuses you of promoting anti-Semitic literature. How're you going to respond to that?' From the best candidates this question would elicit not just a sophisticated understanding of the text, but also an awareness of the subtle diplomacy of dealing with parents: people protective of their children who are paying fees but whom at the same time we might hope respectfully and without condescension to bring with us, to understand and be at ease with the way multiple viewpoints can be held and considered in the teaching of English literature.

Eventually it's down to me to round the conversation off. 'What do you look for in the person who manages your work?' is often revealing, flushing out those who don't want their work managed at all, as well as those who would be unduly needy of praise. Muriel is predictably independent and tactful. She has some routine questions about the school day and about the library, and we are soon shaking hands, with a five-minute gap to change the water glasses before the next candidate arrives.

Many interviewers make the mistake of talking too much and therefore miss the chance to really unpack the interests of the person to whom they should be listening. A good interview has the candidate doing the talking, stimulated with the right prompts. By the end you should feel you have 'met' the person authentically. Only once the artificiality has been dissolved can you begin to imagine what it would be like to work with this person. The candidate can see what kind of people you are too – communicated in so many tiny ways: how you begin and end the conversation, your body language, whether the interviewers listen to each other, whether there is rapport and humour. Muriel would be capable and reliable, we agree – a thoroughly safe pair of hands. Without much time for further conversation now, I make a note saying 'appointable' and we get ready for candidate number two, Luke.

The day passes quickly as we keep to the tight schedule, popping out to make phone calls, answer queries or snatch a quick lunch between interviews (I'm not missing Fred's coconut rice pudding and chocolate sauce), and eventually we move into the larger office, flop down onto the peacock-blue sofas and wait for the rest of the interview team to assemble. Lindy brings tea, and with a pointed 'Don't forget you have to leave for Mercers' Hall at six' over her glasses, closes the connecting door.

There follows a sharing of opinions as we hear how the candidates have fared. I have been looking forward to hearing our director of studies, Andrew, giving his quietly delivered, laser-like analysis of their lessons. Luke interviewed well but his lesson lacked pace: he had underestimated the sophistication of the girls and Jonny had quickly outpaced him in his chosen Pre-U subject of the American novel. Everyone liked Muriel and agreed the department would gain from her experience. But it was Jenny who had totally wowed her class of thirteen-year-olds with a lesson on *Northanger Abbey* and the gothic novel. She had used a variety of activities, had quickly learned all their names and recognised at once the pace and depth possible with a class of eager Paulinas. The bell had rung with everyone longing for more ('She was so cool! It was brilliant . . . are we having her next year?'). What to do? Luke is not suitable. For a safe decision, we would appoint Muriel. But for the greatest excitement and for the greatest future potential, it has to be Jenny. She has much to learn, but is a natural teacher, that's clear: there will be plenty of work for her head of department, helping her settle in and come to grips with being a professional in a school, rather than a PhD student in a library. After an hour, looking at every angle, the balance of skills we already have, our minds are made up and we disperse. Much later that evening, I catch up with Jenny on the phone. She isn't expecting it (the other candidates were so much more experienced) but is delighted to accept. No, she doesn't need to sleep on it! And in this case, neither do I. The next morning, everyone is delighted. Francesca from HR has taken notes, and not forgetting to finish the process, we will find positive and constructive words to offer our two disappointed candidates.

In any good school, teachers move on and new teachers arrive. But school governors and parents watch the rate of teacher turn-over carefully. This is right: too many teachers leaving may well be a sign of an unhappy school and the reasons for departures always need to be clearly understood. But schools where no one ever leaves and there are certain sagging wing chairs in the staffroom which have been occupied by the same tweed-clad individuals for thirty years are at risk of stagnation. There needs to be enough continuity to ensure stability and so that new colleagues can benefit from those who know the habits of the school well. The guardians of tradition, if you like, who can be heard saying: 'Ah . . . Rachel Simms. Yes. Her mother was very bright, I seem to remember . . .' It's also important, however, for the staff team to have the stimulus of new blood, new methodologies and new influences, whether from young teachers fresh from their training or from those in a second career who bring different ways of thinking from other walks of life. A wise school will provide career progression, the chance to take on new responsibility and develop new skills, so as to retain ambitious teachers for longer. Ultimately, the profession is only enriched and developed if teachers move and gain experience elsewhere so as to broaden their skills. A school has a responsibility, I believe, to develop its own staff team but also to contribute to the growth of the teaching profession as a whole, nationally and internationally: we serve not only the children in our own school, but all children. A generous attitude towards providing training and encouraging ambition may result in departures, but it will also ensure there are other talented staff wanting to join your school and help ensure a dynamic, energetic, motivated team of teachers.

In my life as a head, the teachers around me were the professionals upon whom good education depended, which is why I always took great care over the process of appointing them. Like any cast of characters, they were individuals with distinct strengths, interests, talents, personalities and foibles, each bringing their own particular gifts to their work, united by a common commitment to their craft, to their subject, and to the learning of the students.

For many of us, certain of our teachers – loved or loathed – are vividly recalled. Most inspirational to me was tall, rangy, steady-eyed Mrs Gray, in her sensible box-pleated tweed and Fair Isle knits, who strode determinedly along the polished corridors of

Sunny Hill, escaping essay pages flying up in her wake. I scanned eagerly her round, looping writing on my essays, desperate aged fourteen for her to approve what I'd written. Propped at my brown wooden desk, worn into furrows by past generations, listening to her explaining *Jane Eyre* or *Macbeth*, I saw what it was to love your subject and it was Mrs Gray who fired my interest to study English at university. Her successor as our A-level teacher was a more forbidding figure: we respected her sharp intellect, but her temper seemed always at breaking point ('has nobody got a tongue in her head this morning!') so it was a relief that she was paired with the gentler, younger Mrs Freeman. While we admired her slim figure and chic clothes we didn't look up to her in the same way but followed with fascination her engagement and marriage to her blond and handsome fiancé and were even rewarded with a glimpse of him on speech day.

Unsurprisingly my preferences about teachers mirrored my interests. Of livid and resented memory was our short, squat science teacher who had the low centre of gravity of a stable laboratory beaker and presided over our chemistry lessons from the safe distance of a raised dais at the front of the lab. Peering over her slivers of glasses, she would pace the platform, giving instructions in a hectoring monotone and rarely looking at us. Daring only to whisper, we worked in pairs in our green science overalls with embroidered initials, mixing concoctions in test tubes and heating them over naked Bunsen burners until they sizzled and popped. I cannot recall wearing protective goggles but, miraculously, none of us was ever injured. Although I liked the smell of the lab and the colours of some of the chemicals (especially turning copper sulphate blue) and the neatness of my red exercise book where I wrote out the method and the results under carefully ruled headings, at no point did I grasp the point of what we were doing. My attention had clearly drifted off one afternoon, when there was a sudden explosion from behind the teacher's desk and I heard myself sharply referred to: 'There are several puddings in this class. But the arch pudding is Clarissa Farr!' I was shocked into attention. Others threw me sidelong glances. With her parting shot, whispered through her teeth at the door of the room as the class ended – 'You can't be an English student all the time, you know' – that chemistry mistress made me hate her. It took another thirty years for me to find myself at St Paul's and to see, and feel permitted to see (through the work of brilliant teachers and fascinated students) the beauty, purpose and wonder of the world of science.

Not all my teachers had such a traumatising effect and one or two I recall with a certain guilt. The diminutive Latin mistress with her lank hair, heavy square glasses and sensible brogues was the butt of our merciless fifteen-year-olds' humour. Utterly dedicated to her subject and speaking in a precise but barely audible voice, I'm sure she was aware of our passing notes to one another mimicking the stilted style of the translation of Pliny's letters: 'What news is there? None. Otherwise today's holiday would allow more to be written . . .' For all that, Pliny's account of the eruption of Vesuvius remains a vivid memory and I'm grateful now – too late – that we were introduced to those remarkable letters.

PE teachers tend to evoke strong reactions when I ask people to recall them and it's alarming how much they can influence our attitude to sport for the rest of our lives. At age seven, we were taught gymnastics by a compact, muscular man with dark Brylcreemed hair who treated us like an army division and claimed to have been a coach at Tottenham Hotspur. We were impressed. Whether or not this was true, he had a way of building our confidence: we would run up, one after another, at the end-of-term gym display, bouncing and flying head-first over the leather horse into triumphant forward rolls with fearless delight. And the thrill of pride as we all lined up straight as clothes pegs at the end of the mat, breathless and grinning! Later, as a radiator-clinging teenager, the huge windswept hockey pitches carved not quite levelly from the side of the exposed Somerset hill held no allure at all and nor did my PE teachers. The head of games, with her light moustache and carrying voice, who invariably wore a short, red, divided skirt revealing formidably muscular hockey-player's legs, was to be feared. She would pounce on girls like me who found hockey an alarming pastime (the sound of that hard ball against the curved stick always made me think of a skull cracking) and no doubt in order to improve their attitude, put them to play in the positions which would ensure a relentless game. I took to hiding in the changing rooms with my graceful dark-haired friend Shan, who I knew to be too intellectual to stoop to playing sport. We were in our Pre-Raphaelite phase at the time. As the class trooped out to the field, and the locker room fell silent, anxiety about being discovered was almost worse than having to play. Once I became a headmistress and had the chance to appoint games teachers myself, I made certain that no girl was ever going to fear the PE staff and we were not, if I could help it, going to have anyone cowering in the changing rooms.

Teaching must rank as one of the least glamorous of professions – who wants to go back to school? As a pupil I never imagined that I would become a teacher myself, though teaching runs in my family. My paternal grandfather, Harry Farr, was a primary school headmaster at Charlwood in Surrey. He died when I was five and a photograph of him in old age reveals the same thatch of white hair and penetrating blue eyes my father inherited. It must have been at much the same time that my maternal grandmother Trixie Wickham was also working as a teacher in a London suburb. She hadn't liked teaching – couldn't wait to get home at the end of the day, fling down her bag and rush off to the tennis club. Perhaps for her it was more of a relief than a constraint when, on marrying my grandfather after he came back from the first war, she had by law to give up her work. Certainly in the grainy picture I have of them at their Crouch End wedding, emerging from the church to walk beneath a canopy of military swords, she looks as if she has no regrets. But the tradition continued and, in due course, my mother taught dance and I trained as a teacher of English.

It would be more impressive to write that I went into teaching from a selfless desire to enlighten the next generation, but in truth I drifted into it. Unlike the focussed, organised young women I know today, I was in a bit of a world of my own. At an age when others were signing up for law conversion courses or apprenticeships with accountancy firms, I was finishing my MA, wondering how Henry James, a man who deliberately set himself apart from close human relationships, could have such a deep and subtle understanding of the minds of women. Isabel Archer, Milly Theale, Kate Croy, Madame de Vionnet: could the male brain really have thought them up? This and other similar questions were what occupied my mind and as the year came to an end, I decided I would become an English teacher. Books could go on being my close companions and, who knew, I might be able to interest some of my pupils in them as well. I imagined biddable rows of girls, their heads bent over the poems of Thomas Hardy as I wandered up and down in a sunlit room explaining it all to them.

As a West Country girl, cautious about moving too far from home, I signed up for the one-year postgraduate certificate of education at Bristol University. It may be that learning the history and theory of education in a lecture hall from people who have long since escaped from the classroom to the balmier climes of the university world has something to be said for it. You can't just come straight out of university into a school and morph into a teacher instantly: some adjustment is necessary. I don't remember learning much about what was involved in teaching real children, however, until I got in front of some of them on my first teaching practice, which was a lot harder than I expected. As a 'hothouse plant from an independent school', as the first headmaster I worked for would subsequently call me – and I was – being plunged into a city comprehensive school in the early 1980s as a trainee teacher was quite a shock. On one occasion we were 'doing' poetry. Despite being totally exhausted, I had sat up late making decorated work-sheets about Kipling's 'The Way Through the Woods'. Some of the class enjoyed the poem, but I underestimated how much variety was needed in a forty-minute lesson to keep everyone interested. This was not a group of undergraduates swapping anecdotes in an Exeter coffee bar. Soon, at a table at the back of the class, some children happily began making planes out of the worksheets and things deteriorated from there, my voice rising over the growing din as I tried to regain control. Eventually I committed the crucial error of shouting. The teacher who shouts has lost the day and the children know it: it was then that a small, plump, quietly disruptive boy with straight black hair called David made his way to the front. 'There's no point in shouting at us, Miss. Just because you can't control the class and you're not allowed to hit us!'

How to manage your own energies so that the children do the work and you keep calm; how to wait exactly the right length of time for silence; how to ensure that you have the attention of the whole class before starting the lesson; how to vary pace and activity to keep everyone interested and stimulated. How to wrap up and achieve an orderly finish, underlining the learning you wanted them to absorb. It all took a lot of practice. I realised that even-tually I was coming to like the children rather than fear them. A little humour began to creep into my lessons with magical effect. And by the end, I think they were not entirely hostile to me.

I'm often asked what makes a great teacher – what we looked for when appointing teachers to St Paul's. The great teacher can take many forms, all of them appreciated and understood by students, who are quick to spot arrogance or gimmickry, or the person who has mistaken teaching for an easy life because of the long holidays. From a lifetime listening to students talk about their teachers, I pick out here some characteristics which seem to hold as true now as they did a generation ago.

The first quality in a good teacher is compassion, a recent graduate told me a few months ago. He didn't mean being soft, rather being patiently interested in pupils as individual people, listening actively, understanding their potential. One of the unfortunate consequences of the prevalence of safeguarding problems and our highly sensitised attitude to teacher–pupil relationships is that it is now more difficult to assert this without misinterpretation, but a curious and respectful interest in young people and their development is essential to good teaching. I was struck when conversing with a young history teacher at a very distinguished school recently who said over dinner: 'I love teaching. Of course I love my subject, but it's the pupils and their ideas – they're just so interesting. I must admit in the long holidays I sort of miss them. Not in a weird way – I just enjoy their company.' How important to have this genuine and unforced interest, when so much of teaching is being able to create the individual, capable and active learner, someone who can continue to explore ideas and search for new meanings long after leaving school. The great teacher sets aside ego, begins not by parading their own knowledge but by finding out where the students are in their thinking, and starts from that point.

A teacher with this capacity for what my young adviser called compassion, is likely still to be a learner themselves, with an extensive hinterland born of active and continual exploration. But in an age of technology, does subject knowledge count? Information can be sourced at the touch of a button, the argument goes, so what a teacher knows is soon outdated and quicker methods of research and retrieval are available. Who needs a well-stocked mind when you can look up anything you want? Possibly as a result, well-stocked minds are harder to come by. When I was appointing a new head of modern languages some years ago, I realised that the wide-ranging knowledge of European literature and special passion for German poetry of my retiring colleague which had so inspired her students were not a given: more recent graduates I was interviewing had impressive language skills but they just hadn't read as much. (People say much the same thing about the scantily

stocked bookshelves of today's politicians.) Of course, ready access
to online information sources has transformed many aspects of
learning. But in my experience, there is nothing more inspiring
to a class than the authentic mastery and love of subject that a
real-life teacher can convey. A knowledgeable teacher is not a mere
source of information, but someone who can draw upon a fund
of layered and considered experience to form ideas and to make
connections. Importantly, the subject expert of today is still
learning, not simply drawing upon dimly remembered matter from
their own university days, but thinking afresh, keeping abreast of
new developments so as to share their lived passion for art, for
English literature, for languages or for science. Curious students
will ask challenging questions and the good teacher will welcome
this. Pupils will never be told: 'That's not on the syllabus so you
don't need to know it.' Questions may take the teacher beyond
their own knowledge base because that knowledge is questioned
in new ways. The truly great teacher encourages the class to learn
together, coming back to the next lesson with the results of some
research. Teachers who actively listen to their students often learn
from them because the students are seeing the subject with new
eyes. Google may know everything, but in times when pupils are
used to information sources taking inanimate rather than human
form, the inspirational and vivid teacher, who is both knowledgeable and a gifted communicator, as well as still actively learning
themselves, will be admired by their students and remain in the
memory long after any internet search has been forgotten.

If subject knowledge in the twenty-first-century sense has this
dynamism, it follows that a great teacher is ambitious, encouraging
all students to be courageous and aim high. And they should not
be too ready to heap up praise. Encouragement is very important
but the teacher who seeks popularity by freely spreading bland
approval will quickly lose the respect of the class. I'm sorry to say
that research shows students value the praise of male teachers more
than that given by women. Why? Because, in my experience, there

is less of it. These high standards need not be absolute, but each student must be helped to understand where they set the bar for themselves, and that bar or target must be attainable but stretching. A fine line has to be drawn: while encouragement should be regular, praise needs to be more sparing so that each person in the class constantly knows they are continuing to aim higher and finding new levels as their understanding develops. This creative tension is constantly recalibrated by the discerning teacher who will use humour, stories, self-deprecation and many other strategies to keep the students engaged and motivated throughout a carefully designed lesson that is intuitively flexed to the students' needs as they emerge.

We haven't spoken yet about the craft of teaching, or methods. That capacity for flexibility brings me to the fourth quality I have seen appreciated in great teachers, which I would call listening or having a good ear – essential for the mastery of pace and timing. Every good lesson has a structure and the design of a lesson is a skill; how to plan the use of the thirty-five minutes or hour or so allotted to you. The most successful lessons depend not only on having the right scaffolding in place but being able to adapt it as the lesson proceeds, rather like an actor or speaker adjusting pace and tone as they sense the mood of the audience. A lesson should move briskly enough to secure the class's attention and keep the students alert and energised, but not so fast that some get left behind. The start is very important: if you are facing a class who have just come tearing across the school from a PE lesson in a hurly burly of bags, hastily donned uniform and high spirits, you may need to have a calming opening activity. If, on the other hand, your class is the last of the day and the students are tired and listless, they will need something to wake them up. Like the actor, the teacher must engage the class immediately and decisively with their own energy in order to set the tone of the lesson as one of focussed, purposeful activity. I have watched many lessons slump before take-off because the teacher is simply not giving off the light, the wattage, that the students need to engage. There also needs to be variety: even in a lesson of thirty-five minutes there will need to be two or three different activities to keep the class focussed and absorbed. A good teacher knows exactly how to distinguish concentration from boredom, flexing these timings to maintain energy levels. That same instinctive listening comes into play with regard to speech and silence in the classroom, too. I have never forgotten the very experienced teacher who told me at the start of my career that what the students say is always more important than what comes out of the mouth of the teacher. This seemed counter-intuitive to me at the time: after all, I was the one who knew about imagery in Shakespeare, not them: surely it was down to me to tell them about it? But his point was not so much about transferring knowledge, it was about promoting learning: as the students begin to articulate their own thoughts and opinions, guided but not dominated by the teacher, this is how active learning – learning that will last – is shaped. So a great teacher uses their own voice strategically and sparingly, and listens very carefully to the students themselves, guiding, nudging, shaping, encouraging. That same sparing use of the voice is also part of classroom management, or keeping control. Something I learned early in my career, when I had several classes that were barely in my control most of the time, was exactly how long it took waiting quietly at the front for the class to settle and be ready to listen to me. Sometimes it seemed an eternity, but gradually the length of time lessened and I would feel the room coming into focus; conversations and banter gradually dissipated and I had thirty faces actually looking expect-antly at me. (What was she waiting for? Your attention, Mark . . .) That sixth sense about timing and achieving control through quiet waiting never left me, and later, dealing with much less rowdy classes (and even sometimes with a hall full of chatting parents when I was about to give a speech) it remained important. So yes: pace and timing are crucial if your lessons are to go well and no less if you are to survive them without ruining your voice and wasting your energy shouting.

It turns out then that teaching is quite a sophisticated skill, not just a matter of opening a file, dictating notes and setting tests. But why would anyone want to become one? Perhaps because we have all been to school the job seems to hold little mystique: very few of the young people I have taught have wanted to become teachers while still at school themselves. The familiar adage: 'Those who can, do; those who can't, teach' suggests it's a job for the inadequate. Teaching certainly offers no designer glamour – no acres of plate glass or soundless lifts taking you up to the umpteenth floor. Surely one look at most schools with their smell of industrial cleaning products and battered linoleum would make you want to run a mile. In films and TV dramas, teachers are portrayed as tough, overworked idealists, surviving against the odds pursuing a mission in noisy, chaotic surroundings. It's a relentless job that usually gets in the way of having much of a life. The fittest survive through developing a fast patter or repartee with their renegade students, just sharp enough to keep everyone in the room and off the streets. As a young teacher, the sheer demands of being up late every night preparing lessons and marking, teaching my heart out all day and then working half the weekend to catch up with what I'd fallen asleep doing during the week, with an almost permanent throat infection because of the strain on my voice in the classroom, the Christmas holidays were often spent either catatonic with exhaustion or ill in bed. No one who has not done a full-time teaching job has *any idea* of the physical and mental demands it exacts. Nine o'clock start? Not likely. In my first school the headmaster (the same one who called me a hothouse plant . . .) used to stand in the morning at a large pegboard covered with metal polo mints on hooks to see what time you arrived to 'turn your tag' or clock in. Woe betide anyone who was doing that much after eight o'clock. Lunch break? You must be joking. If you had time to eat you did it around constant knocks at the staffroom door by students wanting extra help or otherwise, you were running a club so as to play your proper part in the extra-curricular programme. The drama club I ran at Filton was anarchy, usually attended by volatile boys whose pent-up physical energy from a morning spent chained to a desk was unleashed in the freedom of the school hall. Vainly, I tried to get the children into groups for improvisation. 'Okay everyone. Let's start with a game of statues!' I would call out ineffectually. Nobody took much notice. I just prayed the headmaster would not walk in before the bell released me from my 'break' for afternoon lessons. The days were remorseless. I had (unwisely) gone into teaching to share my love of books. What kind of a life was this?

In my darker moments, I imagined my friend who had opted for the graduate retail management course at Liberty, sipping coffee in an elegant office and considering the relative appeal of different colourways in this season's Tana Lawn cottons. But all was not as it seemed in that world, either. Her feet aching after hours spent on the shop floor and bullied by the controlling woman who was her manager, she said to me one weekend over our glasses of wine: 'They call it retail management. There is nothing wrong with that, but I didn't study all that Shakespeare to spend my life waiting for women to choose their dress material.' Even though teaching can be demanding, underrated, unglamorous, often frustrating, occasionally dirty and also smelly – try teaching a large class of fifteen-year-old boys in a confined space after a PE lesson on a Friday afternoon – it is a job in which you can end your day feeling you have done something worthwhile. For all the challenges of my time at Filton High School, I learned the most from that job and felt huge satisfaction when some of the boys in my bottom set English class did well in their exams. I was in a department store later that summer, and passing through what was then called the 'Hi-Fi Department', heard a voice behind me calling, 'Hey, Miss!' I recognised the boy who had reduced me to tears on at least one occasion, now hailing me warmly, all smiles and proud to tell me he had a regular job. I can't remember when I've felt more satisfaction as a teacher. We had come through a lot together. And my friend in retail? What did she do in the end? She became a teacher, of course, and a very brilliant one.

Surely, the very best graduates should be going into teaching. Apart perhaps from being a doctor and keeping the population healthy, what could be more worthwhile than helping shape the next generation? But while teaching has high status in other countries, in the UK it has remained stubbornly underrated, not even making it onto a recent list of the professions chosen by Oxbridge graduates. Until Teach First happened and reimaged the proposition of being a teacher, that is. Teach First was the idea of ex-McKinsey management consultant Brett Wigdortz. Brett's vision was an ambitious one and in fact, not at all related to the way teaching was perceived. Stepping down in 2017 after running the charity for fifteen years he explained his motivation: 'It's not just about placing teachers; it is about creating a lifetime movement of leaders who will change society. Getting people to teach for two years is a major part of becoming those agents of change.'[1]

Teach First was planned as a platform for creating social change: note that the idea was to teach for two years, not devote a lifetime to it. In fact, while many Teach First pioneers have gone on to pursue other avenues, a number have become 'career' teachers, some even achieving headship while still in their twenties, and the scheme has had a transformational impact on the way teaching is perceived by new graduates. In the space of a few years, teaching has gone from being the thing you did if you didn't have a better idea to something worthy of serious consideration. Ironically, this has been as much *because* teaching is a tough job – in some settings especially – than in spite of it. Teach First trains its recruits in a commando-style six-week course over the summer break (forget the one-year PGCE) before parachuting them into some of the most challenging schools in the country. There, they often have a very tough time – I've spoken to them and to their parents, shocked and impressed by the brutality of what their twenty-one-year-old with a first from Oxford has got themselves into – but they are part of a movement to change the world, to 'disrupt' as a favourite modern term puts it, and they are not going to let it beat them.

I admit I was sceptical about Teach First when it started. It seemed a bit patronising to those of us who had devoted a lifetime to education. Why Teach *First*? First before doing what? Becoming a management consultant or an investment banker? Going on to something better paid and more what grown-ups do? Perhaps as a 'career teacher' I felt a bit threatened by this presumptuous idea that you could train as a teacher in six weeks and then outperform everyone else. A bit like taking a speed course in open heart surgery. Heart Surgery First. No, you wouldn't get that. It takes time to learn it properly, there is specialist skill involved and you have to be committed. Teach First is quite a niche thing still: it accounts for the training of only 1 per cent of those who enter the profession (by contrast almost half take a one-year postgraduate course); it's expensive and comparatively few Teach First 'Ambassadors', as they are called, are still in teaching three years later. But those who do remain have a remarkable career trajectory achieving promotion very fast (I have known at least one become a head within five years) and despite what you might expect, the challenging schools into which these young graduates are parachuted usually welcome them and are keen to take more. Whether those who stay succeed because they are well trained, or because they were rising stars in the first place, and whether the schools welcome them because they are actually good teachers or because the alternative of having supply teachers in shortage subjects is so much worse, must be matters for speculation. But whatever the answer, I can now see that the scheme has been instrumental in changing the image of teaching in the eyes of graduates (I read a little while ago that Teach First is now the second most sought-after graduate employer after PricewaterhouseCoopers – an irony there perhaps) and this can only mean that more people with great potential to make a difference in the world will go into the class-room and inspire the next generation.

Because it's in the classroom there is perhaps the greatest poten-tial for the kind of 'disruption' that Brett Wigdortz and others envisage. And this is what makes teaching such a great job and such an important one. And nowhere do you see this more forcibly expressed than by those people who did not teach first, or before some other career, but who have come to teach afterwards. At St Paul's and in previous schools, I have come across a number of colleagues who have come into teaching late, after a career in management consultancy, or banking, or law. So often these are the greatest advocates of their new profession: it may not have the same financial rewards as their former career, but the personal rewards are much greater. You are working to shape the lives of the next generation – the people who will be making the decisions that affect us all in the future – and from whom we can learn a great deal, as well as teach our subject. In a learning environment, it's accepted that everyone is continually learning – not just the students. And there are few things more enriching (or rejuvenating) than being in an environment where openness to ideas, to the habit of thinking and rethinking, is the norm. To have continual connection with young people and with the great project of shaping the future is to be alive, to be challenged, to be in a constant state of alertness to new possibilities. Complacency is impossible when you are facing the narrowed eyes of sharp fifteen-year-olds every day. Small surprise that Teach First has acquired an older sibling, 'Now Teach', to train exactly those people who after a successful working life in another field are looking for something that gives them a greater sense of purpose. One trainee said that although he had never worked as hard in his life, 'It's one hundred per cent absorbing. When I'm teaching I never think of anything else. It's a flow state – I feel more alive.'

As such experiences attest, teaching is personal: so long as your time is not cluttered with too much unnecessary administration and assessment routines, your work is yours to shape as you build formative relationships of trust with pupils and develop as an individual practitioner. Yonca Brunini, then vice president, marketing for Europe, the Middle East and Asia for Google, summed this up memorably and simply in a talk she gave to the senior girls at St Paul's, in which her theme was pursuing a life of being yourself and being authentic, rather than following the herd and thinking about status. This she captured in the simple exhortation 'be the one you are'. Unlike so much of corporate life where you are encouraged to be a clone of your colleagues (the extensive dress guidance provided to new employees by a Swiss bank recently included specifying the colour of underwear), in teaching you have freedom. There is a craft and a skill in teaching well, of course, and experience makes you better at it, but above all, it is a job in which your essential self, your personality, your interests, your cast of mind and way of speaking, all become integral to that craft.

An exceptional example of teaching presented itself to me recently when, as a fellow of a school to the west of London, I spent my required half-day per year observing lessons. I was first sent to physics – well, you know my record as a scientist at school – so it could only do me good. The laboratory looked Dickensian: dark wood, strange jars and pieces of equipment ranged on shelves, and formal pupils' benches. As the boys appeared, the pre-GCSE year, shuffling into their rows, without ceremony the dark-haired, bespectacled master began, waving a beer can (was it empty?) while striding up and down and declaiming with great force from behind the teacher's bench. It was like listening to someone who had swallowed a loudhailer: did he always speak at this volume? Could he possibly sustain this energy level for over half an hour? The Bunsen burner flamed threateningly (phew, he placed some protective perspex screens on the desk and donned his goggles) and the experiment began. Adding water to the can from a beaker and heating it over the flame, involving the boys by name constantly – 'And the water is going to do *what*, Alex?' – never stopping for a moment his clear and precise explanation (with occasional references to the invention of the steam engine for interest's sake), he finally plunged the heated can into cold water where it spattered satisfyingly and crumpled up. Still speaking, still questioning – 'The molecules in the can are moving more slowly *why*, Henry?' – he held the crumpled can triumphantly aloft in a pair of giant tweezers. The boys could not have been more riveted if they had been watching a circus performer sawing the lady in half: here was science made real, by a teacher who knew this was the most fascinating thing they would discover today, perhaps ever. And not a computer in sight.

But for all that teaching is a varied, challenging and immensely worthwhile job, if we want to attract graduates to do it and retain them then we need a new attitude and a new kind of advocacy to improve its status as a profession. The Metropolitan Police Commissioner, giving a talk at a leading academic school a few years ago, told the pupils, 'The police force will only change when your parents think of it as a suitable career for you.' I can see what he means: both the police force and teaching have yet to become the natural choice for the very brightest and best graduates. Why? Both are associated with long hours, poor pay and a humdrum, lacklustre working environment. Another problem, not so much with recruitment as with retention, is that the career structure it offers is far too limiting and privileges management over teaching. At the moment, there are only one or two routes for teachers who want to advance their careers, and they all involve doing less and less teaching. Typically, you begin as a classroom teacher with no other responsibilities. You gradually decide you would like to take the 'academic' route – becoming a head of department, then a director of studies or academic deputy head, and then finally – for those who want the buck-stops-here job – a head. Alternatively, you take the 'pastoral' route, becoming a head of year or head of section, then a pastoral deputy head and so on. Arguably it's slightly less easy to get to the final stage, headship, following the pastoral route, but there are lots of exceptions and also people who have combined the two routes. I was never head of English, but came to headship via being head of sixth form and then academic deputy head.

Taking on a management position as a head of department (HOD) or head of year (HOY) can be a fascinating new challenge. You have responsibility for the work of a particular part of the school and can also influence the course of the school as a whole, helping shape policy. You will be part of whole-school discussion at heads of department meetings and you will run meetings of your own within the department. The HOD is the conduit between the senior leadership team (SLT) and the rest of the staff. It's a role that demands good organisation and excellent communication skills. It also requires diplomacy: you will be fronting policy decisions that you may not always agree with and sometimes delivering messages you would prefer not to have to deliver. Sandwiched between your team of staff and the SLT, you must be authentic in your dealings with both. And of course you will be the buffer between your departmental colleagues and all that might threaten to derail their work: sooner or later the difficult children (and difficult parents) will be lining up to talk to you. All of this makes for a very interesting working day, but what if you really prefer spending your time in the classroom, doing the thing you trained for?

The promotion ladder at the moment offers little acknowledgement that what you are being promoted to do has only a limited amount to do with teaching, in that it mainly involves managing colleagues. There is no good reason to think that a person who is a brilliant teacher of maths will necessarily be brilliant at managing the work of a team of other maths teachers. It's a job involving lots of administration, coaching, mentoring, possibly managing underperformance, curriculum planning, organisation, chairing meetings, making presentations, liaising between members of the department, senior management and the rest of the school, achieving consensus on policy decisions, recruiting and selecting new teachers, and so on. And of course to do this, the head of department has to have 'remission' – time when they are relieved of teaching to do management work – and therefore spend less time in the classroom. Quite often heads of department are reluctant managers having taken on more responsibility not because they really wanted it but because there was no other way to achieve a sense of career progression. It's more than a decade ago now and things have changed a lot in that time, but I was struck on first arriving at St Paul's to hear my predecessor observe in the lovely, slightly throwaway manner she had: 'Oh, I don't think our heads of department would necessarily see themselves as managers of people . . . no . . . more champions of their subject . . .' Which of course is perfectly right, but there is the little matter of what everyone else in the department might be doing with their time and someone has to take an interest in that if the quality of teaching across the whole school is to be assured.

The core work – the most important work – of any school is not management. Those who love teaching should be encouraged to keep teaching, to contribute to the development of teaching as a craft, to explore how new methodologies can be developed – for example by integrating technology and to pioneer new research into the ever-evolving and fascinating fields of teaching and learning. At present, there is no clear career 'pathway' for those who would like to do this rather than to take on a management role. In higher education, management is largely shunned as grunt work that nobody really wants to do: I remember being surprised that at Exeter, where I studied, being head of department in the School of English was seen as drudgery rather than an honour and had to be passed round year by year: the administration and general tedium of dealing with the central hub of the university's processes just got in the way of the more important callings of research and teaching. The real promotion in higher education is either securing tenure (i.e. job security) or becoming a professor, having a 'chair'. Why should teaching at school level not adopt something similar? I would love to have had a couple of posts as 'chairs' of teaching and learning that I could have assigned, perhaps on a five-year term, to those members of staff whose gifts in the classroom were exceptional and whose knowledge of their subject could be deepened through further research. As it was, some of our most imaginative teachers took short sabbaticals for this sort of purpose: in one case walking the Pennine Way and recording the experience in a literary blog; in another, spending time in Georgia, learning the language and researching the literature and history of the region. These experiences enriched their teaching and would be shared with the students and colleagues on their return.

For the most part, however, there is still no recognised route for the classroom genius who wants to keep teaching at the centre of their career. If the core of a school's work is to be developed, this needs to change. And it matters that we pay attention to the quality of all the teaching in our schools. Teachers are not always as open as they should be about being assessed and monitored: traditionally, your classroom is your domain where you are the only adult and the idea of being observed by another professional is not welcomed. Progressive schools increasingly have a culture of peer-to-peer observation and where there is a genuine interest in pedagogy, teachers are encouraged to buddy up and watch each other working, thereby sharing ideas and strategies both within and across subject boundaries. This is always fruitful, especially if sustained, and can be part of a continuing process of professional development. That said, the best judges of teaching quality are not your colleagues, however experienced, but your pupils. The idea of consulting pupils about teacher quality is an even more sensitive area, but essential if the leadership of the school is to understand where the best work is being done and where there

needs to be improvement or change. In my work with internati[...]
schools since stepping down from headship, I have been impre[...]
by the transparency and detail of the pupil surveys undertaken
where quality has to be assessed; the pupils are given a range of
statements and asked to give them a rating, for example:

My class stays focussed on the work
My teacher explains difficult concepts well
My teacher encourages me to learn
My teacher checks we understand before moving on
My teacher makes lessons interesting.

Students are, in my experience, both astute and fair in their
observations: often their evaluation is entirely in line with the
management's own assessment of how good the teaching is in
certain subject areas or how much it may need improving in others.
All children deserve to be taught well and consistently well, to
experience teachers and lessons which stand out in their memory
and which inspire them to learn more – as a profession we should
be more open to pupil evaluations as no good teacher has anything
to fear from them.

Whatever we decide to do in life, whether we teach first and
then do something else, or come to teaching later, or don't teach
at all, we are, if we have the privilege of choice, searching for the
thing we love to do or, as one colleague put it to me, finding the
hobby in the job: the thing that doesn't feel like work at all because
we are so natural to it. People talk about 'finding their vocation',
literally the thing they are *called* to do, suggesting some compulsion coming from deep within the self. Occupations involving
direct contact with people are more likely to be described in this
way: becoming a nurse or doctor, a university professor, an actor,
a teacher. Millennials anticipating multiple branching careers may
balk at the idea of a job for life – and teaching does not have to
be that: those with other experience bring a great deal to the

classroom and those who go on to different jobs will take with them a grounded sense of the purpose of education that can enrich others. At the same time, bearing in mind the new focus on seeking careers that have social impact, which post-2008 we are told is more important to millennials than to previous generations, it may be that the next generation will come to regard teaching more highly and accord it the significance it deserves.

There are of course those who confidently forecast that as technology advances and artificial intelligence (AI) promises to recalibrate the place of mankind in the world, teaching as we understand it – essentially a human activity – will become obsolete, made redundant because learning itself will increasingly be autonomous. While this is a subject of great fascination to some educational theorists, it is as yet of no great significance to parents, whose interest in education is naturally focussed on what will take place tomorrow, next year and within the next decade or so – the time during which their own child will be in school and university. Of course, setting education strategy globally or nationally requires vision, a sense of the waves of history and is a long-term project (which is why governments should keep out of it as far as possible and stop meddling in five-year bursts), but the individual child is at school *now*. For the parent, the present and the immediate future is all.

There can be little doubt that teaching will have to adapt as new ways of learning evolve and it already has, just as reading habits have adapted to the opportunity offered by e-books. But the excited prediction that 'real' books would become obsolete has not happened, and in fact, book sales have steadily increased alongside the rise of online reading. A casual visit to the ground floor of Waterstones in Piccadilly illustrates a newfound affection for the paper, bindings, weight, smell, proportion and solidity of a material item: call it nostalgia, or call it a timely recognition that experiences located in space and time and involving the full range of human senses seem to be something we care about. Some would go so far as to say our mental health depends upon it. When talking to former students, I have never heard any of them speak with nostalgia about hardware or software: it's their teachers they remember. While we teachers should not bury our heads in the sand and fulfil the clichéd view of us in sweeping robes with Jimmy Edwards handlebar moustaches shedding chalk dust as we walk, and while we should be excited not threatened by the idea that, as technology advances, we will be learning as much from our pupils as they from us, nor should we be afraid to celebrate the vital human dimension of learning and the importance of the living, breathing teacher. Teaching and learning across the generations is as old as humanity itself and if we want to shape education for human health and happiness, as well as for modern efficacy and enlightenment, we need to do it by adapting – and adapting to the new technologies we have created, not being dazzled or obliterated by them.

Notwithstanding this, together with the various baptisms of fire early in my career and the tough lessons that came out of them, I have always believed those of us in teaching are lucky. We are in a position to shape the future. What all this had to do with the novels of Henry James and developing the well-stocked mind is lost in the mists of time. From that rather naive starting point, I went on to pursue a teaching career in a sixth-form college, a large comprehensive, an international school, a grammar school and as head, in two girls' schools. I had some formative experiences, travelled to some fascinating places, taught many inspiring students and worked with great colleagues. Looking back now, I see far more of the rewards than the trials. I may have often gone home feeling exhausted and frustrated, sometimes disappointed and cast down. But I have never gone home feeling my day was wasted. How many people can honestly say that?

FIVE WAYS TO WELLBEING
- Connect
- Be active
- Take notice
- Keep learning
- Give

'To move forward, people ne
be Inspired: they need build
that enhance their creativity
and push them to take their
future into their own hands

– Diebedo Francis Kere (Sen.
Spaces exhibition)

CHAPTER 7

March

Promoting well-being and mental health – a twenty-first-century challenge

March blows in with its gusty winds and as daylight saving begins an end to the long winter evenings. The school is no longer swathed in gathering darkness by 4 p.m., and we can begin to look forward to summer and the feeling of more hours in the day. With this lifting of spirits, we are launching Food Week, with talks from those who have made food their career, including Paulina Tommi Miers, who started the Mexican street-food chain Wahaca – some unusual foods to try in the dining room, including crocodile and ostrich meat – the publication by the girls of a food magazine packed with recipes and tips on healthy eating, and to start things off, an assembly featuring bushtucker trials. The girls are interested in the science – finding new sources of protein in insects – and equally by the spectacle of their teachers sampling grasshoppers. There is wild excitement as the brave head of biology goes up onto the stage and nibbles a few dry, crunchy-looking fragments. 'Rather like Cheerios . . . ?' he muses cautiously. There is rapturous applause.

Promoting happiness, well-being and good health – both mental and physical – alongside promoting the skills needed in modern society such as collaboration and problem-solving, is now no longer a matter left to chance but is an active focus in schools. A surprisingly important part of this is paying attention to food. One way we kept food both interesting and discussable at St Paul's was by having regular food assemblies. I talked at various times about the lemon houses of D. H. Lawrence, the introduction of Mediterranean cooking by Elizabeth David (to whom we owe the existence of the Italian aisle in Tesco), the perils of sugar and the delights of chocolate. I once presumed to challenge former High Mistress Heather Brigstocke's adage that a Paulina 'should be taught to think and not cook' by baking a loaf of bread on the stage in my trusted bread machine (Paulinas can think *and* cook). Luckily I didn't set the school on fire. We made food a subject for wider discussion and debate: the food committee could make suggestions (*more plain food please, and fewer weird sauces. We want our chicken looking like chicken, not enrobed in tarragon sauce or bathed in a tomato reduction*). While encouraging the girls to try new things, our long-suffering chef gritted his teeth and served 'plain chicken'.

We are not a nation of naturally healthy habits where food is concerned. Statistics show that 1 in 3 children in the final year of primary school are overweight or obese and the rates in adults have risen dramatically: in 2015, according to NHS research, 58 per cent of women and 68 per cent of men were in this category. It's a matter both of what we're eating and *not* eating; no surprise that barely a quarter of adults eat the recommended five portions of fruit and vegetables per day. Too-busy lives don't help: I can admit to a few coffee-and-biscuit-heavy, veg-light days myself. And the attempt by celebrity chefs to turn the spotlight on school food has raised awareness but not changed habits: it was dispiriting to hear Jamie Oliver conclude that eating healthily is still a middle-class luxury.

Unsurprisingly, school food has a bad name, though historically more for being unappetising than unhealthy. I remember the plates of grey mashed potato and fish resembling a hairbrush covered in lard (my favourite image from Redmond O'Hanlon's *Into the Heart of Borneo*) of my convent days. Most people of my generation emerged into adulthood with an aversion to some dish recalled from school – usually a milk pudding, semolina in my case – and there are few who can face a plate of boiled cabbage with equanimity, even though, ironically, both might actually be quite healthy compared with the preferred diet of many today. When my brother and I were small children, we delighted in hearing my grandmother talk about the Friday pudding of her own school days which bore the Swiftian nickname 'Dead Baby'. Dead Baby was a suet pudding of long shape and pale colour, served in lumpen slices with a dribble of watered-down jam. By the time my mother was at school, the same pudding was called Dead Man's Leg and still featured regularly on school menus. When first head of a boarding school, I came across some weekly menus from the 1950s. The highlight was Saturday lunch, when pupils could look forward to 'sausage and lettuce'. I have no recollection of those archives giving any quarter to allergies, or even to vegetarians: presumably if you didn't eat meat, your lunch was 'lettuce' supplemented by something out of your tuck box (if you had anything left at the end of the week).

As one of a generation of sweet-eaters, fear of the dentist should have acted as a deterrent to excessive sugar consumption. In my childhood you could go the corner shop on Saturday morning and buy sweets weighed out in paper bags from large jars ranged on high shelves: sherbet lemons, liquorice allsorts, toffees, barley sugar, bulls'-eyes, pear drops. My own children are thankfully indifferent, even disapproving, but my brother and I loved sweets, especially eaten at night under the bedclothes after we had cleaned our teeth. The result was a much-feared six-monthly visit to the surgery of shock-headed Mr Gilbertson, where prone and unanaesthetised, we looked up at the maniacal glasses and explosion of black greasy hair quivering above us as the smell of burning rose from our savaged gums. Nowadays I regularly spend a relaxing hour at the dentist having my teeth flossed while watching on the

ceiling TV the white-headed Francisco di Mosca zooming around
Crete on a motorbike, but even though the worst pain now is the
bill, the smell of the mouthwash can bring the childhood trauma
back with vivid clarity.

With my memories of inedible school meals and that residual
guilt about sugar I was determined as a head that in my schools,
there wasn't going to be any Dead Baby served and neither was
anyone going to leave the table hungry for sweets or with an
untreatable aversion to mashed potato. We would have varied,
nutritious food that the pupils and teachers simply enjoyed. So
we set about completely changing the catering service, putting in
new facilities, rethinking the menus and suppliers, and employing
new key staff. Having stripped back and started from scratch in
two schools, learning a lot in the process, the following, I think,
are the essential ingredients if you want to have great food in a
school.

First, the attitude. You must banish the concept of 'school food'
and all that it connotes: bland, bulky stodge that no adult or child
would actually choose to eat, overcooked vegetables or fast-food
options that fill the corridors with the smell of grease. Just as I
didn't want school drama or school music, neither did I want the
lowered expectations of school catering. We would have appetising
food, every day, with plenty of choice, and we would do it within
a reasonable budget.

Then, the physical resources. Make sure your kitchen is one
that a chef will want to cook in. A school puts resources into its
classrooms, so why not its kitchen? If your ovens are old and
inefficient, there is inadequate ventilation and condensation
running down the walls, you will never be able to attract the
person who can transform what the pupils eat and enjoy the work
enough to stay with you. There needs to be well-ventilated and
well-equipped space in which a chef wants to work – that person
is as important as any teacher – and will be given the freedom to
develop interesting and varied menus. Similarly, the raw materials

need to be of quality and time has to be spent working out how to source ingredients as locally and competitively as possible.

Last and most important, the people. Your team will be headed up by a calm, well-organised, personable manager who can keep everyone happy and smooth over problems when the heat of the kitchen gets too much. In a big school kitchen there will be more than one person cooking and you may have sous chefs with a specialisation: take an interest in them. With my obstinate sweet tooth, I often had conversations with our pastry chef, his floured hands working away on some confection for lunch as we spoke, and regularly took his recipes to try out at home.

It obviously helped that I cared about food and spent time in the kitchen, asking the team about some particularly delicious dish (roasted pork belly was one of my favourites) and taking an interest in the menu. The team loved to show what they could do on special occasions, for example the end-of-term valedictory staff lunch. After serving us with salmon en croute with sour cream and apples or confit of duck, tenderstem broccoli, baby new potatoes, orange chocolate tart with clotted cream, ice cream and fresh fruit, with some reluctance the catering staff would be prised out of the kitchen, wiping hands on aprons, to receive a standing ovation from the teaching staff. A moment of mutual respect: pride and celebration at something well done; skill and generosity acknowledged.

Most important of all, however, are not the special occasions but the lunches eaten every day by the students and staff. And while it takes time to achieve consistent excellence, this does not have to lead to sprawling expenditure. If you regularly nip out of the office to buy a sandwich for lunch at one of the well-known chains, you would be astonished to know that with economies of scale, a well-run school catering department can offer three or four hot-lunch choices plus pudding for considerably less than a round of tuna and rocket on wholemeal. And the benefits go far beyond physical nourishment. In any school or workplace, lunch is influential to morale all day: in the morning, you can look up and see what there is for lunch and chat to your friends in anticipation; when the bell rings you can decide what excuse to come up with in order to jump the queue or game the system and get in before your allotted time; then there is eating the food itself either quickly to get to your next activity or slowly enjoying the company of your classmates; in the afternoon there is the benefit of a good meal to feed the brain and the chance to compare choices with others ('you should have had the steak sandwich, it was *sooo* good!').

The priority given to food at both the schools I've led was deliberately to mitigate as far as possible incipient eating problems by making the simple statement that food is not only our fuel but our friend, to nourish us and to be enjoyed. Food is social: eating with your friends should be a high point in the day – something to anticipate with pleasure. At the heart of that is having an appealing, varied menu each day and coaxing the children to be more adventurous. If you provide pizza and chips, that is what they will choose, so instead, have a traditional meat dish, a fish option, a vegetarian option and plenty of salads, as well as 'food theatre' – tasty stir fries cooked as you watch. There are no 'bad' foods; everything is a matter of balance and proportion. So we would have proper puddings (okay, not 'Dead Baby') – as well as fruit.

In trying to develop that balanced attitude to food, young people are not helped by the conflicting messages they are faced with in the media. On the one hand, amongst those who can afford it, so called 'healthy eating' has become an industry, spawning countless magazines, TV programmes, cafés and restaurants dedicated to telling us with easy-to-digest science what to put into our bodies. The foods we think of as 'healthy' include viscous green shakes like pond sludge containing fruits and vegetables mixed up, hard-core muesli that could work as gravel over bitumen in your driveway, and any number of faddy, oddly textured things that briefly hold sway as the magic solution to our health problems. At the same time, perhaps as part of our harking back to simpler pleasures of the past and the comforts of traditional home life, baking has become a national pastime and favourite topic for reality TV, encouraging us to get into the kitchen and, remembering to weigh our eggs first, produce mountainous confections fit for a celebrity tasting. So do we bake and eat cake, or live off boiled quinoa? I was relieved to see that most girls saw nothing wrong with drinking the occasional kale shake while also enjoying baking. Ever eager to exploit an opportunity, they would happily trip into school bearing cakes in the shape of geographical features (I recall an edible Durdle Door with stack, and a dramatic volcano with chocolate-flake ash) or parts of the body, or historical landmarks, or whatever they were thinking about at the time. Gingerbread houses one year included a scale model of the school, the Portland stone detailing picked out in marshmallow. Cake as wit? Cake as sculpture? Why not.

Despite this, at St Paul's I was frequently challenged by parents about anorexia and eating disorders – these must surely be a seething problem in an academic school? Being in charge of a community of 740 young women it was impossible not to feel concerned about a problem which seemed to affect so many of their generation. Did we have girls with symptoms of anorexia or bulimia? Like every other school, of course we did. Did we have *too many*? According to the charity BEAT, disordered eating affects between 5 per cent and 10 per cent of adolescents, with the most common form being bulimia nervosa. A smaller proportion suffer from anorexia nervosa. With those figures, even taking account of the fact that 89 per cent of sufferers are female, at St Paul's we could have expected to be seeing more than fifty students at any point affected by one of these conditions. The degree to which an individual is affected makes absolute numbers difficult to ascertain, but I very much doubt they were anywhere near this level. But faced with a daughter in the grip of this monster, worried parents naturally look for somewhere to place the blame and school is an easy target, safely away from the sanctum of the family where problems may be much harder to look at.

I am not a doctor, but it doesn't work to make the simplistic assumption that clever girls in an academic environment are going to stop eating, or binge, and get sick. As an educator, my experience of teenagers is that a girl who has an eating disorder is rarely ill for one identifiable reason. Often, there is a constellation of factors which have precipitated the condition, some to do with family, some with school, most with the girl's relationship with herself – her self-image and self-esteem. Sometimes the causes go back many years: it takes time to uncover and look at them. Yes, she might be putting herself under undue academic pressure as part of the need to be in control, but equally, her studies may be a much-needed source of fulfilment and comfort. School is sometimes the theatre in which symptoms are played out: it may also be the place where the particular needs of the girl are best accepted and understood. The root cause may lie elsewhere, in a reaction to loss, for example. Three girls I can recall with eating problems had lost a parent just before starting secondary school. At a time when they needed to stay still and give time to their grieving, they were hurried on into an unknown future that did not include the mourned parent. They were expected to be excited: externalising feelings, making new friends, feeling lucky. To stop eating was to exercise at least some control over their lives, hurtling ahead at too fast a pace in a way so inimical to their feelings.

Perhaps because, historically, eating disorders have been stigmatised, I found it difficult to shift a persistent view outside the school that anorexia was something we hushed up, either because we felt it reflected badly on the school's image or because we were frightened of something we could not ourselves control. It was the guilty secret of a school that was putting undue pressure on its pupils – perhaps, in the minds of some, part of a defensiveness and shutting the world out that a well-known school could afford to do and which perversely even added to its mystique.

Those days, if they ever existed, are over. Not because anorexia and bulimia have gone away, but because we are now seeing them as part of a much more widespread problem: concern about the overall mental health of young people. This discourse is new. When I first became a head in the mid-1990s, I cannot recall ever hearing the term mental health used, other than in exceptional circumstances. The weekly meetings of tutors and those responsible for welfare rarely addressed this issue and certainly no parent ever raised it as a concern with me, though I occasionally had cause to look at the possibility with individual pupils. It was rare. Today, mental illness is openly discussed in the media as another thing that you can get, indeed might, as an adolescent, be quite likely to get. The younger members of the royal family have championed a mental health charity and Prince Harry spoke of his struggle with depression after the death of his mother. Since then, particularly shocking cases of teenage suicide have caused national concern to peak, headlines speaking of the 'epidemic' of mental ill health especially amongst teenagers and young adults. Society has become 'toxic' we are told, and learned academics are invited onto the radio to wonder why.

Knowing the negative press St Paul's sometimes received about pastoral care and the easy assumption that a high-achieving environment must be an unhappy one, I was determined that we were going to be early participants in the conversation on mental health. We would be open about the fact that some girls struggled with depression, or anxiety, with disordered eating sometimes a factor and so try to encourage a more engaged, less defensive and less stigmatised attitude to the subject. If St Paul's was prepared to talk about these problems, then other schools would be too.

Schools cannot cure all society's ills but they can shape thinking about the future. While not negating the fact that there were cases of established mental illness that needed to be treated, we focussed on the positive effort to establish healthy attitudes and practices that could form the foundation of a defence against the creeping symptoms of anxiety and depression. As part of this, working with colleagues and girls, our excellent pastoral deputy head (since lost to Eton) set about creating a policy on mental health and well-being. Practical and user friendly, it lists, for example, some of the elements needed in a healthy life:

1. Proper sleep patterns
2. Time for exercise
3. Eating healthily at regular times
4. Time to relax
5. Emotional resilience – accepting being 'good enough'
6. A sense of humour
7. Firm boundaries
8. Random acts of kindness
9. Walking in fresh air
10. A sense of perspective.

By constantly reiterating and promoting these habits, and encouraging the girls to adopt them individually, as well as supporting one another, we sought to establish a positive culture in the school. The value of community comes in here and within that, nurturing the self-esteem and self-worth of each individual. In a high-achieving environment it's easy to feel you are not good enough. Where the bar is set very high, that can be exciting but also daunting, so we promoted the idea that everyone should set her own high standards for herself to do as well as possible within her own terms, not in comparison with everyone else. The point was to enjoy learning and let the rest follow. Apart from ensuring excellent, stimulating teaching, we paid attention to how we communicated with the girls about their studies. For example, in the early years of school the girls received comments but no grades on their work. They were encouraged to look at the feedback as part of a continuing dialogue about their progress with their teacher. Reports to parents too emphasised qualitative comment over marks. The girls enjoyed external competitions and I spent regular assemblies dishing out prizes to the winners; within school, we generally de-emphasised anything to do with grades or comparisons.

Just as with eating problems, so with the much wider issue of depression where we are only now learning what to look for to see what is ailing a girl. The difficulty can be sorting out those who have a clinical condition from those who suffer from low moods which are no less real for not being exactly an illness. Certainly over my last five years at St Paul's I was aware of a marked increase in cases of girls who were either diagnosed as clinically depressed or struggling with their lives in some way. Some girls were coping with situations that would have tested anyone's stamina while trying to pursue their education – caring for a disabled parent, being left at home alone when parents were travelling, or being caught up with family financial problems. But some have no such presenting reason for their low mood or sadness, and simply feel a non-specific sense of hopelessness or isolation. From my observation of them, I feel that much of what we might call the sub-clinical level of this flatness of spirit has to do with a non-specific anxiety, the sense that life is too open-ended, offers far too much overwhelming choice, and lacks the form and struc- ture of reassuring social connections.

As we know, Generation Z – the post-millennials – are growing up in a society dramatically changed in many ways, especially by technology, which has driven the generations further apart and made it more difficult for adults, parents included, truly to grasp their world view. I was made more aware of how significantly this is affecting them after reading Susan Greenfield's excellent book *Mind Change*. She argues that daily life which revolves round the use of digital devices is changing not only the way we live but, more profoundly, also the way we think about ourselves and about the world. Grasping and coming to terms with this is exacerbated by a crucial generation divide between 'digital immigrants' – those of us who have adopted many aspects of technology but are never going to have total fluency, so parents and teachers – and 'digital natives' – our children, who have known no other way of life than that of the internet, laptop and mobile. Greenfield observes that this makes it harder for parents to know what to do in situations which they instinctively feel are wrong where there is an overuse of technology, and makes children more impatient with their parents who they see as out of touch with the modern, multi-tasking world.

The ubiquity of personal technology in schools has come about very quickly. Virtually all children now own their own smartphone or hand-held device. Not long ago, we were trying to police use of personal devices in school, first by not allowing them at all, then banning them at certain times, then admitting defeat, and finally, embracing them with an acronym: a BYOD (bring your own device) strategy where children were *expected* to have their own smartphone in order to engage with routine classroom activities and which has now become common in many schools. As any parent of a teenage girl knows, it's not uncommon to see a group sitting together, all engrossed by their phones, physically present yet mentally absent, each in her own cyberworld of other virtual connections. Perhaps they are getting some human comfort by being close to other beating hearts, but they appear to be largely ignoring each other.

Greenfield goes on to argue that in its extraordinary plasticity, the human brain is actually adapting to a world of ubiquitous, fleeting, fragmented information, leading to a preference for responding to multiple stimuli but in shorter and shorter bursts of attention. This in itself has worrying social implications, but the phenomenon we were most concerned about in school was the social isolation and objectification of the self through social media and the irresponsibility it enfranchised. Alone in your room online, it's possible to construct a version of yourself that is different from the person who meets her friends in real time, and to say things that you would never normally say. In dealing with occasional friendship problems among my students, I became used to reading transcripts of online conversations between girls splattered with expletives or uncontrolled vitriol that it was impossible to associate with the authors I knew. In the virtual world, young people are experimenting with created identities and with an interactive free-for-all, where the boundaries for normally acceptable behaviour seem to have disappeared – until you find yourself in the headmistress's study, having your words read back to you.

We have on the one hand a rapidly changing world in which global connectedness brings a much greater awareness of the world's problems, while at the same time social habits are isolating us from each other as we become locked into our private, virtual worlds. The effect is that people, especially but not exclusively the young, feel overwhelmed by the sheer enormity and 'uncountability' of their experience, as if they are lost. This is why being at school can be so important. I'm not claiming that school is a cure for mental illness – that is a much bigger issue for society as a whole – but it can promote behaviours which help.

It was when worrying about how to get these clever girls to feel more consistently positive about their abilities that I came across the concept of mindsets and the work of Carol Dweck. This elegant and highly persuasive Stanford psychologist describes in her book two very different ways of looking at life and learning. Recommended reading for businesses, parents, schools and builders of relationships generally, *Mindset* (first published in 2006) is about motivation. Dweck argues with persuasive evidence that the way we think about ourselves and our capability directly impacts the way we live our lives. If we have a fixed mindset, we tend to think that our ability is what we were born with and that it cannot change. We have to constantly seek validation and prove ourselves over and over again. We are unlikely to experiment or take risks, because recognition is what we want most. Those with a growth mindset, in contrast, believe that their abilities can be developed through their efforts. These people are much more likely to experiment or branch out, because for them, life and learning are more of an exploration – and who knows what they may be able to do if they put their mind to it?

Many schools are now adopting the idea of the growth mindset to encourage children's self-esteem and belief in themselves. The growth mindset is not just for school, but for life. I ran a workshop for parents to explain how we were using the concept with their daughters, asking them to write down two activities: one they themselves did well, and one in which they felt they were weak. We then shared them. Many had put down speaking a foreign language as their weak skill, one mother admitting that even though she was married to an Italian, she struggled to get beyond the basics of the language herself. It was all about mindset, we agreed! What was so helpful at St Paul's is that the concept works whatever your intellectual starting point: it was still important for those with exceptional ability to believe in their capacity to improve. I hoped in this way to do away with the well-known Paulina adage: 'If at first you don't succeed, destroy any evidence that you ever tried in the first place.' If only I had had a growth mindset about maths, I thought to myself as the parents left the workshop, on their way home to get out their grammar books . . . my career might have been different.

The idea of the growth mindset could be seen as one facet of a broader movement started by Dr Martin Seligman, director of the Positive Psychology Center at the University of Pennsylvania. Positive psychology, in Seligman's words, is 'founded on the belief that people want to lead meaningful and fulfilling lives, to cultivate what is best within themselves, and to enhance their experiences of love, work and play'.[1] Seligman has written a number of books on the subject of positive psychology and the concept of flourishing – defined as feeling good and doing good. Being a busy headmistress, these were on a long list of books I hadn't read, but I came across his work in an article about the Institute of Positive Education that Seligman had helped found at Geelong Grammar School, near Melbourne in Australia. Seligman's observations about Australian society chimed very much with what I was observing amongst our pupils in the UK: writing in 2008 he notes that, depression having reached epidemic proportions, it is about ten times more common than fifty years ago and that it starts younger: whereas fifty years ago the average age of onset was thirty, the first onset is now below age fifteen. The paradox, he says, is that while so much is materially better in our lives and there has been so much progress in education, the rights of minorities, pollution etc., we are no happier or more satisfied than we ever were, and in fact, less so.

Seligman's response to these conditions has been the development of positive psychology. Careful to position this as a discipline based on empirical research and not 'mere grandmotherly common sense' (though personally I have plenty of time for the latter), he describes its ingredients as the encouraging of positive emotions, seeking experiences which promote what he calls 'flow', or that wonderful sense you have when you lose yourself in something absorbing, forgetting about everything else around you, when capability and challenge are in balance. Finding where your greatest strengths lie leads to giving what you do meaning and purpose, through belonging to and serving something higher than yourself. His contention that positive psychology is not just a nice optimistic idea but can actually be taught was the driving force behind the establishment of the Geelong Institute, which is now well established and running 'Pos Ed' courses for teachers from all over the world as well as promulgating its curriculum for use in schools.

Thinking that this project might have something to teach us at St Paul's, and feeling for various reasons that I could use a bit of positive psychology myself, in the spring of 2014 I set off to

Geelong accompanied by my daughter Isobel to take the teachers'
course. Isobel, admirably independent, would explore Melbourne
while I was in class and we would make a holiday of it by continuing on to Adelaide to stay with friends afterwards. Coming from
the sophisticated, sceptical culture of an intellectual London school,
I knew it might take me a little while to tune in to the relentless,
sunny, Australian positivity. I had that slightly nervous feeling I
also get when attending a communion service and it comes to the
moment where you are invited to exchange a sign of peace. My
boundaries felt a little bit threatened, though in a way I knew
would be good for me.

The sprawling Geelong campus was eerily quiet, it being the
school holidays, but there was nothing low energy about the course.
On day one we were given an enormous file of resources with a
large leafy logo on the front bearing the word 'flourish' – I have
it on my desk now. And thus with the warmest of smiles from
our course leaders, we set forth on a fully immersive, interactive,
positively brimming week. I discovered that the leaves on the logo
each had a dimension of positivity at its tip: positive relationships,
emotion, health, engagement, accomplishment and purpose. Using
ourselves and each other as subjects, we explored them all, finding
out about our core strengths and how we could use them more
(my top three: social intelligence, appreciation of beauty and
excellence, and honesty), learning about building resilience, being
taught the skills of mindfulness and paying attention to the power
of gratitude. My boundaries felt a bit threatened again when we
were invited to write a gratitude letter to someone *and then send
it to them.* I could almost hear the Paulinas rolling their eyes and
murmuring 'cheesy' – but in fact, it was strangely enjoyable to sit
and write a letter to my chosen person (the children's nanny Louise,
who had been with us for the first seven years of their lives. I felt,
and still feel, immense gratitude for the stability, love and sheer
good sense she brought us and it was a pleasure to write it down).
However, in my understated English way I didn't actually post my

letter, though I did resolve to express gratitude more in future. It was a good lesson.

A few weeks later, back beneath the softer spring skies in London, I began thinking about how we would integrate elements of Pos Ed into our pastoral curriculum at the school. Rather like a holiday tan, the vividness of some of the language and the ideas took on a softer appearance back home, and I saw that it would not be easy to transplant this sun-drenched philosophy into St Paul's. Arms might be folded against the idea that this was 'science'. Acknowledging that we might not want to swallow Pos Ed whole, I reassured the staff that I had not been adopted by a cult but believed the ideas were worth our attention. I took it slowly.

Interestingly, five years on, our thinking in the UK has moved much further towards recognising a need for our own brand of Pos Ed. Conferences on resilience and grit abound; mindfulness is being practised not just in schools but in prestigious law firms and there are endless TED Talks on how to bounce not break after setbacks. We don't have to pretend life is perfect, but we need to teach young people to thrive in a modern, fast-moving world.

My most important lesson from Geelong, which has informed so much of my thinking about schools, is the simple idea that deliberately building and reinforcing a positive culture is the best way to address problems – in other words, prevention is better than cure. Or not so much prevention even: if you create the right climate, whether about how we treat one another, or how we manage our time, or how we look after our own mental and physical health, it becomes less likely that problems will develop. Create what is good: eating well, caring for and actively promoting health and well-being, both physical and mental, thinking positively, taking exercise – all these are elements of the broader pastoral responsibilities of a modern school towards its pupils in helping them navigate a teeming, exciting but sometimes hostile and confusing world. We shepherd them, literally: see to it as far as we can that they are happy, that they know how to make friends, that they don't succumb to bullying or become bullies themselves, that they can balance the demands of their lives at school and, in summary, that they are enabled to get the best out of their education. Inevitably, contact with home and parents is a big part of this and in the best schools, a good working relationship is established with a child's family so that what happens at school can complement the home environment. But whose job is that, exactly?

The shepherding, the pastoral care, is the responsibility of all teachers and especially that of the form tutor, who typically registers their form each morning and has oversight of their welfare while in school. In America the term is home-room tutor and the role is exactly that: to provide a parental safe haven within the family of the form, from which the student can branch off into their school life, safe in the knowledge that they have the secure foundation of their tutor and fellow tutees, like a family, at their back.

A good tutor plays a vital part in a pupil's life, drawing together the academic, co-curricular and wider progress and experience of the student as they grow through the school, yet teacher-training programmes pay little attention to this role, which is generally seen as subordinate to the delivery of the academic curriculum. Good tutors are made, not born, and need to spend time developing the skills of active listening, shrewd judgement about incipient problems, diplomacy and tact when communicating with home and infinite patience in seeing a problem through. Your tutor is your champion and your critical friend. As we become more focussed on character education the role of the tutor/adviser comes more and more into the foreground. Both my own children recall their form tutors as formative in their upbringing – instilling values, seeing them through challenging times.

A tutor may be part of a team led by a head of year in a day school, while in boarding, the important unit is the boarding house. The pastoral heroine of my own school days was my housemistress, Miss Wright. Aged fifteen, I was a weekly boarder in her tiny boarding house, 'Wayside': a nondescript bungalow at the edge of the school hockey pitch but very much a home in her hands. Miss Wright walked with an awkward gait on account of childhood polio – but her knowledge of the human character was as straight as a die. When I received a short letter on Basildon Bond from my first boyfriend, ending our relationship after half a term and expressing the hope that we might stay friends, I took my wretchedness to Miss Wright. She sat me by the study fire and opened the drawers in her little low table to reveal a beautiful collection of coloured pebbles. Removing them one by one and placing them in my hands to turn over, she allowed me to unreel my feelings of abandonment, eventually sending me off to bed where, exhausted from all the crying, I quickly fell asleep. That was excellent pastoral care: she was there in the moment of my schoolgirl crisis, she did not laugh at me but gave me time, she found a practical distraction that allowed the feelings to be expressed. She listened without judgement.

Miss Wright's methods would nowadays probably have been described as mindfulness: another facet of positive psychology which is gaining ground, and not only in schools. Businesses and city corporations are searching for ways to reduce stress levels in their employees and one route is to offer training in meditation. Although the conservatism of such organisations means that the scepticism takes time to wear down, Andrew Hill, writing in the *Financial Times* in 2014, reminds us that in the 1950s, the benefit of taking physical exercise (golf or fishing were suggested) was at first regarded as quackery too, and look where we are now.[2] Brain imaging research suggests that meditation – by which lay people often really mean just being quiet, switching off your phone and letting your worries go for a period of time – can indeed alleviate anxiety and depression. The groaning weight of the abundance of self-help books in any bookshop shows that we certainly have a need – how we address it remains personal, but the habit needs to start at school.

Finally, as we think about mitigating the pressures that young people face, while great education can of course happen anywhere, anytime, we shouldn't forget the importance of the physical, built environment a school occupies. Why is it that while in the past, the school might be one of the best and most distinguished buildings in the town, with an impressive entrance and an air of scholarly distinction, nowadays schools are so often nondescript boxes which look if their main purpose is to withstand a battering rather than to enhance learning?

I have always been interested in environmental design and during the period when we were in the process of reimagining the layout of the buildings at St Paul's, which over time had come to feel congested, somewhat illogical in their uses and overcrowded, I attended an exhibition of architecture at the Royal Academy called 'Sensing Spaces'. The timing could not have been better. As the exhibition title suggests, seven architects were asked to consider the question of the impact of architecture on the senses – literally, how the room you're sitting in makes you feel. As the curators put it: 'What is it about the soaring roof of a railway station, the damp odour of a cellar, the feel of worn stone steps beneath your feet, the muffled echo of a cloister or the cosy familiarity of your lounge that elicits glee, misery, fear or contentment?'[3] This was the question the exhibition sought to address. Drifting through the formal galleries of Burlington House the visitor encountered seven immersive, unique architectural installations – including a vast structure of suspended concrete slabs, a maze of delicate reeds, decorative arches echoing the shapes within the building itself, a tunnel of multicoloured straws and a wooden maze like a fairground helter-skelter. Experiencing this made me think about the school and how significant the built surroundings are to mood, the capacity for concentration, and all that goes on in our heads when we are learning. There is no escaping that impact which affects not just what we see, but our entire experience. Grafton, the architects whose founding partners Yvonne Farrell and Shelley McNamara set up their practice in Dublin in 1978 and who were amongst those exhibiting at the RA, had this to say: 'Buildings tell the stories of our lives in built form . . . We walk through and feel spaces with our whole bodies and our senses, not just with our eyes and with our minds. We are fully involved in the experience; this is what makes us human.'[4]

This is not aesthetic dilettantism. Think about the buildings you know that have uplifted or depressed you. I have never forgotten the moment of walking first thing in the morning into the Sagrada Família in Barcelona, Gaudí's cathedral looking from the outside like some vast, fantastic sandcastle and, inside, flooded with jewelled light. Contrast that with the heavy, oppressive menace of any underground car park. You cannot wait to get out of it. Some buildings make us lighter; others weigh upon us with their windowless gloom.

Some public buildings may accrue significance for particular reasons, but a more personal awareness of place is present in most of us. Cast your mind back to childhood: the house where you grew up. Your bedroom there. I can see now the texture and geometric design of my purple curtains, my bed, my books. And then the locations of family holidays: the hotel where we stayed in Cornwall as young children – the rooms, staircases, mysterious doors marked staff only, the way to the beach, the sunny veranda; a certain grown-up smell of lemon slices and tonic water in the teak-lined bar (we were not allowed in: we peeped), the bleached salt smell as you went outside, the cry of gulls and cormorants, the distant gathering and collapse of the waves on shingle. My mind still wanders in those places. It's the same with school: on a visit a few years ago, I was astonished how small the playground seemed at St Cedd's in Chelmsford, an expanse of tarmac that had once seemed a continent. The bike sheds were gone, but if ever I smell the acrid tang of creosote I'm back there, pulling my blue and red bike out of its rack to pedal home for tea. Similarly, when the girls come back to St Paul's after a few years' absence, they rush around eagerly, remapping their special places.

The power of this sense-memory for places and the way environment colours our experience, brought home to me how important it is to pay attention to how we design and build schools in order to promote not just effective learning but essential well-being. My life as a teacher has taken me into some starkly contrasting settings. Most unpropitious, a busy road leading out of the industrial part of Bristol was the location of my second teaching job at Filton High School. There, the flat-roofed main building was functional and drear, the slabs of walls and grid of windows shabby with rain streaks unrelieved by any sense of aesthetics or attempt at cheerfulness. Inside, corridors with patched blue linoleum smelt of sweat and plastic: there was a careless impermanence. Behind the building, an attempt had been made at landscaping a patch of grass, but this too was worn away with only a single, blasted tree surviving the onslaught of short-cutting feet. It was depressing: there was no heart to it. The senior management team would sit hunched in their offices behind what looked like bulletproof glass, as if antici-pating a revolution or a siege. What were they afraid of? The atmosphere felt hectic, tense. These premises, similar to many I visited during teacher training and typical enough, did little to encourage pride and ambition, or to make the children feel they actually mattered. Was this what we thought was good enough for them?

The contrast could not have been greater when I moved to Hong Kong at the end of the 1980s. Admittedly the weather helped: my first view of the school building was of a white oblong sugar loaf set against the bluest sky. I felt exhilarated entering this exotic, pristine world with its palm trees and outside staircases, providing perfect vantage points for looking out over the swaying forest of bamboo scaffolding that was the fast-growing sprawl of Sha Tin. The cool, white building felt orderly and calm despite the restless energy below: thrumming businesses, blocks of flats and shanty restaurants in gutters, the mountains of the New Territories smudging the horizon a soft purple. How different to be a teacher or pupil here, entering the sunlit classrooms with their sweeping views compared with the sticky, clattering corridors of industrial Bristol.

The importance of outdoor space was something I came to understand in the grounds and gardens of Queenswood, where there was room for pupils to let off steam and where it was also easy to find solitude. In my busy job I had people in front of me all day, so I would walk on summer evenings down to the greenhouses, eerily quiet in the fading light, and wander inside to smell the acrid tang of tomatoes growing or see the little trays of seedling plants laid out. It was also hospital to most of the houseplants in the school, which after a term of neglect or abuse were sent to convalesce under the silent and magical gaze of Maurice Hoare, the head gardener. Rumour had it that Maurice, with his white hair and skin as wizened as one of his apples, had not ventured indoors for fifty years, having started as a garden boy aged fifteen. Any plant he nursed returned to vibrant health in a matter of weeks. The many cacti, maidenhair ferns and rubber plants that were thoughtfully given to the girls by their parents for their bedside tables and that flourished in the glass houses, glowing green in the warmth, must have drooped with sadness when they returned to the boarding houses, for another term of being watered with flat Coca-Cola and doused in hairspray. Often on these walks I would be accompanied by our cat, Tiger, then a younger though always somewhat low-slung tabby, who, fancying himself a dog for an hour, would follow me in quick rushes. It was the Siamese in him that made him a talker, people said, and he would suddenly look up and offer a long, plaintive miaow, before another little rush. At the greenhouses he would at once disappear, checking for mice.

To be at school in a setting like Queenswood is undeniably a privilege few enjoy, but it gave me a standard to strive for and a belief that – no less than excellent teaching – a respectful, orderly and aesthetically pleasing environment, with adequate indoor and outdoor space (especially important in cities) should be and can be the expectation of all. Think of the care we put into the design and construction of galleries and museums. Both the V&A and Tate Modern have ambitious new extensions. The British Museum has its graceful enclosed Great Court. The new waterfront Whitney Museum in New York provides beautiful, unexpected vistas of the Hudson River, blending with the impressions of the artworks inside. Recently I made a first visit to the Louvre in Abu Dhabi, where in a semi-open-air setting a vast aluminium canopy allows dappled light to splash through onto the white terraces. Yes, these are spaces whose reason for being is their aesthetic: resources are poured into them and visitors appreciate the setting they provide for the vital if transient activity of contemplating beauty. But they are built to house dumb and eyeless inanimate objects. The Rosetta Stone, however significant, cannot appreciate its surroundings. Why, when these buildings warrant such reverence, should we not accord as much or more importance to schools, where every day, the life of the next generation is being forged and nurtured in our living, breathing, sensing children?

We have to find a way to make school buildings and their surroundings more important, and not just for the privileged few. This does not have to mean uncontrolled expenditure. I have seen private schools where money has been squandered on sterile buildings to no purpose as well as schools run on tighter budgets where there is a true sense of dignity and pride in the surroundings, felt the minute you walk into a school. But how do you tell a cared-for school? One bursar I worked with maintained it was by going into the pupils' washrooms. If children love their school and are proud of it, they don't write on the walls. Filton High in my day was spattered with graffiti, whereas I have seen so-called 'challenging' schools in London where there is nothing on the walls but the honours boards and certificates recognising pupil achievement. Do children write on the walls of the bathroom at home? No. It's a matter of how much they identify with those buildings and their own sense of responsibility. I strongly believe that any well-led school can be a place the pupils feel proud of, and looking after the physical fabric, together, is an important part of that.

A wonderful example of scholastic pride that has certainly not depended on a large budget is the African Science Academy (ASA). Started by inspirational entrepreneur Tom Ilube, the school is currently housed in a residential area in the suburbs of Accra. As yet very small in numbers – only twenty-seven students – ASA operates in what was designed as a large house, which exudes academic purpose, pride and aspiration the minute you step through the door. There is no time to lose in a school where the pupils will only stay for one year, all of them girls, taking demanding A levels in maths and physics after barely ten months of study. Tom Ilube's vision, to change the face of Africa 'one girl at a time' sends these highly motivated young women to study science at universities in Ghana, other parts of Africa and beyond.

We arrived to join an assembly where the new head girl and prefects were being appointed: uniforms, sashes and elaborate rituals all contributing to a sense of esprit de corps and unity. I toured the building where dining rooms and dormitories had been created and was struck by the immaculate tidiness and order of everything. The bedrooms slept six: impossible to tell whether anyone was living there, the beds made smooth and not a slip of clothing betraying a late dash to breakfast. I thought ruefully of the teenage bedrooms I was familiar with at home: here there was no time for adolescent malaise, it was all determined self-discipline and focus. While I was visiting, we drove out into the country, where a piece of land had been purchased to build a permanent school. With some difficulty we found the fence markers in the long grass and I looked up at the low, distant hills on the horizon. There might only be grass and trees there now, but I had no doubt that a new school would soon rise out of the ground. In the meantime, the girls in their temporary home in Accra reminded me that the right environment for learning can be a matter of attitude and imagination as much as bricks and mortar.

The space in which students and teachers spend most of their time is not the entrance hall, or the head's impressive study, but the classroom. A visitor looking round a school (once they have inspected the toilets) can tell a great deal about the culture and priorities by the condition of the classrooms. These vary depending on the level of education but creating an exciting environment for learning is important at any stage. A good teacher will have given thought to what is on the walls, in the way of posters or displays of work, what resources are available to the pupils and how attractively these are presented, as well as to the layout of the furniture in the room. Some believe there should be ample visual stimulation to provoke the imagination, others that clean space is better so as not to clutter the mind. The stage management of the lesson, and the dressing of the space, are all part of the craft of teaching. Most of all, if pupils feel they are walking into a space that has been thought about and cared for, they are more likely to treat it with respect themselves and will settle to focus and concentrate more quickly.

As a head, you have the exciting and daunting responsibility not just for your own classroom but for the entire site and premises. Having worked in such different places as a teacher, I was clear I wanted any school I led to be as pleasing and well maintained an environment as I could make it. At Queenswood, as well as keeping up seemingly endless rounds of bedroom and bathroom refurbishments, we undertook two major building projects: a swimming pool and then the facility closest to my heart, a theatre. The pool with its wave-like roof was much beloved

of the architect and blended naturally into the wooded surroundings. The theatre, cockpit-like, was carved out of the shell of the
former school hall, retaining something of tradition and permanence about it, with a ready-made character. It became an exciting,
intimate performance space, with raked seating and fixed stools
along the sides, somewhat like the Swan Theatre in Stratford-
upon-Avon, where you could lean in towards the action, encircling
the thrust stage. It immediately had theatrical atmosphere – there
was a sense of anticipation when you edged your way into the
muffled purple dark. Why was that? I've sat in many larger school
theatres which never quite overcome a sterile, barn-like quality.
Ours was somehow seasoned, propitious: bringing the cast and
audience into closer relationship and creating the conditions for
that magical experience of suspended disbelief. The success of the
theatre at Queenswood was what made me start thinking about
why one building works and another does not: how significant
proportion, colour, light, material texture and volume can be to
how we feel and therefore to what happens within a certain space.

The needs, practical challenges and opportunities for site development were very different when I moved to the smaller, densely
built, urban campus of St Paul's. On the edge of Brook Green
close to Hammersmith underground station, it is by both location
and character a city school. Its buildings are closer together; its
metronome ticks a bit faster. The original building, designed by
Gerald Horsley for the school's opening in 1904 is elegant and
beautifully proportioned, with the Great Hall at its heart. But
there had been many subsequent additions and that combined
with a growth in pupil numbers made the school feel congested,
exacerbated by a lack of coherence about how everything fitted
together: the flow of people was a problem; it was like a ball of
string that needed untangling. So it was that turning my mind to
the unlocking of that crowded city site I found myself at 'Sensing
Spaces'. The words of the Grafton team made perfect sense, but
it was like seeing something that had been so close up I had missed

it: buildings do indeed tell the story of our lives – they are far
more than a functional way to keep the rain off or the noise out;
our surroundings are an essential part of our experience of school.

Wanting to go deeper into this way of thinking I came across
the work of the Finnish architect Juhani Pallasmaa and his book
The Eyes of the Skin: Architecture and the Senses.[5] You hear it said
that there are certain books, as there are certain people, that change
your life, or more accurately bring it into focus, because when
you come across them for the first time, it's as if you have always
known them. For me, Pallasmaa's *The Eyes of the Skin* was that
book. His observation that, 'We have an innate capacity for remembering and imagining places' lent authority to the connection I
had begun to make between the remembered places of childhood
and the attention we should be paying to the design of schools.
Pallasmaa reveals in intense poetic detail exactly *why* some buildings make you feel uplifted and why others are depressing and
that it has to do not with any one aspect but with the totality of
how we experience them. All of our five senses are potentially
involved in the way we apprehend the spaces and forms around
us, not just our sense of sight; we are affected by scale and proportion, by the balance of detail and simplicity, by the interplay of
light and shadow and by the construction and materiality of a
building. He refers frequently, for example, to the special warmth
and character of natural or worn materials, to wood and especially
to old wood, and the contrasting resistant blankness of sheets of
metal and plate glass in some modern architecture. Touch is a
vital and often neglected sense. As if to emphasise the importance
of our response to what is natural, he invites us to imagine the
'invigorating and healing' quality of a walk through a forest, where
all the senses are invoked together.

Through his deeply considered discussion of architecture and
the role that the built environment plays in our lives, Pallasmaa
also provides insight into what ails us in the technological age.
Talking about the modern privileging of sight over the other senses,

he suggests that the deluge of flat visual imagery we experience
when so much of our perception is filtered through a flattened
screen tends to alienate vision from emotional involvement. He
reminds us that the supremacy of the sense of sight, which we
take for granted today, is comparatively new: in Shakespeare's time
for example, he says, we smelt and sensed the world before we
saw it, whereas now 'the dominance of the eye and the suppression
of the other senses tends to push us into detachment'.[6] I wondered
whether this was part of the answer to why we are seeing such an
increase in depression: perhaps young people are, apart from
anything else, suffering from a kind of sensory deprivation – their
experience flattened out and their true range of senses forgotten
in a half-life of artificial visual perception which leaves them
dissatisfied and empty without knowing why.

This thinking made a valuable touchstone in my mind when
we came together round the grained wooden library table at St
Paul's to think about how to redesign and unlock some of the
problems in our already tightly packed site. It soon became clear
that there was a need for one more building on the main site
(to become a sixth-form centre and teaching block): this would
animate a part of the site that had previously petered out into
the boundary wall and give balance to the imposing science
block that was there already and which it would face across a
landscaped central courtyard. It was a matter of seeing how,
counter-intuitively, adding a building would provide a greater
sense of order and space and reduce congestion. Together with
clever use of glazing and exploiting adjacencies between the
existing buildings, we could create there too a greater sense of
breathing space and better, more logical lines of flow across the
whole site. More and more, I felt this was key: how could the
frenetic atmosphere of this city school, full of animation and
teeming life, be prevented from tangling itself into unhelpful
knots of stress? How could we create oases for thinking and
breathing, for solitude and restoration?

This would come from thinking about the buildings themselves – their shape, proportions, elevations and materiality – but also from thinking about the relationship between indoor and outdoor space. Many city schools have very little green space of the kind the Queenswood girls enjoyed. We've seen that just as contact with wood and stone, with things which are old and have a history as well as things that are new, is key to our well-being, so is the ability to spend time outside. Open space helps balance what can be a frenetic, headlong feeling in a school, restoring a sense of calm. But what is good use of outdoor space when it is limited? There is a way of thinking about this too, I discovered, and about the relationship between what is within and without, between indoor and outdoor space, beautifully illustrated by another influential architect, Christopher Alexander. Here is an image used in his book *A Pattern Language*:[7]

Buildings that create negative, leftover space . . . buildings that create positive outdoor space.

On the left is an image of what is common in so many schools and institutions. Buildings have been added without a planned relationship between the buildings themselves and the outdoor space that surrounds them. This outdoor space appears random, looks 'leftover' and therefore negative. On the right in contrast, the outdoor spaces have a clear relationship to the building and the whole design is thus a totality – it has coherence. I reflected that Oxbridge colleges, with their quadrangles, are the perfect example of indoor and outdoor space working together. If you visit any collegiate university and poke your head in past the porter's lodge to look at a sunlit quadrangle, you will see exactly this principle beautifully at work. From indoors, you look out at elegant, tranquil enclosed space. From outside, you can make sense of the delineated space and enjoy its definition through the architecture rising around you.

Juhani Pallasmaa claims that this relationship with the physical environment not only engages our whole being, it enables us to determine our identity and our place in the world and in the flux of time. If technology has deprived us of that sense of rootedness in the physical world, making us feel lost and bewildered by the apparent endlessness of possibilities in space and time, architecture may be an even more significant element than we think in its restoration. 'Buildings and towns enable us to structure, understand and remember the shapeless flow of reality and, ultimately, to recognise and remember who we are,' he writes. 'Architecture enables us to perceive and understand the dialectics of permanence and change, to settle ourselves in the world, and to place ourselves in the continuum of culture and time.'[8]

Even where resources are scarce, educators must pay attention to this. Until all physical walls dissolve, schools remain physical places where children spend most of their waking hours. They should be designed by the best minds, built with care, made to last and be properly maintained. Those who design and build schools should strive for integrity – the most important quality in any building, as Frank Lloyd Wright asserted in 1954 (at the age of eighty-five). The next generation deserves that respect. Governments are quick to blame school leaders for the culture of demotivation and despondency which leads a school to be 'failing'. But those leaders did not design the premises in which they have to build aspiration and success, which is where pride and positivity can start. As Pallasmaa puts it: 'In memorable experiences of architecture, space, matter and time fuse into one singular dimension, into the basic substance of being, that penetrates our consciousness. We identify ourselves with this space, this place, this moment, and these dimensions become ingredients of our very existence.'[9]

Creating the conditions for flourishing in a school, so that pupils and teachers can find the sense of flow where challenge and capability are in balance, where health of mind and body are held to be important, and where the built environment is conducive both to active learning but also, in a stressful world, to contemplation and calm, is a vital, complex and continual task.

But now there's a knock at my door. A pair of first-year girls have arrived, with a plate of what look like Cheerios for me to try . . .

Impact — Very High / High / Medium / Low / Very Low

Very Low Low Likeli...

I believe it is in our nature to explore, to reach out into the unknown. The only tru failure would be not to explore at all.

– Ernest Shackleton

used by an
to mainta
e area and
Restricti

use of D

PENALTY CHARGE NOTICE (PCN)
TRAFFIC MANAGEMENT ACT 2004

PENALTY CHARGE
NOTICE

WARNING
OFFENCE FOR ANY PERSON
R THAN THE DRIVER TO
MOVE THIS NOTICE

TO DO

- Write risk assessment for camping trip
- Write assembly on resilience
- Remind girls about not taking mobiles into exams
- Pay parking fine

CHAPTER 8

April

When things go wrong – running with risk, facing up to failure, living with loss

April brings the school holidays, a favoured time for expeditions – thirteen of them one year – taking girls to all parts of the world, from Birmingham to Barcelona and from Pompeii to Paris. I calculated that almost half the school was involved (about 360 pupils) which gave us a lot of assembly reports to look forward to at the start of term. As a new headmistress, people asked how I slept at night with so much responsibility for the safety of other people's children. It was one thing when they were all in the building and you could see them, but when they were spread out around the world, how could you know what was going on?

The answer was that you couldn't, personally, so you had systems: a party leader who had planned ahead made a recce of the location and any activities (thankfully no white-water rafting), conscripted enough members of staff to accompany, gathered exhaustive information about each pupil, carried out a formal risk assessment and made provision for repatriating any pupil who became unwell. I would list all the destinations in our final end-of-term assembly, wishing everyone well and exhorting the girls to look after the teachers: all our trips took place in the holidays so as to avoid disrupting formal lessons. But holidays they were not. Looking

after the children of others is a solemn responsibility, as I would
remind parents who were impatient with the formality of our
itineraries and procedures – a school trip is not a family outing.
I had to think about protecting the staff too: without losing all
opportunity for spontaneity, in litigious times, meticulous planning
and a cautious attitude to risk are inevitable.

And because one can never control everything, things sometimes
do go wrong. Glitches may be minor, as occurred at the end of
our tightly packed thirty-six hours at the First World War battle-
fields one year. A visit to the Thiepval Memorial in the snow at
dusk, a windswept walk along Vimy Ridge, a long trudge over
the grassy hummocks that were once trenches and a wander among
the neat rows of aspirin-white headstones at one of the cemeteries
and we were on our way back to Calais when our coach gradually
coasted to a halt. My softly spoken colleague Simon, known for
his charismatic teaching of poetry, went to confer with the driver
who slipped down from his seat and began inspecting the under-
side of the vehicle. Simon joined him. Time ticked by. Other
coaches and cars sped past: whoosh, whoosh. On board the girls
were restless. 'Please, Miss Farr, I need to go to the loo!' said a
small girl with a fringe in the back row. 'So do I!' Pause. 'And
me!' Within five minutes, the coach was a waving forest of hands.
I saw that our only hope was the small grass verge at the edge of
the motorway where we were marooned. 'Okay, girls! Follow me!'
I ordered them off the coach. 'But where are we going to . . .?'
'Right here!' I replied. So we solemnly hunkered down en masse
in full view of the traffic. Somehow the coach got fixed, we caught
our ferry back to Dover and, eventually, delivered the girls to their
parents in the darkened school car park. It was a solemn and
sobering two days, the names on the memorial at Thiepval disap-
pearing up, up as far as the eye can see into the snowy dark. But
that particular trip was remembered also for something discor-
dantly absurd: the Big Wee.

Considerably more alarming was what happened on an expedition I accompanied to Nepal, during my time teaching in Hong Kong in the late 1980s. We were a group of about thirty, with a number of teachers including our party leader, John Freeman. John had worked in Hong Kong for years and had led many trips in different parts of Southeast Asia. A PE teacher turned deputy head with an all-year tan, vigorous moustache and shock of brown hair, John exuded health and an easy confidence. Students and teachers, if you could put up with the occasional cheesy joke, all felt very safe in his hands.

Our ten-day trek involved sleeping in tents, and walking up and down stone tracks for eight hours a day was physically demanding even with Sherpas carrying most of our heavier belongings. One day well into the trip we were looking forward to a break for a picnic lunch and the Sherpa at the head of our group called back that the path was widening: we would stop here. Gratefully slinging down our day packs we sprawled in the sun which glanced through the trees. It was difficult to get a sense of how high we were: the slopes above and below were tree-covered, and you could almost have been in an English wood. Only the faint hum of what sounded like sawing further up the mountain broke the silence. We sipped our green tea floating with a little butter and batted away the occasional fly. It was a perfect scene of rural tranquillity with a few who had been more energetic than others in the morning now gently nodding off, when another teacher said to me casually, 'What's that smoke do you think?'

Events then unfolded so fast I can barely recall the details. John leapt to his feet and shouted in a most un-John-like panic: 'Run, everyone! Spread out!' As he spoke, the 'smoke' which was actually quarry dust overwhelmed us, and behind it, hundreds of tons of freshly broken yellow rock, some pieces the size of small cars, came thundering down the mountain directly where we had been sitting. In the few seconds we had, I had found shelter under a low overhang, still in the middle of the rockfall's path, but cushioned by a bank of turf. I found I had two companions packed in with me there – one a student and another the head of languages – and out of instinct I had my hands and arms stretched out covering both their two heads. How fragile their heads felt, how smooth their hair in this unexpected intimacy, the rocks crashing and bouncing over us as they continued their blind and unstoppable path through the saplings below.

It can only have been a matter of seconds before all fell eerily silent again. We waited. Was there more? We waited again. And then the gradually dawning question: where was everyone else? After some minutes, the silence continuing, we began to creep out from our hiding places. I saw John emerge, covered as we all were in the pale rock dust which had enveloped us. And from memory, for goodness knows where any lists were, he began to call the names. Spencer! Yes, came the reply. Daniel! Yes. Paul! Yes. And so on, until the last one. We were all, somehow, miraculously, safe. By now the path was crowded again, people brushing themselves off, speech gradually returning as we began to ask the Sherpas what had happened. Sitting apart on the tussock of grass that had saved our lives, watching the children gathering in groups, I felt hot tears of shock running down my dusty cheeks.

Later that evening at the next campsite we learned that someone had been blasting with dynamite above our heads in order to carve out a road further up the mountain. Nobody had actually thought to check whether there were any trekkers on the path below. We were the lucky party, the Sherpas said with delight, naming us so in Nepali thereafter. We had cheated death. We had brought good fortune.

An experience like that is not easily forgotten. I can never walk along a mountain path or indeed anywhere where there is the possibility of being hit by something from above (walking under the scaffolding at Russell Square tube station is a problem) without thinking of the rockfall, of John Freeman's voice calling out our names, and the strange closeness of the near-death experience of the lucky party.

Much later I reflected on this as a reminder that in an emergency people will tend to act on instinct, so thinking through the risks beforehand is always a worthwhile exercise. And because of that default to instinct, I saw why teachers are normally not permitted to take their own children on school expeditions when they are responsible for a school party, and why parent helpers should not be used to take the place of members of staff. When danger comes, your deepest instincts, both for survival and protection, take over. Had I been a parent with my own child facing possible death under those tons of stone, I know who I would have tried to protect first.

Hazards when away on school expeditions are one form of risk. The health and safety of children is a priority every day, but as in so many walks of life, the imposition of labyrinthine procedures has undermined the ability of professionals to use their judgement. Today's teachers are often more absorbed by not infringing the rules than by using their eyes and ears to keep children safe. Safeguarding training is a test of jargon and acronyms, not insight. Because they are less confident to act as they know best they are more likely to take a 'by the book' approach which, ironically, may well mean they miss what is most important. The over-complex systems also stagger because there are not the resources needed to deliver them. The pattern is the same: following a high-profile child abuse case which grips the country and puts the government under pressure, new layers of legislation are added. Schools find themselves increasingly disempowered – not trusted to do the thing they do best, which is to understand and protect children – but obliged to pass on any concerns to a tottering and inadequate workforce within the social services. I have on several occasions found myself sitting with the pastoral deputy head on a Friday afternoon (always a Friday afternoon) wrestling with what to do after a girl has disclosed something that doesn't sound right about circumstances at home. Let's say she has been upset by the unwanted attentions of an uncle who has been visiting the family from abroad and has told her tutor she doesn't feel comfortable going home. We know this family; our instinct is to get on the phone at once, bring the parents in and get the thing talked over and sorted out. But no. This is a child protection matter and we must make an immediate referral to the social services. Our telephone call (if answered at all) will almost certainly not result in any action for several days, but having referred, we are not then permitted to take the matter forward ourselves. The pressure to refer may well leave some children more vulnerable, because the sheer weight of cases means that anything not absolutely urgent is left to fester.

Schools are literally drowning in formalised procedure. I recently attended a governors' meeting at an international school where there were twenty-three lengthy attachments to the main agenda. These could have been summarised in one simple question: how do the governors know what is happening in the school? Many schools are so overwhelmed that they appoint compliance officers, just to keep the institution up to date and on the right side of the law. Perhaps this is a reaction to complacency in the past and we needed to become more accountable. Certainly, the tragic cases of child abuse, often perpetrated over decades because they have been left unchecked, prompt revulsion. It saddens me that schools have become mistrusted by association, when in many cases, school is a child's safe haven. If we are going to have confident, capable leaders with good judgement, we need to re-establish our respect for the expertise and responsibility of education professionals. We've seen the importance of trust in creating effective relationships within school: we now need to see trust restored to teachers by the public and the government.

Responsible risk management of health and safety is one thing, but amongst the challenges for high-achieving environments is avoiding too great a risk aversion where education is concerned, making sure that the pressure of staying at the top isn't addressed by a reluctance ever to experiment or change anything about the what and the how of education itself. In terms of the curriculum, the wider education of the school and strategic development generally, a school must always be innovating if it is going to grow and influence society for the better. As individual teachers age, their students don't: a secondary school is always filled with 11–18-year-olds and they must be prepared for the world as it will be, not the world as we know it now or as we remember it from when we were young. The introduction of Mandarin Chinese at St Paul's by my predecessor was a case in point. Nobody knew how the girls would fare learning Mandarin (though given their appetite for anything difficult we were optimistic); nobody knew how it would eventually affect exam results and thus our academic ranking, but offering the language felt important to allow for opportunities in the future and we launched it in 2006. A decade later the department of one had increased to three and Mandarin was established throughout the school, up to and including A level. This was a risk which worked.

Intelligent, courageous yet responsible risk has to be built deliberately into robust strategic planning as well as into the lives of the students. How to take charge of your own learning and being prepared to challenge yourself became a regular conversation at St Paul's. This is especially important in a girls' school because, on the whole, I have found just as girls set themselves extremely high standards, and much as it pains me to write this, they are generally less ready to take risks that may affect their academic credentials than boys. When we gathered in the feedback from Oxford and Cambridge colleges each year about the girls who had not been offered places (which took some interpreting because fear of litigious parents made the remarks committed to paper sometimes noncommittal and bland) if there was a theme at all, it was this: the candidates were reluctant to embark on unfamiliar territory and tended to stay within what they knew rather than allowing themselves to think spontaneously in the moment. We saw the same tendency in the joint university preparation classes held with St Paul's Boys' school. The girls might know as much (or frequently more) but they were less ready to venture an opinion in case it was wrong. Intellectual risk aversion and public confidence are not quite the same thing, but when the winners of the senior scholarship essay competition presented their work as formal papers to a mixed audience of staff and students, the boys, besuited and smart, sounded confident and assured, as if they were already halfway to their management consultancy careers or jobs in the City. The girls tended to read their utterly brilliant and scholarly presentations moving from foot to foot as if they couldn't wait to flee the stage. In front of their peers they didn't have this diffidence and would give superbly researched solo assemblies to a room of 500 people on topics they felt passionate about – I'm thinking of a very brilliant one on the films of Wes Anderson – speaking to the assembled school, with wit, humour and command. Why don't you do it like that at your university interviews? I would sit thinking.

The importance of building girls' self-belief while they are at school is underlined when so many women still report feeling invisible or overlooked in the workplace. We've all seen that cartoon in which the chairman sits at the head of a boardroom table saying to his female PA: 'That's an excellent idea, Miss Twigg. Perhaps one of the men would like to suggest it?' Often, it's not so much that women lack confidence. It's just that reading the room, they refrain from speaking unless what they have to say is accurate, relevant and interesting and, as they silently, instinctively take responsibility for the overall quality and direction of a discussion, they can allow the male voices, untrammelled by such concerns, to dominate. The superior performance of companies with mixed boards shows us that the best ideas emerge when all voices can be heard. Freeing girls to speak out, challenging them to take risks by encouraging lively debate and discussion at school, in the classroom and everywhere else (the ritual of formal debating is great) is vital if women in the future are to have influence, especially in the fields of politics, finance and business. This is why the approach of positive education and the development of the growth mindset are so important for girls: the challenges do not end at school – they are only just beginning.

This chapter is about what to do when things go wrong, but also about how to guard against the ordinary – against things being less good than they could be. This is to do with tackling fear. If as a school you are doing well and measurable outcomes say you are at the top of your game, why do anything differently? Better stick to what works. But a high-achieving environment – an exciting one – can only be created where there is ambition and a leading edge only sustained if there is courage to innovate. A school – any organisation – must constantly check itself for the narrowed thinking that comes from fear. It's not a matter of being reckless, more a refusal to be average. Lasting excellence, as opposed to mere flashes in the pan, depends on a continual balance being struck and restruck between prudence and ambition, especially in a school where so much depends on attitude: that elusive but powerful thing which exists in the motivation and aspirations of staff and students. In the refreshingly business-like world of for-profit education that I am now getting to know, the drive is always for business efficiency – the raw teacher–pupil ratios that you can see on a spreadsheet. The staffing must be tight. Yes, but these neat numbers hide enormous variations of quality and therefore of outcomes: if your teacher is unambitious and unmotivated, and sits in front of the class checking their emails while the children wade through a worksheet (I have seen it many times) it costs the same amount as paying a brilliant professional to ignite the passion of the class. Which of these you find as you walk the corridors of your school and the value delivered depends on good, efficient recruitment and husbandry of resources, but also on leadership and culture – forging that energetic ethos where constructive risk-taking, delegated responsibility and the power to

exercise judgement keep the teachers and students always stimulated, alive and reaching towards the edge of their capability. There
is so much more to optimal performance than just having the
staffing budget right.

At St Paul's, where being different is much prized and where
the intellectual appetites of girls and staff are naturally strong,
there was usually enough sand in our shoes to create a bit of
friction, to keep us asking why, to maintain a sense of active choice
and freedom. Take the no-uniform policy. People were often
surprised the girls could wear whatever they liked (how did you
ensure there wasn't competition? How did you set the boundaries?
How did you prevent these clever girls taking advantage?) but to
me this showed they didn't understand the school. Yes, there were
some girls who liked to dress eccentrically (fairy wings; eighteenth-century costume; panda outfits) – and really, why not, if it
didn't cause offence, represent a risk to health or hinder them
doing their work? If you can't try out your identity through your
clothes when at school, when can you? Others took next to no
interest apart from being comfortable and that was okay too. For
me it was an absolute joy not to have to undertake the tedium of
pulling people up on their skirt length, or untucked shirt, or
laddered tights. Unless you are in the armed services or the police,
there are surely few walks of life where wearing outdated formal
clothes in order to be identified is required. A girl would soon
learn about dress codes in society – that it wasn't sensible to turn
up for an internship assessment at an investment bank wearing a
bustier (we did warn her). Overall, this was a freedom, a refusal
to be average, which they learned to manage extremely well. A
risk? Perhaps. And well worth it.

Letting them choose what to wear was all of a piece with my
predecessor's warning to me (as I now see it) that: 'The girls don't
accept anything just because you say it. Everything has to be
argued intellectually.' By the end of a decade, I certainly knew
what she meant; the relentless dialectic may be exhausting at times

but important, because coasting, in the sense of working too much within everyone's comfort zone for fear of difficulty, failure or conflict, can creep up on you. Especially, if I dare risk saying this, where there is too much emphasis on the sentimental pursuit of happiness. Schools which focus on happiness as an end in itself (the more times I see the word, the more I feel as if I have just drunk a too-large glass of very sweet banana milkshake) can find themselves on an insidious downward path. Well-being is most important, and we've looked at how to promote that. But if we are constantly guarding against putting pressure on the children or having the staff lose that much sought-after perfect work–life balance (who with any passion for work or life ever managed that?) the danger is that they deliquesce into a warm fuzzy world of under-expectation. And nobody *really* feels happy about that.

Of course, where there is an appetite for risk there is bound to come failure. It has become normal to be more open about failure because it's also now widely recognised that young people *need* to confront failure in order to develop resilience for the modern world – the ability to bounce back when things go wrong. There is the messy sort of failure that doesn't seem to have an upside at the time – and nowadays also designer failure. We are virtually falling over successful entrepreneurs who, wearing slouchy jeans and trainers, pace up and down speaking self-deprecatingly about what it was like before they had their big break and were still driving a three-wheeler. This is failure viewed through the lens of casually worn success: a comfortable enough perspective but not resonating with most people. The real challenge is how you deal with failure not recollected in tranquillity but while it's happening. I had been told that in the case of Paulinas, the answer was not well.

One of my first images of the school was seeing a girl lying face down on the long marble concourse crying her eyes out having just received her GCSE results. You know what's coming. When the slip of paper with the offending news was prised out of her hand, it emerged that she had achieved ten A* grades. What could be the problem? It was the eleventh result – only an A. Disaster! If you have won a place at St Paul's at age eleven, you are automatically a high-achiever and the temptation is to expect that you will attain all your goals thereafter. But life isn't like that. I realised gradually that many of the girls were under pressure from home (consciously or not) to do brilliantly all the time. So I mentioned this tendency in my introductory talk to parents. A place at St Paul's is not an automatic ticket to world domination, I reminded them. The girls have to learn that they will *not* always ace everything and in fact, not achieving what you want is an important life lesson that every person needs to learn. Unfortunately, in one sense, the girls were so talented that often they did ace *almost* everything, facing perceived failure for the first time when they were rejected from Oxford or Cambridge in their final year. Often it was parents who 'could not accept' the rejection and expected the school to cause the university to change its mind (can't you use your influence, Ms Farr?). Only time brings perspective: a few years later, it was possible for one very gifted Paulina to look back and see that reading medicine at Birmingham rather than Oxford had led to an equally successful and perhaps even better-grounded career. What had all that anguish been about?

One of the ways I tried to help the girls manage their sense of failure was by talking about my own mistakes. Self-disclosure can be powerful if you don't overdo it. Becoming high mistress was a fairly daunting prospect for anyone: that title for a start, never mind the critical or charismatic line of predecessors. Being exposed on a pedestal for the gimlet-eyed consideration of that fiercely intellectual, mane-tossing set of adolescents – never mind the staff – was not something to be contemplated lightly. How to get over my own bad case of imposter syndrome? When it became obvious (as it soon did) that most of my colleagues and pupils were considerably more talented than I was, for me to be completely honest and never pretend to knowledge I didn't have seemed the only way. I made a sort of virtue out of it, sometimes going out of my way to demonstrate my own limitations, mistakes and weaknesses, and I've always stuck to it. This was not to curry favour or insure myself against unforeseen intellectual traps where my jack-of-all-trades, master-of-none brain would be exposed – more to present myself as a normal, fallible person. If the high mistress can make mistakes, they would surely reason, then it's okay if sometimes I make mistakes too. When I parked momentarily outside my own front door in west London, for example, rushed inside the house to collect shopping bags leaving the engine running, and came out to see the car being driven away, this was beyond a mistake – it was just completely stupid. A week of pounding the streets later, I was lucky enough to find the car abandoned and garnished with a sheaf of parking tickets no more than a few streets away. My first thought (honestly) was that it would make a good assembly, which it did. Then there were the inevitable stories of my failures at school: my undistinguished A levels, my failure ever to get selected for a sports team, my terminal incompetence in chemistry, my inability to impress the inscrutable, whiskered woman who interviewed me at St Hilda's College, Oxford (*a sweet, virginal young girl, but alas . . .*) and what it felt like being cast into outer darkness when I went to Exeter University instead. Well, life didn't end, did it?

Some experiences I turned to good account when advising colleagues about their careers. I believe fate plays a hand in our lives – which is another way of saying things often make more sense when read backwards rather than forwards. There have been occasions when I've felt disappointed not to get a particular job. But the feeling often lessens after some new turn in the road, a different opportunity presenting itself, enabling me to see how the failure was, after all, part of the preparation for what turned out to be. That fluffed question about how to deal with the angry parent: I was ready for it next time. How glad I was, in hindsight, not to be selected for a teaching role at a more comfortable school in Bristol: I might never have gone to Hong Kong. How fortunate to come second in the race to be the next head of another leading London girls' school – I wouldn't have become High Mistress of St Paul's a few months later. And so on. It's not true to say that there is no value in being wise after the event. Often we are wise *because* of the event, so how could that not be helpful, if you take the longer view of things?

Clearly, the Paulina sense of failure would to most people be unrecognisable as failure at all. That doesn't make it insignificant for those highly ambitious young women. Success and failure are relative and have as much to do with how we feel as with the facts. The important thing in a school is to be ambitious for *all* children and encourage them to be ambitious for themselves. This has not always informed national curriculum planning where the aim of ensuring flattering results has been allowed to influence subject content. The shameful disapplication of modern foreign languages had more to do with shying away from something difficult than with thin arguments about freedom of choice. I often think of my former pupil working in the hi-fi section of a department store in Bristol. A world away from sobbing over a lost A*, he was feeling the thrill of success having found the springboard for his life in his first job: what a great start.

But how do we grow that ability to pick ourselves up without losing all sensitivity? Resilience and grit – those popular buzzwords – summon up images of digitally created, bionic men and women with cascading locks, racing through hostile landscapes dealing out justice to marauding monsters and emerging from hair's-breadth escapes hardly out of breath, surveying the horizon in eager anticipation of the next adventure. Resilience has a glamorous, pugilistic, external image. And of course to a certain generation, grit will always be embodied by John Wayne – *True Grit*. Rather than being a battle to be won, recovery from failure is often much more a matter of developing a quiet inner strength and the unfashionable virtue of patience; drawing what lessons we can from a thing that was painful or difficult or messy, or just less than we hoped for, and finding the resolve to move forward, even if the transformational lesson that the experience will surely deliver is not immediately clear. School life provides students with myriad opportunities to develop this ability: if you don't get selected for the netball team or the school play you can try again next term; if you find a subject difficult, with a growth mindset you can do better; if you fall out with your friend you can learn how to listen better and even say sorry: a friendship can be mended. Moving schools can be traumatic but you can make new friends in another school, especially if you take an interest in others; if you miss your place at your preferred university because you didn't get the grades, you can try again if you want to, but there is more than one place to be happy and get a good degree. So many experiences of failure or disappointment look different with the passage of time. More and more, I see patience as the most important skill – call it a virtue – that we should be teaching our students. We shouldn't shield children from all unwelcome experiences in the mistaken belief that being temporarily unhappy is bad for you.

The real problem, new to us in education, is that technology and the communication revolution have insidiously planted the idea that speed is the ultimate virtue trumping accuracy and with it detail, nuance and truth. What is fake news if not a product of the obsession with speed and the soundbite? We are constantly absorbing (and writing) thousands of characters on our hand-held devices (our children will text the equivalent of the complete works of Shakespeare twice in their lifetimes). The world has hit fast-forward and this is the enemy to true inner strength and stamina. No wonder we are hearing about the epidemic of so-called depression in children and the 'medicalisation of adolescence', with record numbers of young people being prescribed drugs to mitigate their state of mind. If we thought more about teaching them to live with disappointment, even boredom, and about the value of giving some of life's problems the requisite time to come right, we might have fewer woozy students in our classrooms with a more realistic outlook on life.

In my experience children are often much more naturally resilient and adaptable than we think and can cope with major changes in their lives better than many adults, even if they have the occasional meltdown about lesser things. I've seen remarkable courage and fortitude in children who are facing bereavement, for example. I have in mind two girls who were coping with the extended illness and then the death of a parent. Each one faced this differently, according to her personality, but their ability to be entirely present for that parent yet at the same time pursue a full and fruitful life at school (school perhaps a special blessing at this time for its normality), to be immersed in academic work and in the community, was humbling to see. I'm visualising now two very different funerals, one in a west London church, the other in a Jewish cemetery, each of them for a father. On both occasions, I watched a teenage daughter, my student, conduct herself with restrained self-possession, dignity and strength, showing the public face which, despite hiding such pain, was a sign of promise – embodying that capacity for courage and self-determination which came from deep within herself. How proud those two fathers would have been.

Schools are touched by all aspects of human life and death. When being interviewed for the headship of another leading girls' school I was asked the following question: 'You answer a telephone call one morning in your office, just as the bell for assembly is ringing. It's the police telling you that one of your pupils has had a fatal car accident on the way to school. What do you do?' This question took me unawares, as it was meant to, and I ventured something about getting the senior team together and activating the crisis management plan. The fact is that when someone dies, there is nothing you *can* do. However experienced you are, you can't solve or undo the situation. Your work as a head is instead to channel and manage reactions: shock, fear, grief, disbelief, anger – a process which begins at once and then goes on for weeks, months and perhaps years.

The first time I had to manage the aftermath of a death was in the early part of my headship at Queenswood. It was a quiet Sunday afternoon and many of the older girls had gone home or were spending the day in London. I was working at my desk on the next day's assembly. The phone rang and it was the mother of a girl in the sixth form. She and her husband had been travelling abroad on business and on returning to their hotel, he had collapsed and died the previous evening of a heart attack. He was a healthy man in his mid-forties. It was a complete shock. She had four children at boarding school in England. How was she to tell them? The eldest, Fiona, was with me. Would I tell her, the mother asked? There was so much to attend to, and at least she could hear it from a real person rather than a disembodied voice down the phone. No, she wouldn't prefer to do it herself. She really must go. Would I do it straight away? She would call and speak to her daughter later that evening . . . her voice drifted away; she had hung up.

I sat for a time at my desk. That poor, brave woman. Less than twenty-four hours after losing her husband she was trying to cope with the practicalities of repatriating his body and she had four children to worry about. I must think how to help her and the first thing was to tell Fiona. Feeling my mind drop down into a state of cool clarity (as fortunately it seems naturally to do in a crisis) I confided in the housemistress and waited for the girls to come back from their day out in London. Fiona would be sent to see me on some pretext and I would tell her.

The study fell silent, waiting. All that permanence – the wood-panelling, the lawn rolling away outside. Peaceful and reassuring. But now this. An hour later, I heard her light steps tripping down my corridor and turning round, saw her hover in the doorway, her fair hair hanging down her back and her cheeks pink from running. Her eyes were anxious – what did the principal want with her on a Sunday afternoon? As I looked at her, I felt the most terrible sense of responsibility – almost guilt. Here was this lovely young woman, back from her carefree day, and now I must break her heart.

Fiona. Come in. I stood up. My dear, I'm afraid I have something very painful to tell you. Come over here a little . . . My hand was held out. Your mother has just called me to say that your father has had a sudden heart attack. Fiona, I'm so sorry to have to say this to you, but he has died . . . my words petered out. After a dreadful moment of silent disbelief I shall never forget, she collapsed into my outstretched arms and we found ourselves sitting on my carpeted floor, the sunlight splashing around us. She rocked there for what seemed like a long time. Eventually, she recovered enough for me to call two friends who escorted her up to her room in the boarding house. Others closer to her would take over from this point and my role in the terrible breaking of news was done, for now. Over the succeeding weeks and months, with the help of friends especially and a very experienced and sympathetic housemistress, Fiona came gradually to terms with what had happened. She went to university, eventually started her own design business and, years later, wrote to me that she was grateful I had been the one to tell her. I was surprised and touched that she could feel gratitude to the person who had imparted such devastating news. That had been, in different ways, a life-changing moment for us both.

The death of a parent is one thing. The loss of a pupil, a friend to others and a member of the school community, is different in its impact and a great test for any school.

At Queenswood, a girl in her GCSE year died in hospital after a series of respiratory complications. She was a quiet girl who had not been in school for some time. Marion, the school secretary, walked into my office having just taken the news over the phone from her father. He had sounded tired, but been completely calm, she said. The sense of shock and responsibility poor Marion felt, as the bearer of such news, was only one of the many things which had to be considered that afternoon. I called the chaplain over and we sat thinking about what to do and in what order: telling the girls, telling the staff, providing space and time for the feelings that would come to be expressed and managed. On another occasion at St Paul's, a final-year student died a week after experiencing a severe anaphylactic shock brought on by a nut allergy. In this case, there was a week in which she lay peacefully in a white hospital bed, her parents keeping vigil. Eventually it was clear that there was no possibility of a recovery and her extraordinarily brave and dignified parents took the agonising decision to withdraw the life support. A tall, dark-haired, sensitive and talented girl who loved music, she was their only child.

There have been other occasions, each marked by the highly personal nature of the circumstances. One extraordinary girl at St Paul's who was passionate about film made a highly watchable documentary of herself in hospital, full of humour, showing her optimism and determination to vanquish cancer. Her courage and positivity were felt by everyone in the school when this was showed in an assembly and when she died, the synagogue overflowed with the young people come to honour her. I have enduring respect and sympathy as I think of her parents and indeed of each of those families. No child should die before her parents and the loss of a young life leaves a family in disbelief, bereft and devastated. As a mother myself, I could barely imagine it. But as headmistress I needed to separate myself somewhat from the effect of empathy and think practically – first about how to convey the news to the communities of which the girls had been a part. Some might think such rationality unfeeling, but I've found it essential when you are dealing with others who may not be in command of their emotions or behaviour and when it's necessary to create a framework within which to manage erratic emotions as they develop and change over first hours, then days and weeks. I'm grateful for that clarity which seems to come over me in a crisis, giving me unusual certainty about what to do and when.

There is obviously no right way to go about informing a community of a death. What I saw mattered in each case was that I should tell people myself and tell them all together, which meant addressing the girls and staff at an assembly. 'Girls, I have something very sad to tell you today and I need you to be very brave . . .'

I recall on one occasion coming to the end of my short address and pausing. The shocked silence of a large body of young people hearing that one of their number has died is poignant; you feel their trust in the rightness of things, in the safety and security of the adult world that can surely make all well, blown suddenly off course. How can this be? There is disbelief. They stand together, eyes widened, supporting one another instinctively. But they also stand alone; for every individual, the impact is unique. There are those for whom death is already a familiar thing, because they have lost someone close to them. They feel their private loss freshen. Others feel a vaguer fear – could this happen to them, or to one of their close friends? And for some, there is a curious blankness. This was an older girl they did not know, but she has gone. They should be feeling something big – but what? They have only a sense of a vague wrongness having come over the day. The comfortable certainties shudder, as time is momentarily suspended in the silent air of the school hall.

At such times the strength and authenticity of a school community are tested. There are so many needs to think about. The girl's close friends. Those in the same form or tutor group. Her particular teachers. And of course the parents – in many ways beyond the help of the school, but needing to know that the school is still there, doing the right thing, and will continue to remember and care, as their sense of their lost child as a pupil and member of that community imperceptibly begins to sink in. There are the needs of the first few days: to come together, to share feelings, to express something of the shock and to keep the pupil present in memories and anecdotes. 'Do you remember when we all dressed up to raise money for sending books to Africa and she put on a gorilla suit . . .' And then there are the needs that continue, when life has picked up and moved on for the majority, for those few at the centre for whom the recovery and acceptance will take much longer.

For the head, trying to orchestrate all this, sensing the needs and the right timings for everything is critically important. There is often the desire for some form of ritual or process to channel feelings. What felt right was to set aside a quiet space where people could go throughout the day to sit and reflect, with a place to light a candle if they wanted. This wasn't necessarily religious, though we offered a time for prayers led by the chaplain for those who wanted it. Many drifted to the place, the school library, during the day. In form time, with the form group coming together, every girl could take a white card on which to write any thoughts or feelings she wished. Gradually, as the days unfolded, in one case it became clear that those close to the girl who had died wanted to hold an event to celebrate her life and all the talents she had. They came to me angry at first. Not enough had been done. Did I not have any idea how they felt? What had been the point of prayers in the library? It was just a pathetic attempt to make them move on. I saw the anger as a natural expression of their sense of loss. It would help them if the energy it took could be focussed on the organisation of a short event in words and music about this talented girl. It was important that this came from them, and when they had recovered from the shock enough to use the energy of that anger for action. Would her parents come? They did, and sat with great restraint and dignity to watch what had been so lovingly prepared and rehearsed out of the fierce grief of the friends. I wondered how the parents managed it: the whole experience must have been an agony for them. And yet they serenely watched and graciously thanked everyone at the end, seeing perhaps how this homespun ritual, amongst many others, was somehow helping to move us all forward. They left quietly and without fuss, walking carefully hand in hand down the stone steps, taking their grief home.

For parents who have suffered in this way, life is irrevocably altered and any recovery takes a very long time. A woman who had lost a son many years before to blood cancer once told me that while she had never got over it, she had learned to live with it. In the end she survived both her sons, living to be over a hundred. Whenever I look at the little gold fox cufflinks she thoughtfully left me, I think of the model she showed the world of patient, loving, maternal fortitude. Parenthood will always be at once the most responsible yet vulnerable of states. For a school community, recovering from loss, eventually the welling up of hope and the momentum of always looking forward that is the habit of young people means there is renewal. This is a natural and gradual process which in no sense weakens or renders insincere the intensity of the emotions felt in the raw first days of the aftermath. Perhaps because the population of students is always in flux, every year new ones joining and at the top of the school another generation leaving to go to university, the shared memories shift. Inevitably, there are now no current students who remember those girls as their contemporary.

Working through difficult or tragic events is an inevitable part of the life of a school and I have marvelled again and again at the ability of a community to unite in sadness over a loss but then, also together, to pick itself up and move forward. Something to do with the essential vitality and optimism of young people: hope and happiness well up again. It's a natural process.

Some of the talk about resilience may be a little oversimplified and cartoonish, but schools today are generally more pragmatic, compassionate places than a generation ago. Good that we can talk about failure and what it teaches us, even if it has become a bit irritating in the mouths of people who are demonstrably successful. This more human and realistic approach helps mitigate against perfectionism from which so many girls (even discriminating, smart Paulinas) sometimes suffer. You don't have to be perfect. You just have to work each day to be the best version of yourself that you can.

And with that I notice a particularly beautiful cherry tree which will soon be in blossom outside my window. A memorial tree, planted in memory of one of our students. A sign of renewal.

Dear Sir

Congratulations to *The Sunday Times* on highlighting the hitherto largely neglected opportunity offered to companies by shared parental leave. As any new mother returning to work knows, early parenthood teaches resilience, flexibility and patience, while building stamina and resourcefulness. Why would we deny men the chance to get better at these highly transferable skills too?

Shared parental leave can not only give the strong

With Adam
in the jogging
stroller,
Queenswood
1998

☐ ✉ ⚑ ↦ **Good morning.** Have the High Mistress ring me at once.

TO DO
- Revise parent handbook
- write talk for parents
  re. exam week
- Thank lost property Mums
- Isobel – new trainers
- Return permission form for

CHAPTER 9

May

Creating the triangle of trust – working with today's parents

As April turns to May, I see exam timetables already being posted neatly with four pins on corridor noticeboards. A busy time, not just for the school but also for parents: there's the exam period to get through and then the long summer holiday to plan for. Parents have been appearing frequently as extras in the foregoing chapters; here I want to devote time to them specifically.

My emblematic image of the schoolchild's parent is of a figure hovering beyond tall school gates, looking somewhat uncertain, standing on the brink of a world that isn't theirs. As students come streaming out at the end of their day, eyes search for that one dear, familiar face to emerge from school, the face that stands out from all the others. Or in the mist of a summer morning, the same eyes watch as the figure disappears into the hubbub and chatter of the school, to resume a life of friends, habits and discovery within a landscape that the parent on the sidelines will never really know.

Habitually hovering at the gate, on the brink of your child's special world, how do you get to know what is actually going on at school and feel included and informed about your child's education?

One obvious way to keep yourself informed is via the formal parent consultation evenings – these go on throughout the year and today, with the summer term in full swing, I've been doing a refresher session with a group of new teachers about how to prepare. Let's pause a moment to see how those occasions are handled from the inside.

This evening, with the long light making the day stretch out, the school's Great Hall will be laid out with rows of the small, square desks normally used for exams, each with a chair placed neatly behind and a pair of chairs in front. On each desk, the deputy head will stand a card bearing the teacher's name. There the teacher will sit, mark book or laptop open ready as aide-memoire, as wave after wave of parents sit and, leaning forward a little, incline their heads eagerly to hear how their daughter is progressing. From the outside it might seem like an exercise in speed dating: amid the constant scraping of chairs, exchanging as much information as five minutes will allow and moving on.

It's worth remembering that for teachers who have been in front of lively classes all day, a parents' evening holds some challenges. First you have to keep to time: with anything from twenty to forty sets of parents to see, it's impossible to linger over the talents and individual needs of any one pupil for too long, or an impatient queue will start developing. Worse, this will bring the deputy head to hover over you. What to do if the parents, oblivious of the queue forming behind them and eager for every last pearl that will fall from your lips, want to settle in for a much longer conversation? 'I studied *Tess of the D'Urbervilles* myself at school, Miss Hardy, actually. I must say it's been fascinating reading your comments on Emily's essays. I was always especially interested in that image of the playing card – what do you think it means . . . ?' This one could go on all evening.

Or there are those who are combative and have a broader agenda they want to pursue . . . 'Frankly, Miss Cribbs, your account of

Harriet's efforts this term isn't good enough. Teacher after teacher is saying she isn't doing enough work. Why haven't we been told this before? [*Because this is the parents' evening.*] I've cut short an important meeting in the City to be here and I don't like the inference that my daughter is lazy. My question is: what are you doing about it? I admit I never did much work myself at school – it hasn't held me back of course – but I'm not paying fees so Harriet can waste her time on Facebook . . .'

Going over possible scenarios, I coach the new teachers in how to bring a conversation to a close, firmly but politely, by standing up, holding out their hand and looking the parent in the eye with the words: 'Thank you, Mr Sacks . . . Dr Sacks . . . I'm glad we are working together on this and of course there will be a written report coming home at the end of term . . .'

Sitting at the small desk, you work your way down the list of names in your mark book, ticking them off, until there are only two left to go. A fascinating if tiring insight into family resemblance and heredity, filling out your knowledge of your pupils as only a glimpse of home can. But now it's half past seven and the deputy head is patrolling again, ready to encourage latecomers to finish their conversations and leave. You are just settling your papers, thinking you'll call those last two on the phone in the morning, when both arrive breathless: 'So sorry . . . you were probably thinking we weren't coming! We had to collect our other daughter from a match and it went on later than expected. Would it be all right for us to have just a short chat . . . ?' And visualising the pile of marking waiting for you later at the end of the District Line, you sit down again.

I have been on both sides of the desk, as teacher and also as parent. The interaction is necessarily brief – a mere snapshot of progress – and you might not think much could be achieved, but a good teacher will have a clear idea of the profile of each student and will have given careful thought to what needs to be communicated. It's all in the preparation. As a parent, whether you get confirmation of what you expected or a revelation of something you did not (and the school will try to avoid unwelcome surprises) this is an opportunity to sit face to face with the person your child has often mentioned at home and of whom you can now form your own connection. My husband John and I had it well planned: he took down shorthand like the seasoned journalist he is while I listened. I often found myself comparing the reality with the impressions – usually hilarious and affectionate – that the children had treated us to at home, concentrating on not calling Mr Smith 'Badger' or whatever name it was they had for him.

What teachers may miss, however, is that we parents can feel vulnerable. We may well barely recognise the child being described (*but she's not at all like that at home!*). It's wonderful to hear that favourite and most unique person (your daughter) praised, but somehow an affront to you personally if it is tactfully mentioned that motivation could be better. And anyway, as parent, we are not used to being told about *our* child as audience rather than participant: whether or not our children welcome it, we want to feel involved in this complex experience that is our child's formal education. So looking for the right role to play, many parents ask: 'How can we help at home?'

Being very practical, my advice as a head would be as follows.

First, be well informed about your child's schooling by reading the information you are sent (it's axiomatic in schools that parents have to be told everything in at least three ways before they take it in. Be the exception!). Turn up to those parent consultation evenings ready to listen and enjoy supporting as much as you can at school matches or other events (not beating yourself up if you can't do all that many – your child will appreciate it all the more when you do). But then, especially when your child arrives at secondary school, be prepared to step back and *let the school get on with its work*. You wouldn't tell a surgeon how to take out your appendix, so why would you think teachers need your advice on how to teach? Don't hover endlessly over every detail of the curriculum: your over-attention will not be welcomed when your child is trying to make their own way, and sometimes even make their own mistakes, without you knowing about every detail. Put your trust in the school (if you are fortunate you will have chosen it) and respect the boundaries your child sets as she gradually finds her place and relaxes there. Practise some healthy neglect: your unhindered child will be relieved and become more independent as a result.

We've talked about the educational benefits of allowing failure to happen, so while our instinct to protect our children is natural, try to refrain from micromanaging and taking away all the obstacles. Even, perhaps especially, in our achievement-driven, maxed-out society, children learn from weathering disappointments and from sometimes making mistakes and need to be allowed to experience this without being rescued constantly by their parents. Don't be a snow plough, sweeping away every problem and turning your child into a melting snowflake herself. Instead, within reason, allow her to dig herself out of the snowdrift because she will be the stronger for it. Children have to learn not just to overcome difficulty but to be bored, to kick themselves when they know they could have done better and to go after their own aspirations and dreams, not the ones you would set for them.

Your child is learning all the time, and will also be watching you and what you do, as well as hearing – and sometimes heeding, if you're lucky – what you say. Is it actually *you* who can't put the iPhone down and is constantly distracted when your child is trying to speak to you? Rather than obsessing about the homework schedule, continue to be a learner yourself – be curious and create an environment at home that invites curiosity. Sit down and read. You deserve it after the day you've had! Let your children see you reading for pleasure. Make time to go to films and plays, see exhibitions, take walks together, cook together, have interesting conversations at meals and don't allow any technology at the table.

Don't monitor school too closely; concentrate instead on making home an interesting and unpressured place to be. Education is happening all the time, not just at school. Better to play your own part in that experience for your child than to try to helicopter over the school.

Homework. This exercises parents a great deal. *How can I persuade my child to actually start it and then help them get it done?* Or sometimes: *How do I stop my child doing too much homework?* However tempting, don't do their homework for them (even if you do actually understand it) but, as far as possible, support the skill of independent study by providing space and quiet at home. Whether the homework is to consolidate learning or prepare material for the next lesson, it is better done without your intervention. Ask what the homework is, but after that, don't show too much interest unless invited. Instead, model the skill of quiet concentration. If you study yourself, great! Or open that novel you wanted to finish. They can learn good habits from you. Agree what time homework will finish and make it well before bedtime, so that they can do something to relax (not screen-based) before going to bed. Your role is not to badger but to create the conditions in which the study can be done.

The same goes for revising for exams. Encourage your child to have a revision timetable and to divide their time sensibly into manageable chunks of perhaps half an hour to an hour. Not longer – frequent breaks aid concentration. Provide the cups of tea and the meals. Again, be available but don't hover and especially don't get stressed yourself. As with doing homework, one aim of any good revision programme is guilt-free leisure: your role can be to see that your child takes breaks and is refreshed for the next revision period.

If you're like me, you are probably worried in a vague kind of way about your child's use of technology and what they might be doing online. It seems only yesterday that my husband John was striding into our sitting room at Queenswood at the end of a twenty-minute episode of *Postman Pat* ordering 'television off!' and actually prevailing. Now it seems as if the train has left the station: you will now never be able to catch up with the technology revolution and as the claims for the possibilities of technology to transform the way we live become ever more extraordinary, a little bit of you is stubbornly resisting and reasserting the importance of real-time, face-to-face experience over what is virtual and artificial. As the digital immigrant parents of today's digital native children, however much we are impressed that a computer will soon write sonnets better than Shakespeare (I actually heard an IT guru claim this with joy at a seminar recently), is there also a bit of us which questions the desirability, the trustworthiness of all this? With echoes of Mary Shelley's *Frankenstein*, technology has opened up prospects that are both exhilarating and alarming. Our children, who have never known a world without the iPhone and the iPad see only possibility. But you are not so old-fashioned if you are keeping healthily sceptical. You may even be ahead of your time. It's obvious to most parents that the majority of usage by many young people today – I say the majority, not all – is not life-enhancing. Rather, as Susan Greenfield dares to say, it is 'solitary, passive and unspectacular'. As a parent you should not feel you are being a dinosaur – in fact you should know that you are joining a new wave of thinking – by challenging the ubiquity of technology and encouraging your children to enjoy themselves through sport, through drama, through doing things together with their friends and with you, whether through conversation, or cooking, or being outside, or through playing games as a family. (Is there a website for 'funnest family games'? There should be. They are going to make a comeback, just like knitting.)

In short, your children's well-being, their mental health, depends on you providing opportunities for sustained interaction with real people, both with other children and with older generations. I heard an inspirational speech-day address at a school in Brussels a few months ago where the young speaker, himself an alumnus of the school pursuing an enviable career in the theatre, very much a digital native himself, advised the graduating class to put away their iPhones and get to know their parents. There was a different kind of attention in the packed sports hall, where those same parents, wilting in the June heat, brightened visibly at the thought of their newfound appeal. He might have added grandparents too – so often a wonderful fund of stories and images – who are often marginalised as we continue to be in thrall to the idea of youth as the most interesting stage of life. And if you think this emphasis on the role of parents in promoting human contact is just convenient cod psychology, read Susan Pinker's *The Village Effect*, where she argues about the vital importance of intergenerational human contact from evidence gathered in a Sardinian village:

Face-to-face contact is crucial for learning, happiness, resilience and longevity. From birth to death, human beings are hard-wired to connect to other human beings. Face-to-face contact matters: tight bonds of friendship and love heal us, help children learn, extend our lives and make us happy. Looser in-person bonds matter, too, combining with our close relationships to form a personal 'village' around us, one that exerts unique effects. Not just any social networks will do: we need the real, in-the-flesh encounters that tie human families, groups of friends and communities together . . . [1]

In summary the school parent should: support through judicious but not claustrophobic interest; model the behaviour you want to encourage, and live at peace with technology through offering many other appealing forms of social communication.

And finally, keep open good channels of communication with the school not about what it is doing, but what you are doing. What you don't tell the school, the school cannot help your child to manage. Even if it may be difficult to pick up the phone and call the deputy head to explain something personal about the family, the more open you are about any issues that, may arise at home, the more the school can support and be sensitive as needed. Whatever is happening in your family, the school will have experience that can help your child. Several times I saw what courage it took for a parent to come to see me alone to tell me, for example, that a marriage was breaking up and that, inevitably, children would be affected. As a result of that courage we could help the child much better. Without intruding, the more a school knows about a family on the whole, the better for the child and for the suffering parents too: those already greatly burdened by their own feelings and responsibilities are often grateful simply to rely on the school to look after the child – all made so much easier if that relationship of trust is there from the start.

In the course of a child's secondary school career there will inevitably be storms to weather. Friendship issues, or problems with behaviour or academic motivation (mostly just a normal part of growing through the teenage years) require home and school to be aligned in their approach and can be navigated much more easily if the relationship with home has been established firmly. Things don't go well by accident: what matters is that there is mutual respect and a commitment to open communication where the best interests of the student are always paramount.

That doesn't mean it is always easy. I remember a meeting with a father whose clever teenage daughter had decided not to work hard at school, to squander her considerable musical talent, and to amuse herself at home by pushing all her father's buttons until, beside himself with rage, he had lashed out at her physically (fortunately he missed). This large, bewildered man, his crumpled suit betraying a hurried journey, used to being a success and telling other people what to do, was now sitting opposite me in my office. He looked most unhappy: why couldn't the school get some good history essays out of his daughter? He had never come across such inefficiency. He huffed and puffed, but at the same time he was shamefaced, looking as if he had been sent to see the headmistress himself, which in a way, he had. I had a sudden glimpse of the little boy at school, probably just as idle and rebellious then as his maddening daughter. He was cross, he was not used to being remonstrated with, especially by a woman, and he was waiting for me to come up with answers: to his daughter – her attitude, her work, her relationship with him. His relationship with his wife probably too, who was blaming him for all the shouting in the house. Offering tea, I waited and listened. You cannot get anywhere with a person who has things to get off their chest until they have said everything they need: it takes as long as it takes. Eventually his exasperated monologue began to peter out – the arguments, the ruined family meals, the forgotten bassoon, the Saturday night curfew defiance. It had all got too much and he admitted he had gone for the nuclear option of cancelling her iPhone contract.

I looked at him, twisting his fingers in his lap. A sympathetic silence grew in the space between us: 'This must all be very difficult for you,' I ventured. 'You're busy trying to do the best for your daughter. I can see how exasperating you must find it!' He looked up. He thought a little. We sat. The suggestion of a smile of relief began to appear at the corners of his mouth. 'Well, yes, Mrs Farr. I can see you understand something about this. Young women . . . well . . . I suppose you do see them. Maybe I haven't helped the situation. Do you think we can perhaps get her to at least go to orchestra practice?'

This was a small turning point: the recognition that we were both on the same side, there to work together to help his daughter come to terms with herself and her own growing up, and settle to her school and home lives more positively. Which in time, she did.

One of the many reasons leading schools is such interesting

and delicate work and why the human side of leadership is so obvious that we might miss it: when you are dealing with children and their parents, it is not like dealing with any other kind of client. Children are their own, glorious, unpredictable and remarkable selves; parents, while they may be ruling the world as their day job, are often at their most vulnerable and irrational where their own children are concerned. Try telling any parent that the university aspirations they have for their child are unrealistic. I have frequently had to tell parents – even in a very high-achieving school – that for their daughter to apply only to Cambridge, Harvard and Yale may be setting the hurdle too high. They would look as if they had been personally insulted. With all interactions so potentially vulnerable to emotion and irrationality, it matters that, as the head, you are able to maintain a calm, measured and pragmatic approach, not judgemental and informed by empathy.

Often I came to know parents well because together we had weathered some storm. There was one Russian family with whom I had had bitterly difficult exchanges early in the girl's career when I wouldn't let her go on a school visit to Italy because she had a recurring leg injury. I judged it too much of a risk that she wouldn't cope and the trip would be compromised for the rest of the group. Her father was furious: this was hopelessly weak thinking – I was denying his daughter an educational opportunity! Later, when his angelic daughter became a talented and difficult teenager and he didn't know how to get through to her, we had much more companionable talks in my office. By the time she left, mutual respect was very much restored and I counted that family as amongst our most supportive. It had just taken time.

Not all the difficult interactions ended in a conciliatory manner, however, and I have come across some spectacularly angry people and sustained some memorable verbal assaults: 'If that's the best you can come up with then I'll stop wasting my morning,' flung dismissively over the shoulder while sweeping out of the room (I had declined to overrule the head coach by insisting the girl played for the first netball team). This was never going to leave a bruise, but early on in my life as head at Queenswood I had a slightly more dramatic escape. I had agreed to see a father whom I had not met before, whose second daughter had been denied a place at the school. It was a simple enough situation and not all that unusual: the elder daughter had passed the entrance exam and was thriving in her second year, but her younger sister had different educational needs that meant the school was not the right place for her. I made it clear that while we looked sympathetically on applications from siblings, a place was not guaranteed. All children needed to be in the right setting to thrive. This father was angry in the way that only a parent who rarely takes an interest in the education of his children can be. His wife had received my letter and, I imagined, telephoning him in a state of distress, recalled him from a business trip to Spain. A large thickset man, he arrived in my office with an air of nonchalant swagger, clearly determined that this decision was going to be reversed. After a short and brittle conversation, he rose from his chair and lunged towards me (I was not experienced in feeling physically threatened). Retreating behind my desk I wondered how I was going to undo the window to escape when by some fortunate chance, the bursar appeared in my doorway. 'Ah! Mr Norman. Would you mind if we continued the conversation in my office? I think Miss Farr may have another appointment . . .'

Although it was alarming at the time, I learned from this. Here was a man quite unused to being thwarted but who was completely unable to accept authority in female form or indeed to accept any decision that he did not like. The authority of the school came head to head with his sense of his rights as a paying parent. Although this was the only time I have ever come close to a physical assault (so far) I saw it as a worthwhile lesson in family dynamics and how to deal with a volatile personality.

There are cases where you are unable to win people over, but generally a rewarding part of headship is to work not just with the child in your care but to get to know the whole family. Parents whose children are happy at school are your greatest advocates and many are prepared to give of their own time – I don't mean by getting too involved in the education of their own child, but by volunteering in the school to help make things happen. In both the schools I've led there has been a lively parents' association at the heart of this, which has provided unstinting support. An active parents' group is a sign of a happy school and provides a channel for involvement which benefits both sides.

It's something of an aside but in a book chiefly about educating girls, I must say this aspect of my job also gave me a window into the exceptional organisational ability of women. Take the planning of the Christmas fair at St Paul's, for example. If you've ever wondered why the corporate world lacks something – and I often have – it's because many of the women who should be running it are busy planning school events up and down the country. Picture a warm, book-lined school library on a weekday evening. A dozen or so women are seated around the large oak table. Conversation is quiet but purposeful. Nobody is checking their emails under the table, planning a golfing weekend or just waiting for the person currently speaking to stop so they can say something more impressive. People are listening to each other. Roles have been assigned without fuss: reports are being heard, help is being offered, deadlines are being tweaked, the to-do list is being recalibrated and obstacles planned away. At the end, there are words of appreciation and encouragement from the chair. It's all wrapped up in an hour and the team goes away to get more things done as the big day approaches.

On a bleak Saturday morning, the school festooned with garlands and that huge tree stabilised and suitably bedecked, the doors opened promptly at nine. By then, the committee members had found another gear, the mothers having spent the previous day taking over and setting up. Now, nothing but a few more hours' hard work and relentless good cheer stood between them and a tidy profit for the school charities and the bursary fund. At the end of a long term, it was all I could do to resist inviting them in to take over the day-to-day running of the school itself.

Where relationships are strong and founded on trust and respect, parents are delighted to be included as part of the community, to give of their time where they can, without crossing that invisible line into management matters. A parent body that is busy, welcomed, engaged and appreciated does not worry away at policy matters or individual matters of concern, rightly using the proper management channels for such conversations. I count myself blessed never to have had a militant PTA to contend with. But on reflection, perhaps it wasn't entirely an accident.

So from working with the school to working parenthood itself. At the time I became a working mother who was running a school, this was unusual enough to warrant a photograph in *The Times* of me running through the chapel cloister with Adam in the jogging stroller (of which more anon). In the early days, living the slightly strange, institutional life of the principal of a boarding school meant that having a toddler (Isobel stole the show by taking her first, wobbly steps right on cue on our first day at Queenswood) and soon after that a baby (Adam arrived towards the end of the first year), was not as impossible to combine with a seventy-hour working week as it might have been. Life was also made if not easier then less stressful for me because my office was two floors below our flat where we lived, and not only did I therefore waste no time commuting, but even on a day which started with meetings at 7.30 a.m. and ended with a concert finishing at 10 p.m., I could run upstairs, even play a quick hand of Happy Families, and be back in time for my next meeting. The very fact that my children were close by, and I could see them occasionally, made all the difference. And as I've said, children are very adaptable.

When later I asked Isobel whether they had been unsettled by my brief visits to the land of Postman Pat and Fireman Sam during the day, she showed (with a roll of her brown eyes) that they had learned by my clothes how long I would be staying: suit and heels meant Office-Mum, who didn't stay long and couldn't be used as a table napkin; tracksuit meant Weekend-Mum who, with any luck, would listen to your poem or song right through.

In a work context now, whatever arrangements new mothers make, I want to see that they work for the mum as well as they do for the child. Based on my own experience that nurseries or crèches which are near to the mother's place of work are preferable to leaving the children with a childminder on the other side of town. But not all agree. A member of my senior team who had a longed-for first baby in her late thirties was very happy to come back to work knowing that her little boy was in his own home with a nanny, able to take a nap in his own cot in the afternoon. Whatever the solution, a mother needs to be emotionally ready to come back to work and have arrangements in place that she can feel calm about. Employers who want the new mothers to be fully concentrating on return need to pay plenty of attention to this, and go on taking an interest in how things are working out long after the first week is over.

For the new mother, the first days and weeks of that return can be incredibly hard. Of course, an understanding and supportive partner is key and I was immensely fortunate in that too: John, having come to fatherhood at the age of fifty-two, was utterly devoted to being a practical, hands-on dad, even though he was still working long hours as a journalist, where in the pressured, insecure world of newspapers, he was fond of reminding me, you are only as good as your last story. The children's bedtime routines were for him a way to unwind after a stressful day and I can never once recall him – a light sleeper then admittedly – objecting to getting up in the night to a wakeful baby. Now, shared parental leave means that fathers can, in theory at least, participate more fully. I look forward to evidence that they are choosing to do so, which so far has been slower coming. However, much of the practical responsibility for the arrangements for returning to work still falls to mothers, who then live in a state of constant anxiety about the childcare arrangements breaking down – when the nanny is ill or doesn't turn up, when the baby is ill, when the childminder lets you down, when your own mother and father who normally do Thursdays cannot make it because the boiler has blown up, when the car won't start, etc.

Working parenthood often relies on a whole network of support which may mean you find your family extending, not just by one, but by the number of people on whom you depend to keep the show on the road. Although my own parents lived too far away (and were by that stage too infirm to take on childcare duties) we were very fortunate to find Louise – or Weezy as she is to this day, now married and with her own family – who came to us when she was twenty-one and stayed seven years. I don't know what star was shining on me the day she walked briskly into our lives with her strong and steady gaze, her bobbed auburn hair and her air of freshly laundered whites, but it was Louise who made it not just possible for me to work, but – I argued to myself then and now – even better for my children than having me as a stay-at-home mother. There's an art in blending someone else into the household who will have authority over your children but for me this was one of many small acts of letting go essential in the orchestration of complicated responsibilities. True, I remember feeling a pang of jealousy when a friend described how her howling infant had to be peeled off her at the door of the nursery – I was much more often assailed with a chorus of 'Why are you here? We want Weezy!' – but I learned to be grateful for the way my children, growing up in a community of pupils and teachers who worked, ate and often socialised together, were able to form natural, trusting relationships not just with their nanny but with other assorted adults too.

Louise and I were a great partnership. I remember one particularly hectic day towards the end of the autumn term when the
children were small and we were living at Queenswood. The rain
was swirling about the building, I had hundreds of end-of-term
reports to write (it could equally well have been the summer term)
but we were already into the annual wind tunnel of carol services,
plays, concerts and Christmas parties. At about 4.30 p.m., my
own children hurtled through the door from school in the usual
hail of half-made paper chains and Thomas the Tank Engine
lunchboxes. Adam (he must have been about seven) stopped
abruptly, looked up at me and said: 'You've got to make a sheep
costume. I'm a sheep in the nativity play! You've got to do it now.
The play's tomorrow.' If you're old enough to remember Shari
Lewis and Lamb Chop, you'll understand why at first I cleverly
tried to get away with suggesting an odd white sock and a pair
of false eyelashes, but we were talking a proper, full-body costume
here, not some glove puppet. Suffice it to say, the rest of the
evening was spent taking apart an old bath mat and being creative
with all the cotton-wool eye make-up removal pads that Louise
and I could rustle up between us. The show went on, the sheep
was in sheep's clothing, and somehow the reports all got written.
And no, I never did remonstrate with the headmaster about reasonable notice for costume production (or flapjack making, or
sunflower growing – there was always that sneaking suspicion that
I'd missed some letter at the bottom of the school bag). Somehow,
once term ended, it all slipped my mind. And Adam made such
a dear little sheep . . .

Funny in recollection, but managing work which involves long
hours and responsibility alongside bringing up children is hard.
Women have to cope with being judged as lacking in the proper
maternal instincts – even the strongest and most modern working
mothers at St Paul's would sound slightly apologetic about the
hours they were out of the house. Just as the idea of 'having it all'
grates – as if combining work and motherhood were an act of

egregious selfishness – I also dislike the pressurising term 'super-woman', making women feel that they are not 'super' if they cannot handle all this pressure and make everything work without chipping their nail varnish. I've seen enough tearful mums who eventually give up their jobs because they just can't square the circle any more to feel that we could do without the pressure of this label now. We need instead to unpack the positives about parenthood so that they can be seen and admired, making it understood that this momentous change in anyone's life is an experience which actually enhances professional capability rather than diminishes it.

We should start by celebrating the fact that like many difficult tasks, parenting is educative. New parents learn fast some important transferable skills: stamina, flexibility, adaptability, patience, problem-solving, empathy, resourcefulness, courage, optimism, commitment, inner strength. Which employer would not want these skills in their managers and leaders? Yet which companies ever acknowledge this or take time to capture and develop the learning that is naturally being added to their organisation when young fathers and mothers return to work? Very few. Women returners have long felt that far from increasing their professional profile, maternity leave attracts an unspoken expectation of gratitude: how lucky they were to have been granted leave, had their job kept open and been welcomed back! Aware of this in the air, they spend the next few months trying to prove that their new family has absolutely no negative effect on their ability to do their job. In fact, although there are many very tiring aspects to new parenthood (if you need eight hours unbroken sleep a night get ready to feel constantly jet-lagged) it may well in the longer term make them *better* at their job. But this is rarely noticed, let alone celebrated. And in the case of men, who are less likely to have taken parental leave and who therefore do not return but are just there as before, the new, life-changing experience they are having is largely ignored. When speaking to a group of executives recently at a PR company about parenthood,

I asked the men how many of them had experienced any interest being shown in the fact that they had become fathers. The answer was not one.

How as a working person do you weather those early months when the whole thing is just a blur of sleep deprivation and wiping sick off your lapels? One of the pieces of kit which enabled me to survive with a baby and a full-on career was composed of a simple triangle of red canvas, some powerful suspension and three rubber wheels. The jogging stroller was an American invention, and mine arrived packed flat for travel courtesy of my Seattle-dwelling brother, Richard. Richard is two years younger than me and although I was horrible to him as a child because I believed my mother preferred him (and why wouldn't she have done, kindness personified as he is?), he seemed willing to forgive me the glancing blow on the head with a golf club in the garden when no one was looking, and other such jealous acts. In adulthood, we are the firmest of friends. Richard is one of those people who has the knack of thinking of the very thing you need just before you think of it yourself (call it empathy), so it was no surprise he intuited my need for a jogging stroller. At the end (or more often at the start) of a long day I would strap Isobel into the red canvas cockpit, lace up my running shoes and off we would go, bowling lightly across the garden and into the summer woods for our outing.

The jogging stroller was an early opportunity to kill not two but three or four birds with one stone. I could take Isobel out for a spin in the fresh air and watch her pointing: 'Look! Ears!' at the many rabbits nibbling the verdant lawns; I could stop and speak to people along the way (excellent management by walking about); I could stretch my limbs and get the exercise I needed after too long spent at my desk; and I could show that being a mum and working at the same time are not incompatible. London parks today are littered with athletic-looking young mums and dads in Lycra doing exactly the same, though they sometimes look a bit too focussed on their mileage. I hope that the exercise-bird hasn't trumped the delight of an adventure with their child, with the world rushing past at just the right exhilarating degree of speed, and the fun of stopping to point and look when something catches the eye.

Given my empathy with other working parents I should have been more alive, sooner, to the pressures this can create once your children go to school. Schools have not always been as quick as they might have been to adapt to the needs of families, where both parents work, and need to do better. I once had a very polite but emphatic email from a mother, wanting to know in what universe did I think she and her husband could both attend a parents' evening (however well drilled the staff) to discuss their daughter's progress when they both had demanding jobs and the event began at 4.30 p.m. I could hear the stress of the working mum (the email had been written close to midnight) behind her words. She had a point: I had managed things thinking first about the welfare of the staff, who, having taught all day, would in any case not get away from school until 7.30 p.m., and then face a commute with possibly a thick pile of marking to tackle after that.

As the working parent, I know from experience there will be times when you simply can't win: you either have to neglect your work or neglect your children – there is no middle way and a painful choice has to be made. This is where your patience and ability to see the longer view come in, and your capacity to live with things that don't always work out neatly. And incidentally to forgive yourself. One particular occasion is etched indelibly on my conscience. When we moved to London, Adam won a place at the junior school of St Paul's boys' and was asked at the end of his first term to read in the school carol service. What an honour! For any mother, this was a moment to anticipate with great pride, and even more so because of the special invitation (I hadn't missed this one) to sit in a special pew at the front with the headmaster and parents of other readers. All was excited anticipation and rehearsals, except that when I checked my diary I realised that the date was the same as my own school's carol service, where I would be required to stand in front of 400 people and Unfold the Mystery of the Incarnation: giving the reading from John's Gospel, Chapter 1. Whatever Adam's mother might have preferred, there was clearly no choice but to fulfil my responsibilities as High Mistress of St Paul's. The reading from John 1 is indeed mysterious: I have given it in total twenty-one times and am no more sure that I grasp its meaning now than I did on the first occasion; this was number eleven. At the same time, I did hope that somewhere I was being forgiven for missing Adam's moment of glory in his first term, the other parents no doubt noting my absence and its confirmation that I was, as everyone suspected, a workaholic whose children were neglected and dragging themselves up as best they could. My mother, when I was fretting about this incident and generally about working too many hours and getting the balance wrong (I know all about that guilt), would often say wisely: 'Look at them, Clarissa: they're perfectly all right. And so will you be. Your job is to make your children independent of you – as soon as possible.' This from someone who had been sent away to boarding school aged five – while my grandmother nursed my grandfather through post-traumatic stress disorder after the First World War – had a sad poignancy about it. But she was right.

To be a parent is to be at once responsible, untrained, conflicted, subjective and vulnerable. It can push you off balance. No other relationship in life has the power to floor us or leave us so unprepared to manage the feelings it evokes. Young mothers on the teaching staff at school might tell me of the difficulty of that first morning at nursery school. Later, at the start of primary school, there is another watershed moment, and so on, through secondary school and eventually you see them depart with duvet and sprawling piles of books to university. But the balance changes. By this stage you are lucky to receive a backward glance coupled with 'Oh, can you put £50 in my bank account and I need a new duvet cover and kettle?' These jolts are, as time goes on, harder for us than for them, and are all part of the whole paradoxical process: make yourself entirely vulnerable to another human being and then watch as they separate themselves from you.

You would think that for the increasing number of time-starved working parents, being gently told by the headmistress to back off a little, encourage independence and let your children make their own decisions wouldn't be entirely bad news. But working parents, who perhaps feel an underlying guilt about the amount of time they are able to spend with their children, are often the most resistant to these messages and the most inclined to hover over the school, sending rushed and tense emails demanding information. Parenting is about doing things, creating the right conditions, but also about *refraining* from doing things: this is the counter-intuitive part we need to give ourselves permission to accept. If you are the working parent of a child at school, cut yourself some slack. Welcome the exhortations to independence for the benefit to your child and to you.

From the point of view of a school, to be entrusted with the care and education of another person's child is an enormous privilege and requires mutual trust. That's why it's essential to treat with understanding and compassion, as far as possible, anything that gets thrown at you by the family. A rude or aggressive parent is often feeling vulnerable because they are up against something they cannot control or explain. Building effective relationships with parents therefore increases their confidence, helps the child in your care and strengthens the sense of the school as a community. I have always felt it was well worth weathering the few difficult individuals for the reward of the many very positive and supportive relationships that form. Understanding and compassion are as much needed by adults as children, and if a school can extend its care to parents too, understanding the many pressures they face, then so much the better.

And now, having just had a chat with a girl who has dip-dyed her hair electric blue (and who now looks like a rather exotic bird) about how she and her mother might be reconciled on the matter, a to-do list reminder has just popped up on my screen: it's half term already! Both my own children are on holiday with revision to be done for GCSEs and A levels: the year of the public exam double whammy in our household. Time to put my own advice into action, close the office door, switch off my emails, try a new banana bread recipe and spread domestic calm. Let's see if I can keep that up for a week.

There is an internal landscape,
a geography of the soul; we search for
its outlines all our lives. Those who
are lucky enough to find it ease like
water over a stone, onto its fluid
contours, and are home. Some find it
in the place of their birth; others
may leave a seaside town, parched,
and find themselves refreshed in the
desert. There are those born in rolling
countryside who are really only at ease
in the intense and busy loneliness of
the city. For some, the search is for
the imprint of another; a child or a
mother, a grandfather or a brother,
a lover, a husband, a wife, or a foe.
We may go through our lives happy or
unhappy, successful or unfulfilled,
loved or unloved, without ever standing
cold with the shock of recognition,
without ever feeling the agony as
the twisted iron in our soul unlocks
itself and we slip at last into place.

- Josephine Hart

CHAPTER 10

June

Valediction and looking to the future

June ushers in the second half of the summer term, a time associated for me since childhood with the smell of mown grass and with exams. Growing up in the long, stone Somerset cottage that was Heron's Pond, we spent our summers outside and often in the water. Not in the eponymous pond itself, because, despite being large enough to scull across in a small rubber dinghy, its waters were shallow and brackish at this time of year. Instead we swam in the freezing outdoor pool at my brother's prep school, a short walk across the fields. When our grandparents came to stay my grandfather – Punjah to us – would stand ramrod straight on the dry, lichen-covered edge and then fall slowly backwards, letting out a sharp warrior's cry against the cold shock of the water, the same sound he made when taking his cold shower in the morning. We were somehow made aware of a lifetime of self-discipline we could only wonder at. Later, when A levels loomed, pretending to revise, I used to lie on the grass and, looking up, feel the light splashing through the leaves of the pear trees in our garden, eventually forcing myself indoors because there was serious work to be tackled. I still have my schoolgirl copy of *Hamlet* with its rhetorical marginalia: 'Hamlet's inaction?' or 'symbolism?' and many lines of text marked for learning by heart as quotations – no open-book exams then. People say you will never know any text better than those you study for A level and certainly there was an exhilarating feeling of mastery as, back at school, I wandered up and down in pyjamas on the open flat roof of my boarding house in the long weekday evenings, spouting to the green Somerset hills 'To be, or not to be . . .'. Thankfully no one had thought of doing a risk assessment to spare us from stumbling over the forty-foot drop to the ground, so we enjoyed this wonderful vista unencumbered. I think all school children in the summer term must be torn: longing to be outside in the long light days, but with the looming prospect of exams drawing them reluctantly back to their books.

I have no recollection of what I wrote about Hamlet's excruciating inability to avenge his father's murder, but the setting – the gymnasium, smelling faintly of bare feet, laid out with its dust sheets and rows of temporary desks and dominated by a large exam clock – is still vivid (and in fact, on a recent visit, I found it more or less unchanged). There were the invigilators (the word prompting slight butterflies) distributing white writing paper and looking oddly distant as everyone settled wordlessly into their seats. Hands up if you have a wobbly desk! Squares of special blue paper were folded up and wedged expertly under a desk leg here and there. Are there any questions? A pause, a glance at the clock, an intake of breath and – you may begin! In a rustle of simultaneously turned, yellow papers, the exam got underway. Now only the click of heels and the scratch of pens (the mowing outside having been suspended) broke the silence as the sun settled on the walls and the long morning began.

What is the point of exams and how much has the whole ritual changed? The problem of how we measure learning, both knowledge and skills, has always been there. Assessment for learning has become a subject in itself with many MA theses on the subject toiled over by ambitious teachers. We are now much more aware that a mark or grade is not enough; much better to create continuing dialogue with students which challenges and stimulates new learning. We have experimented with assessing them continuously, the obverse of the formal, now-or-never exam, and have found both benefits and drawbacks. Where formal exams are still used, there is a tendency to set shorter ones, reflecting the shrinking capacity for sustained concentration (and writing by hand) that technology has caused: there is rarely the requirement now to sit down and write solidly for three hours. But still at the end of a course or stage as a way of determining what level can be recorded for posterity as having been achieved, the formal, handwritten exam persists. Why?

First, for all our ability to automate processes, we haven't yet come up with a better way of measuring the unaided capacity for recalling, understanding and applying a certain body of knowledge than through formal written exams. And although of course cheating is possible with the aid of technology, it really just requires some simple policing. The prohibition of hand-held devices in the exam room and the disqualification risks candidates run if they even inadvertently have their mobile on them strikes terror into the heart. Warning notices rather like the skull with the red cross which indicates poison adorn the exam hall. While if not a reason for retaining exams then a happy by-product, they are an exercise in memory. Respect for the use of memory has largely gone from education because so much information is right there on the screen (children rarely experience the pleasure of learning poems by heart, for example), but formal exams still require the ability to absorb and retain material and represent it in a coherent form. To me this is healthy mind gym: exercise for the brain which may stave off senility later and in the meantime is a useful, transferable skill. (How often have you been introduced to a circle of influential people in a work context and instantly forgotten all their names? A well-oiled memory is worth having.) And with thoughtful question-setting, revision need not be mere dull rote learning for regurgitation. I was impressed that my son, when revising for his university finals in English literature, set himself to learn new material and construct new lines of argument so that he could adapt the deliberately broad questions, using his skills of analysis and comparison in fresh ways. Rigorous and creative challenge can be – and should be – part of any exam system. And beyond that, before we draw the conclusion that exams really have had their day, bear in mind the sheer discipline, the sheer nerve required to concentrate and craft coherent answers and proofs in a formal setting within a tight time limit. In an era of ever-softening academic expectations this is a way of honing mental organisation – many students enjoy it and some become extremely good at it.

The expert examinee is symbolised for me by the steely girls of a particular Cheshire grammar school, none of whom I ever met. As a young teacher, I took on batches of exam marking and every day for a week or two in the late summer term got up early in the mornings to work my way through a hundred or so A-level English literature scripts. I remember marvelling at the answers of the candidates from one particular school. These girls were professionals: they could turn out four beautifully crafted essays, moving effortlessly from Thomas Hardy's *The Mayor of Casterbridge*, to George Eliot's *Silas Marner*, to John Webster's *The Duchess of Malfi* and the poetry of John Donne in the space of three hours. The controlled, round handwriting never changed or faltered. Without hesitation I gave several of them full marks: they deserved it after pulling off such a feat of intellectual stamina. I've often wondered what those highly capable young women are doing now: whatever it is, thanks to their exams they have steady nerves, limpid minds and the ability to marshal an argument fluently; they would not be outfaced by circumstances which tested them under pressure of time. Not unhelpful skills for adult life.

Exams may require skill, but they are associated with pressure and, with so much concern today about depression and mental illness, we are wary of experiences which could give rise to stress. Recent coverage of the alarming rise in cases of self-harm, for example, cites the pressure from social media but also from the expectations of measurable academic success as reasons for this. The former, yes, but the latter – really? In my experience, schools today spend most of their time trying to keep exams in their proper perspective. As a school pupil in the 1970s, I don't remember being given much guidance on how to prepare for exams. There were certainly no talks on how to manage exam nerves, mindfulness sessions or workshops for parents on how to support your daughter at home. My parents did support me, mainly by not taking too much notice beyond giving me regular meals and encouraging me to get enough fresh air and go to bed in good time.

Today there is much more in place to help students and their parents limber up for the challenge. Our approach at St Paul's, where there was more likelihood of the girls overworking than underpreparing, was (as with so many things) to be purveyors of calm, achieve a balanced attitude and, where necessary, bring the temperature down. Whatever the worry, get it talked about, get it into proportion. The girls were taught how to make their revision timetable and plan well ahead (but not too far . . .), the director of studies would send a careful letter to parents, emphasising that exams for the younger girls were *practice* for later on and that it was important for them to get used to writing under formal timed conditions. They should be following their revision timetable with the help of their tutor, they should not be staying up late at night to revise or going to a private tutor on Saturday mornings . . .

My contribution would be my annual, slightly tongue-in-cheek exam assembly, reminding the girls of the history of exams and how lucky they were that they could now take them. What a privilege! And they would stare back at me with that slightly hooded, withering, we-will-tolerate-this-but-keep-it-short look that teenagers do so well. I introduced them to social historian Jane Robinson, who recounts in her wonderful book *Bluestockings* how a number of ambitious women, including the redoubtable Trixie Pearson and her friend Constance Maynard, having grubbed for an education themselves, badgered their parents to let them attend university. And how another pioneer, Emily Davies of the Langham Place group, persuaded the authorities in the 1860s that girls should be able to participate in the qualifying exams for higher education, first Junior Locals (the precursors of GCSE) and then Higher Locals, which eventually turned into A levels. How much we owe to those determined women!

The girls were still looking at me. It was ten minutes until they would be lining up for their first exam. How long was she going to go on? Time for a little advice, I continued: examiners are not looking for mistakes but for opportunities to give credit (so make your points clearly); reading the instructions is important (so don't do as I did in one of my finals papers and answer the wrong number of questions – mild consternation here); timing matters (each question has allocated marks and you can't get more than full marks on each one) and finally – concentrate on your own work! Your friend writing a mile a minute next to you doesn't necessarily mean she knows more than you do.

And with that, I gathered my papers at the lectern and ended with some light, almost certainly apocryphal, exam howlers:

The greatest writer of the Renaissance was William Shakespeare. He was born in the year 1564, supposedly on his birthday. He never made much money and is famous only because of his plays . . .

An expression of the values of our times perhaps? Or this for scientists, clearly from a bored candidate wanting to stir things up:

Question: Explain one of the processes by which water can be made safe to drink.

Answer: Flirtation makes water safe to drink, because it removes large pollutants like grit, sand, dead sheep and canoeists . . .

They were looking at one another smiling – with me or at me? It didn't matter today. Time to send them off to start their exams.

I have discovered that more or less everyone needs the chance to get their own exam experiences off their chest. One year, preparing for assembly and curious as to whether the staff remembered their own exams as I recalled mine, I sent round the unforgivable global email and was deluged with anecdotes. There was the lady from the office who had dyed her hair with henna (this was the 1970s) only to wake up with it having turned bright orange the day of her first exam; the science teacher who had thought she could revise for a paper on animal behaviour at university simply by watching David Attenborough documentaries; the music teacher who had never recovered from scoring 13 per cent in his first maths test; the maths teacher whose chemistry equipment had exploded in the middle of a practical exam giving him a lifelong fear of volatile substances . . . So they went on. This was confirmation that our exam experiences stay with us: all the more reason to make the process as manageable and as normal for the students as possible. It may well be that with advances in technology this anachronistic, formal challenge of handwriting answers from memory under a strict time limit will become a rarer thing. In the meantime, even though so much that is most important about what we learn in school, and what through being at school we become, will never be captured and distilled in an exam room, I defend them. Exams are a test of memory, of mental organisation and of nerve – all skills worth having in the twenty-first century.

But there is more to the summer term than this. As the school settles quietly into its second-half rhythm, the girls checking their names off each morning as they arrive before making their way to the sports hall, in more celebratory mood we are preparing to bring the academic year to its conclusion: to celebrate achievement and to mark the leave-taking of our top year. Getting up from my desk to go and give the girls some support by seeing the next exam start, I see various blocks of time have appeared in my diary marked 'Speech'. Just as I would begin every year by speaking to the staff and giving that first welcome assembly, at the end of every one of my twenty-one years of headship I have made a speech to the students and their parents. There hasn't been too much recycling – last year's words are last year's words – so Lindy knows I will need quiet time to think and carefully protects this.

In schools, naturally places of ritual and structure, the set-piece valedictory event takes many forms. At Queenswood, a traditional speech day involved the whole school community, including parents, and was held in a large marquee. The reek of canvas flapping in the summer afternoon, the rows of dressed-up people with their picnics gave it all the feeling of a large wedding. My predecessor Audrey Butler told me: 'This is the only time you have all the parents together. If you want to get across anything *important* to them, this is the moment.' In the early years, I tended to follow convention: details of the competitions, matches, plays, concerts, expeditions etc. in which the girls had taken part were gathered and stitched together, with congratulations and thanks for parental support. Later, with such information circulating in regular colourful newsletters, I used the opportunity instead to speak about the school, about education and about the challenges ahead for the students, especially those on the brink of leaving. That focus developed further at St Paul's where 'Valediction', held in Horsley's Great Hall (doors propped open in the hope of some stirring of the air) was purely for the leaving year group and their parents. A time to say goodbye, a rite of passage: a time to reflect on what school life had meant and look to the future.

Speeches of this kind are normally given in large hot spaces to people who are feeling the significance of the moment but don't want to hear a long improving monologue from the head. At the same time, I remembered Audrey's words about not losing the chance to have their attention one more time. Seven brief years had passed since the girls' arrival: then I had opened the door on their lives as Paulinas, welcomed them in, started the process of managing expectations. Now it was time to open another door in their minds, this time leading them out of the school into a wider world. What would that world be like, and how well had we prepared them for it? What last thoughts did I want to express? Rather than extemporise on some famous quotation, I would often root my remarks in the words of a speaker the girls had heard as part of the Friday lecture programme. In 2014, for example, Lord Green of Hurstpierpoint, then Minister for Trade and Investment, had spoken about the globalised world of work and how the rousing call of the nineteenth century to ambitious youth 'Go West, young man!' has its echo now in 'Go East, young person!', predicting that not the USA but Asia, China and Africa would be where economic influence and opportunity would concentrate for their generation. This was an exciting perspective for a graduating class, many of whom had learned Mandarin Chinese, stimulating them to think about how – and where – they would make their contribution on a global stage. I often also found myself in these speeches drawing on Gillian Stamp's wisdom about leadership: the need to acknowledge the complexity of the challenges ahead, to encourage the girls not to be afraid to exercise judgement and be independent and flexible in their thinking, as the working environments of the future would require. With the early practice in these skills they had received at school, they would test them in the wider world.

Given the driven, achievement-oriented nature of Paulinas, I also reminded them of the need to find a healthy equilibrium in their lives, as well as to be ready to be blown off course occasionally by the unexpected:

While work is important and can be very rewarding don't allow it to dominate your entire life because that will stifle your creativity. Our generation has tended to work far too much and it's a mistake. Cultivate your great capacity for light-heartedness and play: it will be at the most unlikely times that you will have your best ideas. Do things you enjoy for their own sake and have fun.

Talented though you all are, life will throw at you unexpected challenges and there will be times when things don't go according to plan. At least I hope there will be. Some of you are scarily focussed and organised – I feel I can hardly wait for it all to go pear-shaped because you have fallen in love or discovered a passion for making sushi.

In a hyperactive, perpetually connected world, remember also to have time on your own to think. It's only when we are alone that we actually have thoughts which are wholly ours: the rest of the time we often are just responding to other people.

Earlier the same year, 2014, Maya Angelou died. She definitely belonged to that expanding cadre of women we loved to identify who 'should have been a Paulina' (though was about as far from being one as it's possible to be) and I ended my speech with two of her characteristic pieces of advice: to 'grab the world by the lapels' and the surprisingly useful 'never make someone a priority when all you are to them is an option'.

So, a draft written at least, and with a list of the staff I needed to thank carefully appended by Lindy in order of length of service, I could put speech-writing aside, let it mull in the back of my mind and turn to other aspects of the event and the ritual of leave-taking. For students leaving a school where they have been happy (which on the whole, the Paulinas I knew were) there is a feeling of loss, as well as of excitement. School draws to a close and they look forward to life beyond. However much pupils might balk at the idea of formality, there is a place for ritual to mark that rite of passage with celebration as well as with solemnity. Those who have been part of a school community for seven years need a way to channel their emotions on leaving and resolve their sense of the experience as a totality, and careful thought needs to be given to the opportunities they have to do so.

In an age where informality is so much prized, how do you forge ritual and what are the ingredients needed to mark a rite of passage in the human heart? When I first arrived at St Paul's, where formality, convention and any whiff of stealthy agency capture were regarded with much healthy Paulina suspicion, there was scepticism – resistance even – to any event to mark the end of the final year. I was dismayed to find that the girls finished their exams and then just drifted off, either to holiday destinations (mental note to avoid Turkey this summer) or to summer jobs – the whole thing more or less petered out. What an anticlimax to seven defining years. When I suggested we arrange something to mark their leaving, I was told it would never work – they wouldn't want to come. They were done with school. And they probably were, judging from the rather awkward and resentful way in which they drifted back at the end of the following term, to be seated in by now unfamiliar rows to receive their A-level certificates in the gloomy December twilight. It didn't work.

There had to be a better way to conclude. I asked the girls and staff about how we might mark this time, and I listened. They already had 'muck-up day', when a certain amount of (usually good-natured) misrule was allowed, something we managed over time to modify (though I wasn't one of those heads who felt the need to ban it). But all the more reason for some more formal counterweight to that. Eventually we designed two special events, the first of which was a formal dinner, for which everyone dressed up and to which the girls invited their tutors as an opportunity to say thank you and goodbye. There was a careful table plan designed by the girls, then short speeches and an entertainment by the Pink Slips. This had nothing to do with petticoats but was a hastily assembled rock band, led by the head of maths and named after the St Paul's sanction for poor work or behaviour. The girls loved the Pink Slips, who provided the necessary ingredient of staff revealing their other talents while slightly aiming off, as adults trying to be hipsters are bound to do. While this is excruciatingly embarrassing when it's your parents (I should know), your teachers doing it is apparently adorable. The girls quickly came to anticipate this event with great excitement. Leavers' dinner was very soon something not to miss.

The second and final event was Valediction. It was difficult in a school where all the girls were so talented to have prizes, and we had comparatively few. Valediction was rather a chance to celebrate the contribution of each of the leavers, regardless of prizes, and say a few words about each girl too: what she had been studying and what she hoped to do at university. The focus was on each girl as an individual. Everyone received a copy of the same book – we chose something different each year that would be of broad appeal – and a silver replica of the St Paul's emblem, as a welcome to the lifelong community of Paulinas. The parents, each seeing their daughter walk across the stage in her best clothes, just looked delighted with everything. And at the end we spilled out onto the grass for tea and fond farewells.

I eventually returned to my office at about 6 p.m., shutting the door quietly behind me. Lindy was still there, cup of tea in hand, having produced another list of people who would need thank-you letters. I saved these for you, she said, producing a plate of small chocolate cakes and strawberry tarts that she had retrieved from the dining room. And, with a grateful sigh, we kicked off our shoes, sat down on the sofa and tucked in.

Valediction and the leavers' dinner are now firmly established, eagerly anticipated traditions. Even in a highly individualistic community naturally suspicious of anything that feels conventional, there is an underlying human need to mark occasions and rites of passage. You just have to find the right structure. The success of Valediction as a way of channelling emotion and recognising a time of significance came down to listening, involving the girls in its design, emphasising celebration for all rather than success for a few and ensuring that the head girl herself had the last word as she addressed her peers, their parents and their teachers. Each year, I listened in different terms as an eighteen-year-old young woman modelled for us all how to meet an ending with her full self and how to embrace a new beginning. She summed up for them all what school had meant and how being a Paulina would continue to be part of their lives in the future: invariably there was much about the importance of friendship, the excitement of intellectual discovery and the confidence which had grown through the experience of community. It was the being together in that particular place with those particular people that had mattered. But then it really was goodbye, with the tears coming from sadness or excitement they couldn't tell.

Had we prepared them well enough for that next step? It was a question I often asked myself, especially when they came drifting back in December with tales of their first term. Having nurtured them so carefully, left no stone unturned to ensure their success, supported them through difficulties, had we done enough to ensure they could stand on their own two feet at university? Had we encouraged enough the resilience needed to bounce back, and the growth mindset that would serve them when the intellectual pace heated up and they were simply left more to their own devices to make university life work?

Much of what came to be known at St Paul's as 'Lifeworks' – preparation for university and beyond – was practical. The director of higher education and careers had the application process for university finely tuned and this worked well for most resourceful and independent Paulinas, matching the girl to the right course and ensuring she achieved her required grades. But there's more to it than getting them there. They then have to survive and thrive in higher education, taking charge of their lives not just from the academic point of view but coping with all the practicalities of life away from home, often for the first time.

Overall, schools and universities could do more to connect with each other in paving the way for this major transition. While they may have turned eighteen, undergraduates do not become adults overnight. Yes, we can teach them independence and resilience at school, but being suddenly expected to function like an independent adult takes a significant adjustment. I saw the challenge of this from the parental point of view when my daughter went to university at the other end of the country. Determined and independent, she nevertheless found it tough settling in and when she sought help, there was very little support for her. She eventually came home at the end of the first term, took a year out and started again on a London-based course which she much preferred. Both my children have a number of friends who have 'rusticated' and taken a year out because they are simply not managing academically or socially, or both. Some even drop out of education altogether. While more universities are now developing better counselling provision (led at Cambridge University by the remaining women's colleges) the phenomenon of rustication is surely a wasteful and distressing shame which ought to be addressed with better pastoral vigilance for all these emerging young adults. And attrition rates should be part of the statistics universities are obliged to publish. Too many students, it seems, receive barely any teaching and are left to sink or swim in the vast ocean of the university library where, unsurprisingly, they sometimes begin to feel lost and depressed.

The school–university disconnect has other facets. For example, there is a gulf in understanding about what matters in education, between what is seen as important in a rounded school and the qualifications needed for access to university – in this country at least. For the leading UK universities, we had it from a senior admissions tutor that his university was more or less uninterested in co-curricular achievements or wishy-washy stuff like your character – beyond your capacity for hard work and teachability. If you happened to have grade 8 violin and had been volunteering to read to a blind person in your area for two years, this was all very laudable but of no real importance to your application to read English.

American universities would give a very different view, however. As a candidate for the US higher education system, your talent for leadership, your versatility and wider experience are central to your proposition, making application a different kind of challenge. American and Canadian universities deliberately set out to populate a class or year group with individuals who have diverse talents to build a stimulating community. They don't simply think of applicants in isolation. This always seemed to me a sensible approach (except when they inexplicably turned down some of the multitalented girls that we were sending them) and more consistent with the view of education we had. True, the competitive nature of the top US universities meant that the profiles of determined candidates preparing to jump this hurdle were somewhat extraordinary. Surely there was something a little unnatural about a candidate who had founded a charity at the age of ten, was writing her fourth play prior to taking it on an international tour and was in discussion with world leaders about climate change? I wondered about the true team-working powers and basic likeability of these omnicompetent, unblinking eighteen-year-olds. But the idea that university life was going to offer more in the way of broader development and that there was an approach to education that valued more than narrow academic achievement – as their school had done – undoubtedly drew Paulinas to apply. Currently, fees at such universities are very high, and finance therefore a big barrier. But with more and more offering scholarships and financial aid, the UK will see the numbers of applicants to the US rise and rise.

University takes some getting used to, it seems, and not all manage the adjustment. But is university, wherever in the world, the best or only route for all bright eighteen-year-olds? For governments, a rising proportion of young people going to university is a measure of success. It is still the case that the majority of school leavers aspire to take a degree – 74 per cent according to the Sutton Trust's 2017 poll of 2,600 teenagers – but looking over time this figure is at its lowest since 2009, attributable mainly to concerns about cost and the burden of paying back debt. Alongside this, the percentage of the same cohort saying that they are positively unlikely to go – largely for the same reasons – has risen to 14 per cent from 8 per cent over the past five years. What conclusions do we draw from this? I've rehearsed the argument that it's important to protect education from becoming unduly instrumental, a means only to secure lucrative employment and national profitability, depriving the next generation of the richer education as human beings and citizens that they need to build a better, more peaceful world. And a university education as we understand it now is surely intended to be that, conferring as John Henry Newman so eloquently puts it in his 1852 lectures published as *The Idea of a University*, 'a special illumination and largeness of mind and freedom and self-possession'.[1] But with escalating fees and the prospect of young people launching on long-term debt, uncertain job prospects and sofa-surfing, it shouldn't surprise us that they themselves are asking the question: is this what we want and is it worth it? Why should we be shocked at the logical suggestion that degree courses might be fitted into two rather than three years of study? Are we rather out of touch thinking that somehow our children just need to be 'in school' until the still-symbolic age of twenty-one, which hasn't been the age of majority since 1970?

There are clearly those for whom a deep and rich intellectual education at university is valuable and just the right thing – many Paulinas are in that category. As a champion of learning for its own sake within the particular context of a highly academic school, an academic degree which is of real substance and which develops the mind in the way Newman envisaged is a wonderful opportunity, including those courses such as law and medicine with a specifically vocational bent. However, other possibilities are opening up now for bright eighteen-year-olds in the form of apprenticeships and work-based training, which may be as stimulating, as educative in a broad sense and conducive to their development in ways which, while targeted at specific work, go beyond the narrowly instrumental. If the choices are multiplying, so much the better. In a world where patterns of employment and the kinds of skills needed are changing so rapidly, schools and universities will need to work hard to keep pace, because having simply been to university for three years will no longer be seen as a proxy for employability unless you can demonstrate the ability to be a flexible, creative thinker, applying your knowledge and skills in new situations and working collaboratively with others. These are the capabilities that will count and employers will care less about where you acquired them than that they test out in practice.

'Lifeworks' at St Paul's therefore increasingly sought to prepare girls not simply for higher education, in whatever form, but for the world of work beyond, thinking from an early age not just about academic subject preferences but about identifying their strengths and developing capability. As thirteen-year-olds they went to spend a day at work with a parent and from that starting point were encouraged to build up work-shadowing placements and internships, often helped by the powerful network of former pupils spread across the world. Many Paulinas were already showing signs of entrepreneurial talent while at school, starting and publishing magazines, organising charity events, or setting up small businesses online selling their baking or handmade jewellery. It always impressed me how they never wasted any time. We were aware that the world of work for them would be different: more branches to their careers, less linearity and certainty, more moving from one thing to another. With the arrival of artificial intelligence there would be less paid work and more volunteering over a life-time. So their social engagement and work in their local communities was something we encouraged too. All the time, we needed to be listening, adjusting, adapting. These girls would not spend forty years doing more or less the same thing, as I have. Nothing could have driven this home more forcibly than attending a conference of young entrepreneurs setting up new businesses, one in fashion and another harnessing the appeal of handwritten messages to personalise marketing for big companies. These twenty-somethings were confident they would be 'financially free' by the age of twenty-seven. And, listening to them, I found myself thinking of all the imaginative ways in which they would be able to contribute to society after that.

I was in conversation recently with friends of my own generation, comparing our experiences of 1970s undergraduate life in 'Russell Group universities'. We had all had a good time, made friends, grown up a bit, drunk liberally of the subsidised beer in the university bars, read some books and received an indifferent intellectual education at the hands of academics most of whom took only a passing interest in their students (though there were notable excep-tions). In effect, it had been three years more growing-up time before starting work. How much more we would make of that opportunity if we could have it now! How we would drink in the lectures rather than the beer, how we would relish the seminar discussions, the time to read and think! It had been wasted on us then. Now, we reflected, our own children in their twenties and thirties are facing a very different world to which the traditional degree course with its one hour of teaching a week is in many ways equally if differently inapplicable. I would not cling too vehemently to the idea of the three-year academic degree as an irreplaceable life-enhancing experience for eighteen-year-olds. It is for some, but not all. I would be active in rethinking the pathways post-secondary school. We could be much more open to a continuation of education in a work-based setting and meanwhile, we could repurpose the academic degree to target people of any age who are ready and right for it: those with a strong work ethic born of experience who yet have many years of active life ahead and perhaps a new contribution to make to society might make equally apt undergraduates. We talk about lifelong learning: let's live it and let our children get on with engaging with the real issues for our planet sooner.

All education is focussed on preparing for what is to come, which is what makes it exciting, but as I reflect on the professional responsibility I have had for the rising generation, full of potential, I often think about what I owe to the previous generation – and my own parents, especially at this time of year when I lost my father. Why is it that as children we only appreciate our parents when it is too late to tell them? Mine were both as exasperated and mystified by my behaviour and interests as a maddening sixteen-year-old, then monopolising the landline with its three-digit number (North Cadbury 317) as many of the parents I see today. Just like today's Dads4Daughters champions too, my father took a great interest in my career, was thrilled beyond words when I became a headmistress and would often give me sound advice over problems I was facing. He was in his late eighties by then, and over the next few years his health and mobility declined.

I recall vividly the June morning in 2001 when my mother phoned me to say that he had died. Another ending, a momentous

one, as the academic year drew to a close. I was looking out at
the garden and thinking (as usual) about an assembly when I
received the call: it was a beautiful day and as I picked up the
receiver, I noticed the sun on the grass outside. My mother said
simply: 'It's Daddy.' Silence. It was about 8.30 a.m. The conversation was practical: she sounded calm; perhaps just tired. I walked
away from my desk and out into the hall. I had an assembly to
take, so I took it. I had a lesson to teach; mechanically, I taught
it. It wasn't until several hours later when I was sitting making
conversation with two visiting nuns from a local prep school over
lunch that I suddenly thought: What am I doing here? My father
has just died, my mother is being comforted by a neighbour and
I'm still going through the mechanics of my working day before
driving down to be with her because somehow I believe that's
what the principal should do. I bid the nuns farewell and got into
the car.

Looking back, my decision not to go to my mother at once
that morning was wrong – how very obvious from this distance
– and I feel ashamed. It had to do not with indifference but a
very strong sense of duty towards the job and the feeling that as
the person in charge, it was simply not okay for me to do anything
which showed a sudden outpouring of emotion or which allowed
people to see my worlds colliding and out of balance. After all,
my father was a very old man. It's not tragic, exactly, that a man
in his ninety-second year wakes on a summer's morning and
peacefully dies in his bed, his wife at his side. Yet to lose a parent,
at whatever age you are, is a watershed moment. In the weeks
that followed I realised I had often silently consulted him,
wondering what would he say about this or that thing I was about
to do, and finding the answer coming to me silently. It was as if
I was a tent on a windy hill, on which one of the guy ropes had
suddenly been pulled up. Part of me was flapping, untethered. It
would take many months before, gradually, I was able to secure
that part of myself again. I know better now than to underestimate

the importance of being able to give time, as an adult child, whether in the closing weeks of a person's life or afterwards, to the changing and passing of that relationship. And I try to be more compassionate with those I work with than I was towards myself. A decade later, when my mother was declining in a nursing home in Castle Cary, I made sure that I took time to go down each weekend and see her. Frail though she was, and though our conversation was limited to the crossword clues, those Saturday afternoons together were some of the happiest I can remember. I had time to thank her, to appreciate her, to laugh with her. And in the end, in both our minds, to go with her to the very end of the garden, even though the gate she was approaching was hers to go through alone.

Plenty has been thought and written about the highs and lows of working motherhood, but what about working daughterhood? In my family, the generations are stretched out. My parents married late, having met while appearing together in an amateur production of the Noël Coward comedy, *Relative Values*, in 1956, a story I always found highly romantic. Unusually for that time, although not so now, my mother had her children when she was nearly forty. History has a way of repeating itself: like my mother, I married someone older and we became parents at the ages of thirty-seven and fifty-two respectively. This meant that in my early years as principal of Queenswood, I not only had a baby and a toddler but a mother of nearly eighty and a ninety-year-old father to think about. Nor were they on our doorstep: they lived in a creaking old Somerset house, a good three hours' drive away from us.

Many women (and men) are juggling not just career and children, but career, children and ageing parents too. We are apparently the 'sandwich generation'. Indeed, there are times when I have longed for the leisure actually to both make and eat a sandwich, but the sense of being in the middle of two demanding domestic forces, each unpredictable and tugging hard on the emotions, will be familiar to many. The difference is that while bringing up children and arranging childcare is recognised as a responsibility by employers, and there is law protecting the expectant mother and parents with young children so that they can give time to their parental responsibilities without guilt or discrimination, in theory anyway, no such formal provision exists for those managing the care of the older generation. Yet as we all know, just as you never stop being a parent, you also never stop being a child. This much less talked about and less cooed-over role is every bit as demanding as looking after toddlers and a growing family. And, for those trying to care for parents who are frail or unwell, or perhaps reaching the end of their lives, this is also often beset by sadness.

The great practical difficulty for working people facing the decline of their parents at the end of life is that nobody knows the timeframe they are working to. No one dares articulate the question: how long? And of course there is no answer. Employers need to think about their duty to people in these circumstances, have clear policies on compassionate leave and help those trying to second-guess how much leave they should take and when, especially if parents are a long distance away. These can be agonising decisions. Now, talking with colleagues caring for elderly parents, it's important to give no less consideration and even to think in the same way as with those who are wondering about how long to spend at home with a baby. People must, within reason, take the time they need. Because whether you are preparing for the ending of a life that is dear to you, or laying the foundations for a new life you have created, you will want to look back on this liminal time, knowing that you did all you could. These are days that will not come again.

So, as June now deepens into July, the last farewells have been said and the school year draws to a close. The leavers, taken unawares by the welling sense of a poignant ending, full of half-understood emotion, are sad at a loss yet at the same time excited by the new vistas opening. We have finally said all the goodbyes (my face aching from the smiling and my palms stiff from shaking so many hands) and now, carrying the sum of all their experiences, the girls are departed, scattered like seeds across the world. The teaching staff, breathing a sigh after something successfully completed, have packed up their mark books to begin that period of decompression that precedes some much-needed relaxation. The buildings, momentarily bereft of purpose, fall strangely quiet, though not for long: soon teams of overalled workmen will appear to start the summer maintenance jobs of decorating and repairing, while a different set of international students will be using the facilities for language, sport or music courses. I remember how at Queenswood, writing my end-of-year reports at this time, I would look down on the lawn where people from the marquee company deftly dismantled the great canvas tent in which speech day had taken place, leaving a large bleached cross-shape on the grass. It looked like the spot where a great spacecraft had momentarily landed. But the event was over now, the girls once more dispersed, to continue their journeys in another place.

How do we prepare our students – minds and hearts – for what lies ahead? What are going to be the challenges for them? We ask ourselves that question constantly. Some notable contemporary commentators take a bleak view. In his Nobel lecture, delivered in Stockholm in December 2017, prizewinning author Kazuo Ishiguro, whose great respect for his (and my) parents' generation is keenly felt, writes: 'We watched our elders successfully transform Europe from a place of totalitarian regimes, genocide and historically unprecedented carnage to a much envied region of liberal democracies living in near-borderless friendship.' But the landscape we have allowed to emerge since is very different from that vision: he points to the enormous inequalities of wealth and opportunity, both within and between countries, the far-reaching effects of the economic crash of a decade ago and the rise of racism like something waking and stirring beneath our city streets. The advances in technology, especially current discoveries in artificial intelligence and robotics he sees as just as likely to bring 'savage meritocracies' as 'life-saving benefits'.[2] While I cannot argue with Ishiguro's world view – too many others have pointed to the same characteristics which make the contemporary world a worrying and uncertain place – his apparent pessimism, due to our lack of a cause or a mission to give coherence and focus to our aspirations for the future, I do not share.

Yes, this is the world we have created and which we hand on to the next generation. We may not have earned the same gratitude from them that we owe our own parents. Indeed, many would say we have much to answer for. Certainly there are huge challenges to be addressed: I have been writing this book through the longest, most searingly hot summer that anyone can recall, where London parks are nothing but brown dust and temperatures in parts of temperate Europe have reached 47 degrees. Surely even the naysayers must concede now that we are on the brink of destroying our own habitat irreparably. It is not us, but our children and today's young people who will find that unifying, rejuvenating cause, that Ishiguro says we lack. Having spent a working life amongst the young from many different backgrounds and cultures and witnessed their courage, adaptability and intelligence, their gift for friendship, generosity and humour, their capacity for hope and their thirst for renewal which is never dampened for long, I cannot help but be optimistic about the future in their hands.

For each of them, school will have been just part of an education which is, like our own, lifelong, but a most important and formative part. A school should not be a pressure cooker but a laboratory in which to discover skills, explore new interests, culture values and refine personality. Making mistakes and learning from them will always be an important part of that. Especially, school should be a place where living in community, our fundamental need to nourish and express our being in human relationships, can never be sidelined or replaced. Beautifully designed, well-led schools are not a luxury, or an anachronism, but our greatest hope in countering the negative effects on mental health of isolation in the cyber wilderness. Above all, schools should be at the centre of the most important debate of all: how to forge a peaceful, equitable and collaborative world in the future. A number of international schools now place the achievement of peace amongst their key educational goals. Students learn the lessons of history and the skills of dialogue, negotiation and diplomacy. With recent, unanticipated changes in the international political landscape making it almost unrecognisable to many, there can never have been a time when this is more important than today.

I often think about one particular Paulina, a bright-eyed, dark-haired mathematician, sharp and focussed as a piece of jet, who came to the school on a full bursary and said of her education that it had been 'the most incredible and life-changing gift I have ever received'. We should not be satisfied until all children can look back and say that about their education, shaping the future, one young life at a time.

As I finish the last few reports, I look up at the large oil painting on my wall, the work of one of the girls, long gone now. It shows an ant struggling along a horizontal branch carrying a huge leaf. Suddenly, I am that ant. I should start to think about taking a break myself. A headmistress who is worn out because she hasn't had a proper summer break is no role model for staff and students come September. I'm looking forward to getting out the list of books entitled 'must read that' which has been lengthening during the year. In only a few short weeks, we will begin again with a new generation being welcomed in, the waves of the future coming up to meet the shore inexorably.

So with the sense of something not ended, but paused, I find the final lines of 'The Whitsun Weddings' rising in my mind:

. . . And as we raced across
Bright knots of rail
Past standing Pullmans, walls of blackened moss
Came close, and it was nearly done, this frail
Travelling coincidence; and what it held
Stood ready to be loosed with all the power
That being changed can give. We slowed again,
And as the tightened brakes took hold, there swelled
A sense of falling, like an arrow-shower
Sent out of sight, somewhere becoming rain.[3]

And now, somewhere from within the house a voice is calling:
Mum? . . . *Mum?* . . . *Muuum!!*

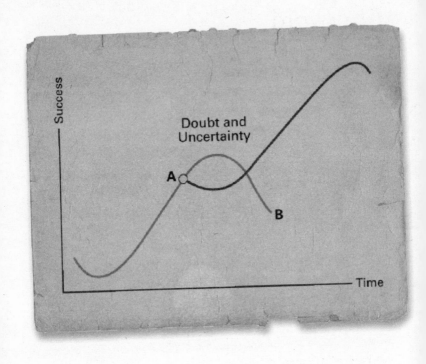

Afterword

In the autumn of 2016, after ten years at St Paul's, it came to me quite suddenly that my work there was finished and it was time to do something else. As with other big changes in my life, a restlessness had been stirring in me and I had felt the moment would come when it was ready. It did. As I sat listening to our choir and orchestra playing at the annual joint concert with St Paul's boys' school on a soft September evening, enjoying the wonderful achievements of our two directors of music, I realised that I had brought everything I could to the job. It was time to make way for a new leader and there was, somewhere, a new challenge beckoning me. I didn't know what it was yet . . . that would come. So I went into school the next morning and wrote my resignation letter.

Change in a community is often unwelcome at first. The senior girls I met with every week were a little dismayed; didn't I like them any more? I explained my thinking in terms of the sigmoid curve. In any episode of your life or work, after the effortful start-up period, there is a gradual escalation of capability until eventually, you reach a peak. After that, watch out: your effectiveness, because you have become complacent, or too native to the culture, or bored, begins to fall away. The skill is to find the point on the upward curve when you have made a satisfying and significant contribution but have *not yet reached* the point where you have done all your work – where there is still more you could have done. This is the point to make the change. That act may feel reckless, frightening: what will you be, *who* will you be, when you have walked away from that all-consuming, all-defining role? You have stepped out onto a new curve and at first, it may dip downwards, into uncertainty and confusion. But gradually you will find your feet, and new growth will be possible, which can take you up and beyond, onto another path.

The girls listened thoughtfully while I explained this. They looked at each other and I could see it made sense to them. 'So, it's a bit like when David Tennant left *Doctor Who*?' one ventured. 'Exactly,' I said. 'You've got it.'

Like many of my generation now, I don't think of a career ending but of a new one starting: a new period of working life which for me, involves writing, speaking, working as a non-executive director, adviser or governor for four schools and a museum, and bringing my experience of educational leadership to the development of a fast-growing international schools group. One former head who has helped me work out how to design this next phase of life explained she had found it helpful to think in terms of three things: learning, earning and giving. I am learning about the world of museums and the world of business – the one very similar and the other very different from what I have known before – earning my living through advisory work and giving back through board involvement in the charity sector. Getting the balance of these elements right is a challenge and may take longer – I am only a year into this new 'portfolio' life – but thus far the exploration is stimulating, energising and challenging.

'How is retirement?' well-meaning people younger than me ask, with the assumption that after a long phase of working life in a high-profile role, you must somehow slacken into doing less, that you are in decline. I think of Millament's wonderfully ironic line in Congreve's *The Way of the World* when she undertakes to '*dwindle into a wife*'. I see this not as an afterthought but as a new beginning, and for all the difference in our ages, feel more affinity with the girls stepping away from school into their new lives than with those in mid-career. Nothing is certain and the sad loss of several friends of my generation in recent years is sobering; ill health can strike at any time, putting an abrupt stop to it all. But all the more reason to use the energy and experience you have as fully as possible.

Wherever it takes place – in a parent's arms, in the classroom, on a mountain path or on the football pitch – our education is the story of the growth of our human capability, of the making and remaking of ourselves, a process which begins with our parents, is explored through our schooling and which continues throughout our lives. For all that our school life is formative, we ourselves are the principal instruments of that process. We all, and especially those of us who work in education, with its endless pouring out of the self, have to remember to pay attention to our own development by creating for ourselves – as we do for others – enough challenge, but stopping short of what might overwhelm us. In this way, we can continually grow in our capability, to find and follow the true grain of our being, to become the best – the only – version of ourselves that we can be. That may face us with difficulty from time to time, and is a ceaseless task.

Gillian Stamp introduced me to the words of the third-century philosopher Plotinus, much revered by John Colet, who, using the image of the carver in stone, describes the duty of care to tend the self: 'Withdraw into yourself and look. And if you do not find yourself beautiful yet, act as does the creator of a statue that is to be made beautiful; he cuts away here, he smooths there, he makes this line lighter, this other purer until a lovely face has grown on his work. So do you also . . . never cease chiselling your statue.'

I hope one day to have time to go back to sculpture: I have so much still to learn.

Acknowledgements

Once, when thanking leaving teachers in the end-of-year assembly, I accidentally left out a very cheerful PE teacher who had given a lot to the school and was returning home to Australia. I felt dreadful listening to her afterwards saying bravely, 'It doesn't matter,' when it clearly did. Since then, as someone who believes in showing appreciation, I have had a recurring fear of omitting some vital person from any such announcement. The 'acknowledgments' page of this book has therefore given me more anxiety than any other.

And since there are genuinely far too many people who deserve recognition here to name them all, I am going to keep it short. First, warm thanks to my colleagues, especially the senior leadership teams at Queenswood and St Paul's. It has been a pleasure working with you and learning from you, and seeing you continue to fly onward in your careers. The wise counsel of governors and fellow heads of school during twenty-one years of headship has improved my work in myriad ways. Each year I reflected that as girls left the school, I would equally miss their parents. Thank you to the many families who extended their warmth and care to supporting their daughters' education, as well as so much more. And the girls: surprising, funny, clever, inspiring, humbling, maddening – if not for you, then what would it have all been about?

It was the generous introduction provided by David Bodanis to Patrick Walsh at PEW Literary, who in turn convinced me I could write and led me to meet Arabella Pike at HarperCollins, that enabled me to publish this book. While all the mistakes in the book are entirely mine, my gratitude is due to them all.

Finally and most importantly to my family. My brother Richard, a real writer, listened patiently and gave me countless ways to bring the book back on track when I was stuck. John, who gave unwavering support during the years of my two headships, taught me to have a nose for a story and was the first to encourage me to write a book. And our children Isobel and Adam not only patiently tolerated having a working mother but were – are – ever ready with that levelling remark: 'You're not high mistress here, you know!'

Notes

Chapter 1

1. Philip Larkin, 'Days', *Whitsun Weddings*, Faber, 1964.

Chapter 2

1. JoAnn Deak and Teresa Barker, *Girls Will Be Girls: Raising Confident and Courageous Daughters*, Hyperion, 2002, pp. 42–3.
2. Cordelia Fine, *Delusions of Gender: The Real Science Behind Sex Differences*, W. W. Norton and Company Inc., New York, 2010, p. 81.

Chapter 3

1. Ethel Strudwick, 'The School and Life', in E. Strudwick, *The Headmistress Speaks*, originally published in 1937, John Catt Educational Ltd, 1993, pp. 113–118.
2. M. G. Clarke, 'Feminine Challenge in Education', in Strudwick, *Headmistress Speaks*, pp. 35–42.
3. 'Judgement and Decision Making': http://www.bioss.ac.uk/.
4. *Fortune* magazine and Hay Group, *Lighting the Path to Success*: report covering fifteen years of research analysing the best practices of *Fortune* magazine's World's Most Admired Companies, 2012 (see http://www.haygroup.com/fortune/downloads/2012-FORTUNE-Lighting-the-path-to-success.pdf).

5. Tom Stoppard, *Every Good Boy Deserves Favour* and *Professional Foul*, Faber and Faber, 1977.

Chapter 4
1. Philip Larkin, 'The Whitsun Weddings', *Whitsun Weddings*, Faber, 1964.
2. Jonathan Smith, *The Learning Game: A Teacher's Inspirational Story*, Hachette, 2000.
3. Poem by Sir Cecil Spring-Rice, '*Urbs Dei*' ('The City of God'), *c*.1908 or 1912, set to music in 1921 by Gustav Holst to the tune 'Thaxted'. The poem described how a Christian owes his loyalties to both his homeland and the heavenly kingdom.
4. Virginia Woolf, *Mrs Dalloway*, Hogarth Press, 1925.
5. A. N. Wilson, 'Church bells ring the soundtrack of Britain', *Independent*, 29 April 2012.
6. T. S. Eliot, *The Dry Salvages*, Faber and Faber, 1941.

Chapter 5
1. Martha Nussbaum, *Not for Profit: Why Democracy Needs the Humanities*, Princeton University Press, 2010.
2. Neil MacGregor, (BBC Radio 4 Podcast) *A History of the World in 100 Objects*.
3. Mary Oliver, *Wild Geese*, Bloodaxe World Poets, 2004.
4. Nussbaum, *Not for Profit*.
5. Rainer Maria Rilke, *Letters to a Young Poet*, first published 1929, Penguin Classics, 2016; translation copyright Charlie Louth, 2011.

Chapter 6
1. Interview with charity Teach First, *Frontline*, October 2017.

Chapter 7

1. Website of the Positive Psychology Center.
2. Andrew Hill, *Financial Times*, University of Pennsylvania, 2014.
3. Royal Academy of Arts, *Sensing Space – Architecture Reimagined*, 25 Jan – 6 April, 2014
4. Ibid.
5. Juhani Pallasmaa, *The Eyes of the Skin: Architecture and the Senses*, John Wiley & Sons Ltd., 2005.
6. Ibid., p. 22.
7. Christopher Alexander, Laura Ishikama and Murray Silverstein, *A Pattern Language*, OUP, 1977
8. Pallasmaa, *Eyes of the Skin*.
9. Ibid.

Chapter 9

1. See https://www.susanpinker.com/the-village-effect/.

Chapter 10

1. John Henry Newman, *The Idea of a University*, 1852
2. Kazuo Ishiguro, *My Twentieth Century Evening and Other Small Breakthroughs*, Faber & Faber, 2017
3. Philip Larkin, 'The Whitsun Weddings', *Whitsun Weddings*, Faber, 1964.